THE SOUTH WALES DERBIES

A History of Cardiff City versus Swansea City

DEAN P. HAYES

The Parrs Wood Press
MANCHESTER

First Published 2003

THE PARRS WOOD PRESS

St Wilfrid's Enterprise Centre
Royce Road, Manchester, M15 5BJ
www.parrswoodpress.com

© **Dean P. Hayes 2003**

ISBN: 1 903158 43 5

Printed by Newton Printing Ltd. of London
www.newtonprinting.com

CONTENTS

ACKNOWLEDGEMENTS

The following organisations helped me considerably in the compilation of this book:

Cardiff City Football Club, Swansea City Football Club, The National Library of Wales and in particular Rhydian Davies and the Central Reference Libraries of Cardiff, Carmarthen, Llanelli and Swansea.
Thanks also to Richard Shepherd for providing the majority of the photographs in this book.

INTRODUCTION

THERE IS CERTAINLY no love lost between Cardiff City and Swansea City and we have to go back over ninety years to find the origins of this rivalry.

The establishment of a first-class professional football club in a rugby stronghold such as Cardiff is due to the members of the Riverside club, formed in 1899 out of a cricket club of that name. The original idea was to form a football team in order to keep all the cricketers fit during the winter months. After a disappointing turn-out at the inaugural meeting, the idea was scotched, but when a second meeting was arranged there was a much better response and the Riverside AFC was formed.

The interest in soccer in Swansea had grown to such an extent that it was decided to form a senior club in the town. One of the main obstacles was the availability of a central ground but all was resolved in 1912 when the Swansea Gaslight Company failed to get Parliamentary permission to develop the Vetch Field site after strong opposition from the residents of Sandfields. On 14th June 1912, a meeting was held at the Royal Hotel and the new club was formed.

Cardiff City were Swansea's opponents in their first competitive game on 7th September 1912 at the Vetch Field. It was Swansea's first-ever game as a professional outfit and they drew 1-1 on the clinker surface. The return at Ninian Park later in the season was goalless.

The two clubs first met in the Football League on 5th October 1929 at Ninian Park in a game that was also without a goal. The Swans won the return at the Vetch on 8th February 1930, 1-0. Cardiff's first League victory over Swansea came on 27th December 1930 when a Leslie Jones goal separated the teams.

Swansea's biggest victory over Cardiff City came at the Vetch on Christmas Eve 1949 when goals from Billy Lucas (2), Jackie O'Driscoll (2) and Sam McCrory helped the Swans win 5-1 in front of a crowd of 27,264. Cardiff's revenge came in 1964-65 when in one of the final games of that campaign, they won 5-0 with Ivor Allchurch scoring a hat-trick and John Charles the other two goals.

The clubs have met twice in the FA Cup with the Swans winning on both occasions.

THE SOUTH WALES DERBIES

Cardiff have also played Swansea in the Welsh Cup on numerous occasions, many of the meetings producing memorable games. On 25th February 1960, the Bluebirds fielded their reserve team in a sixth round tie at the Vetch Field because the Welsh FA refused to change the date of the match, even though Cardiff had an important League game at Leyton Orient two days later. Swansea fielded their full-strength line-up but soon fell behind to a Steve Mokone goal. As the game wore on, tempers became frayed and the tackles more vigorous, but to the Swans' dismay, Harry Knowles put the Bluebirds 2-0 up with just a quarter of an hour to play. The Swans pulled a goal back before Colin Hudson was sent off for dangerous play. A few minutes later, Cardiff were reduced to nine men when Mokone and Swansea's Harry Griffiths were dismissed after throwing mud at each other! The Bluebirds hung on to win 2-1 but they were fined £350 by the Welsh FA and ordered to play their strongest side in the Welsh Cup in future.

In the 1965-66 Welsh Cup competition, the teams had drawn 2-2 at the Vetch and returned to Ninian Park for the fifth round replay. With just eight minutes of the second half played, Cardiff led 3-0 and seemed to be coasting into the next round. However, in the 64th minute the game turned on its head when Don Murray received his marching orders. Within a minute the Swans had pulled a goal back through Todd, who later netted a second and, after Herbie Williams equalised, the game went into extra-time. Further goals from McLaughlin and Evans gave the Swans a remarkable 5-3 win.

One of the most emotional meetings between the two clubs as far as Swansea supporters are concerned was the first-ever meeting in the Third Division on Boxing Day 1985, after the Vetch Field club had escaped the clutches of the Official Receiver. Had that game not been played then Swansea City FC would not exist today. Though the Swans lost an evenly fought match to a late goal, every Swansea fan went home happy because the club was alive again!

Now with the Bluebirds just having won promotion to the First Division via the play-offs, and Swansea winning their last game of the season and so avoiding dropping out of the Nationwide League, it means it will at least be another two seasons before the two South Wales clubs could meet in the League!

THE GROUNDS

NINIAN PARK

In February 1910, Cardiff City were offered an area of waste ground which had been used as a rubbish tip, between Sloper Road and the Taff Vale railway. Offered a seven-year lease by the Corporation, the club had to provide guarantees for an annual rent of £90. After one of the club's backers withdrew, Lord Ninian Crichton-Stuart came to the rescue. Thus the ground, which was provisionally called Sloper Park, was named in honour of his Lordship's contribution.

Aston Villa, the Football League champions, played a friendly at Ninian Park on 1st September 1910 with the official kick-off being performed by Lord Ninian Crichton-Stuart. Approximately 7,000 saw Villa win 2-1 but the honour of scoring Cardiff City's first goal at Ninian Park went to Jack Evans.

A small 200-seat wooden grandstand with a canvas roof was built on the Sloper Road side of the ground with a dressing room erected in the corner. Though the ground was to remain basic for a good number of years, it replaced the Arms Park as Cardiff's football international venue and, in March 1911, staged the first game against Scotland.

In 1920 the Canton Stand, which was named after the district, was built behind the north goal. After City had won the FA Cup in 1927, the profits of their triumphs funded a second large roof being erected over the Grangetown End terrace in 1928.

On 18th January 1937 the Main Stand was burnt down, the result of thieves trying to blast open the club's safe, which they wrongly believed to contain gate money from the FA Cup tie against Grimsby Town played two days earlier. The old structure was replaced by a stand of brick and steel. The ground remained like this until 1947 when the terrace in front of the Main Stand was extended and, in 1958, the Bob Bank was enlarged and a roof erected over its new rear section. Floodlights were installed in the summer of 1960.

On 14th October 1961, Ninian Park's all-time highest gate was recorded when 61,566 witnessed the Wales v England international.

In 1972-73 the club spent £225,000 on extending the Main Stand to seat nearly 4,500 but, in 1977, Ninian Park was designated under the Safety of Sports Grounds Act, as a result of which the South Glamorgan authorities reduced the ground's capacity from 46,000 to 10,000 until the repairs were carried out. It cost the club £600,000 of which £200,000 came from the Football Grounds Improvement Trust and £27,000 from the Welsh FA.

Perhaps the most significant of the changes enforced by the Safety Act was the demolition of the Grangetown End roof in 1977 and the cutting down of its banking.

As the years unfolded, the Arms Park began to host the majority of international games following doubts about Ninian Park's safety. In 1990 City owed their landlords, Cardiff City Council, for unpaid loan repayments and three areas of the ground had been closed to save policing costs. Ninian Park was by now a sorry state and in February 1991 just 1,629 fans turned up to see City beaten 3-1 by Aldershot.

The club needed a miracle and found one in the form of millionaire Rick Wright, who though he said he didn't like football, put £2million into the club just 48 hours before a final winding up order.

In late 1991, 2,100 seats were installed on the Main Stand paddock. They were covered by a roof extension, while the terracing under the Bob Bank roof was converted to hold 5,330 seats. At the same time, the Grangetown End was restored and the Canton Stand refurbished to allow extra seating for 1,761.

In the summer of 1995, Samesh Kumar took over as chairman of Cardiff City and there was talk of the club moving to Cardiff Bay and the involvement of David Sullivan and the Millennium Stadium. Now with former Wimbledon chairman Sam Hammam in charge of the club, the Bluebirds continue to play their home games at Ninian Park, which now has a ground capacity of 20,000.

VETCH FIELD

Also known as the Old Town Ditch Field, the site was first used by Swansea Villa during the 1880s before being opened as a sports ground on Whit Monday 1891. At that time, it had a circular running track and a grass track for horses.

When the Southern League expanded into South Wales in 1909, the Vetch Field was seen as the most suitable choice for Swansea's ground, but it was by then owned by the Gas Light Company who were planning to build a gasworks. However, after their plans were rejected, the new Swansea club which had been formed in June 1912 secured a £75 a year lease on the ground.

They played their first competitive match at the Vetch Field against Cardiff City in a Southern League game on 7th September 1912, a game that ended all-square at 1-1. Throughout that first season, Vetch Field had no grass and the players had to wear knee pads on the hard surface of clinker. When they embarked on their second season of League football in 1913-14, they were not only able to play on grass but also had a new 1,100-seater stand designed by local architect Benjamin Jones. The stand, however, only ran for two-thirds of the pitch and in the corner a tall Territorial Army drill hall overlooked a small area of terrace. When the Vetch Field club entered the Football League in 1920-21, a small corner stand was erected in front of the drill hall.

In April 1921, the Vetch Field staged its first international match when Wales played Ireland.

When the Swans were promoted in 1924-25, the local Vetch Field Infants School was demolished to allow for the expansion of the North Bank and a double-decker stand at the Richardson End of the ground was built at a cost of £5,540. It was opened in 1927 and the upper tier seated 2,120.

During the Second World War Swansea's ground was used as an ant-aircraft post and, after renting St Helens, the club returned to the Vetch Field in 1944. In 1958 the Supporters Club donated £16,000 to the cost of covering the North Bank and the following year the fans also helped to fund the club's floodlights, which were first switched on for the visit of Hearts in September 1960.

In 1974, with the club experiencing financial difficulties, the Vetch Field was sold to the council for just £50,000 despite the site being valued at a later date at £1 million. The club were granted a five-year lease at a cost of £3,000 per year but with the proviso that if the Swans were ever to drop out of the Football League, the Vetch Field would be lost altogether!

Despite having to apply for re-election in 1974-75, the club won promotion to the Third Division three seasons later. Within 12 months the club had gained promotion to the Second Division, but the Vetch Field then became designated under the Safety of Sports Grounds Act, resulting in a bill of £700,000 to cover the costs needed to repair the dreadful state of the ground. In 1980, work began on the uncovered East Stand and was completed in January 1981 at a cost of around £800,000.

During the 1985-86 season, the club somehow survived a number of winding-up orders in the High Court as they struggled to cope with the massive debts from the ground works. Following the fire at Bradford City's Valley Parade, further safety checks led to the closure of the club's West Stand upper tier which was eventually demolished in 1990.

Though there were hopes to move into a new ground at Morfa, the Swans still occupy the Vetch Field, where the current capacity is 10,402.

THE MATCHES

The period covered by this book starts with the very first meeting in the Southern League between the Bluebirds and the Swans on 7th September 1912 and ends with the FAW Premier Cup Final on 13th May 2002 - a total of 150 games in a variety of competitions; Football League, FA Cup, League Cup, Associate Members Cup, Welsh Cup, South League, Wartime and Friendlies.

During the early years of the derby matches, attendance statistics are estimates made by the regular local reporter on the game such as the Citizen, Cygnus, Clubman or Crusader, though the Football League attendances are those recorded in the ledgers of the Football League headquarters.

All teams and scorers have been checked at least twice from the pages of the Western Mail and South Wales Echo. Where the information was not reported in either, or there was a doubt or conflict, then the registers held in the Football League headquarters has been consulted.

Match reports for the games played in the wartime regional Football League and Cup competitions, which operated over the seven seasons of 1939-40 to 1945-46, do not include line-ups as a preponderance of 'guest' players and, on occasions, players plucked from the crowd at the last minute, altered the original selections!

Honours even in first meeting

7th September 1912
Southern League Division 2

SWANSEA TOWN 1 CARDIFF CITY 1

The game was Swansea's first Southern League match and, on a Vetch Field pitch of pressed clinker, they shared the points with Cardiff City in a game in which each side scored once.

The Swans had the better of the opening exchanges and Cardiff were seldom out of their own half! Both Ball and Coleman came close before the former netted for Swansea. This came on 20 minutes and was the result of Coleman's long-range shot coming back off the post and into the path of Billy **BALL,** who made no mistake from close range. The Swans then went in search of a second goal and Nicholas tried his luck from fully 30 yards out, only to see his shot strike the woodwork and bounce to safety. Kneeshaw then saved well from Swansea goalscorer Ball before Cardiff drew level in what was virtually their first attack of the game. Tracey's cross was met by the head of Jack Evans, who laid the ball into the path of Cardiff skipper Jack **BURTON** to easily place past Whittaker.

The game thereafter was contested keenly with both sides going in search of a winning goal. Cardiff's Featherstone saw his shot turned round the post by Whittaker before Keggins headed wide with only the Swansea keeper to beat.

In the closing stages of the game Swansea almost grabbed the winner but, with Jack Kneeshaw beaten, Hardy kicked Coleman's goalbound shot against the post and away to safety!

SWANSEA TOWN: W.Whittaker, A.Cleverley, J.Nicholas, J.Duffy, J.Hamilton, S.Jepp, W.Messer, J.Coleman, W.Ball, R.Grierson, J.Swarbrick.
CARDIFF CITY: J.Kneeshaw, R.Croft, R.Leah, H.Harvey, P.Cassidy, W.Hardy, H.Tracey, J.Burton, H.Featherstone, H.Keggins, J.Evans.

Scorers: Swansea Town (Ball)
Cardiff City (Burton)
Attendance: 8,000

Grierson sparks amazing comeback

15th February 1913
Welsh Cup semi-final

CARDIFF CITY 2 SWANSEA TOWN 4

Up to the interval, the home side thoroughly deserved their two-goal lead but early in the second half they were reduced to nine men and the Swans took advantage!

The Bluebirds took the lead on 20 minutes when Devlin, clean through on goal, was brought down from behind by Cleverley. The referee had no hesitation in awarding a penalty and though Fisher got his hands to **CASSIDY's** spot-kick, he couldn't prevent it crossing the line. In the last minute of the first half, the home side were awarded a second penalty when Nicholas pulled back Featherstone as he shaped to shoot. Tracey took this kick but blazed the ball high and wide of the target. From the resultant goal-kick, Cassidy crossed the ball high into the Swansea area where **BURTON** scored with a spectacular scissors-kick. Even Swansea's players shook Burton by the hand, a sporting tribute rarely seen on a football ground!

No sooner had the second half got underway when Featherstone had to leave the field with a serious leg injury. Within a minute, Swansea had reduced the arrears through **GRIERSON** who headed home Ball's cross. Then Evans was also forced to hobble off, leaving Cardiff with nine men. The Swans were all over the home side and drew level through **BALL**, who converted a penalty awarded for handball against Doncaster. Midway through the half, the visitors took the lead when **COLEMAN's** shot from the edge of the area hit the inside of the post before nestling in the back of the net.

At the other end, a snap shot by Burton almost caught Fisher unawares, but Swansea made the game safe in the last minute as **BALL** netted his second goal to take the Swans into the Welsh Cup Final.

SWANSEA TOWN: E.Fisher, A.Cleverley, J.Nicholas, J.Duffy, J.Hamilton, S.Jepp, W.Messer, J.Coleman, W.Ball, R.Grierson, J.Swarbrick.
CARDIFF CITY: J.Kneeshaw, T.Doncaster, R.Leah, H.Harvey, P.Cassidy, W.Hardy, H.Tracey, W.Devlin, H.Featherstone, J.Burton, J.Evans.

Scorers: Swansea Town (Ball 2; 1 pen, Grierson, Coleman)
Cardiff City (Cassidy pen, Burton)
Attendance: 12,000

Swansea defence holds firm

15th March 1913
Southern League Division 2

CARDIFF CITY 0 SWANSEA TOWN 0

A win for leaders Cardiff City over third placed Swansea Town would have given the Bluebirds the Southern League Second Division Championship. Unbeaten at Ninian Park all season, there was little danger of the home side losing that record, although Jack Kneeshaw had to be alert on more than one occasion.

Though play was spoilt by a high wind which blew across the ground and more than one player - on both sides - was blamed for the lack of control he possessed, the game didn't lack excitement.

Only three minutes had been played when Jack Kneeshaw failed to gather a long shot from Messer but, recovering, he threw himself full length at the ball and managed to turn it round the post. From the corner, Coleman had a header kicked off the line by Harvey. At the other end, Cardiff had strong claims for a penalty waved away after Devlin had been upended in the six-yard box.

Swansea's only goalbound shot of the second half came on the hour when Ball's snap shot from the edge of the area grazed the outside of Kneeshaw's right-hand upright.

Cardiff hit back strongly with Burton hitting the crossbar from fully 30 yards out and both Holt and Devlin bringing fine saves out of Fisher. The Bluebirds dominated the majority of the game and should have won handsomely but for the heroics of Fisher and the woodwork that came to his rescue on a number of occasions, most notably from a powerful Clarke header in the closing minutes.

SWANSEA TOWN: E.Fisher, A.Cleverley, J.Nicholas, J.Duffy, J.Hamilton, S.Jepp, W.Messer, J.Coleman, W.Ball, R.Grierson, J.Swarbrick.
CARDIFF CITY: J.Kneeshaw, T.Doncaster, R.Leah, H.Harvey, P.Cassidy W.Hardy, A.Holt, G.Burton, W.Devlin, J.Clarke, J.Evans.

Scorers: Swansea Town (-)
Cardiff City (-)
Attendance:10,000

Opportunist goals give Swans the edge

29th November 1913
FA Cup 4th Qualifying Round

SWANSEA TOWN 2 CARDIFF CITY 0

The much improved Vetch Field was packed for this FA Cup 4th qualifying round tie, which saw the home side deservedly win by two clear goals.

Cardiff could offer no excuse, though they played for most of the game with ten men following a knee injury to Dr McBean, an amateur signed from Scottish club Queen's Park. They were also reduced to nine men for a period of ten minutes midway through the first half when Bennett needed treatment following a clash with Nicholas. He returned and played the rest of the game with a broken collarbone, the full extent of his injury not being discovered until after the game.

Swansea took the lead just before half-time when Bassett rolled a free-kick to **MESSER**. His first time shot took a deflection off full-back Doncaster and completely wrong-footed Cardiff keeper Jack Kneeshaw. The Swans almost extended their lead but Weir's shot-cum-cross rolled agonisingly along the goal-line with Kneeshaw beaten before Harvey cleared the danger.

The Swans' second goal midway through the second half was as a result of Robertson needing too much time on the ball. Nicholas dispossessed him and crossed for **WEIR** to shoot past the advancing Kneeshaw.

Cardiff threw caution to the wind in an effort to reduce the arrears, but this left gaps at the back and Kneeshaw was forced into making a couple of brave saves at the feet of the onrushing Swansea forwards Ball and Grier.

A game that was remarkable for the number of stoppages, Swansea went on to beat Merthyr in the first round proper before losing to Queens Park Rangers.

SWANSEA TOWN: E.Storey, A.Allman, J.Nicholas, J.Duffy, S.Bassett, S.Cubberley, W.Messer, D.Anderson, J.Weir, W.Ball, R.Grier.
CARDIFF CITY: J.Kneeshaw, T.Doncaster, Dr J.L.McBean, H.Harvey, P.Cassidy, W.Hardy, K.Bennett, J.Henderson, T.Robertson, J.Burton, J.Evans.

Scorers: Swansea Town (Messer, Weir)
Cardiff City (-)
Attendance: 12,000

Swans on top in Good Friday clash

18th April 1919
Wartime Friendly

SWANSEA TOWN 2 CARDIFF CITY 0

The Bluebirds had the better of the early stages of this Good Friday encounter with both Grimshaw and Evans going close. Denoon in the Swansea goal then made a good save at the foot of the post from a Devlin header. The Swans' first attack saw them awarded a penalty when Smith was adjudged to have handled the ball right under the referee's nose. Hewitt saved well from Brown's spot-kick but two Cardiff defenders encroached into the penalty area and from the re-taken penalty **BROWN** this time sent the Cardiff keeper the wrong way.

Cardiff then created a host of chances before half-time with Beare missing the easiest from the edge of the six-yard box. Johnson then kicked Evans' goalbound shot off the line before

Swansea, through Brown and Mortimer, almost extended their lead, the latter shooting into the side-netting when it seemed easier to score.

Early in the second half, Nicholas burst through the Cardiff defence but shot against the post with Hewitt beaten. Hale, Swansea's best forward on the day, also struck the woodwork before a slip by Smith allowed **HALE** to net a second goal for the home side.

Cardiff went straight down the other end and Beare should have done better with a chance created for him by Evans, but he too shot against the post.

Scorers: Swansea Town (Brown pen, Hall)
Cardiff City (-)
Attendance: 12,000

Revenge is sweet!

21st April 1919
Wartime Friendly

CARDIFF CITY 3 SWANSEA TOWN 0

Both clubs were strongly represented for this wartime friendly with Bolton Wanderers and Wales wing-half Billy Jennings 'guesting' for Swansea. He was later to become Cardiff City manager!

Play in the opening quarter of an hour was both fast and furious and though Grimshaw and Evans both came close, the Bluebirds had to wait until the 20th minute before netting the goal their play warranted. Cassidy took a free-kick from wide on the right, flighting the ball perfectly for **RUTHERFORD** to outjump a static Swansea defence. Beare then scraped the outside of Johnson's right-hand post with a swerving shot before **WEST** doubled Cardiff's lead on the stroke of half-time with a well struck drive from just outside the area.

Cardiff again dominated the opening exchanges of the second half though Hole almost reduced the arrears, beating Kneeshaw but seeing Brittan clear off the line. At the other end, Johnson saved well from Evans before Beare again hit the woodwork. The Cardiff winger had the beating of Jule who was 'guesting' from

Dundee and forced three corners in quick succession off the Scottish left-back. The Swansea goal had a miraculous escape when Harvey's long-range shot took a deflection and hit the post before Hewitt cleared the danger. The Cardiff youngster wasn't to be denied though and in the 88th minute, **HARVEY** scored from close range following good work by Evans.

Scorers: Swansea Town (-)
Cardiff City (Rutherford, West, Harvey)
Attendance: 18,000

Swans win fully deserved

27th September 1919
Southern League Division 1

SWANSEA TOWN 2 CARDIFF CITY 1

Cardiff's visit to the Vetch Field attracted the Swans' best gate of the season. A crowd of 15,500 saw a fast, open game, which, if it did not reach the highest standard, was always interesting.

The first half was goalless though Swansea, who had suffered four defeats in succession - three of which were at home - came closest to breaking the deadlock. Sheldon's header from Evans' cross beat Kneeshaw but grazed the crossbar.

The visitors took the lead early in the second half when Hewitt failed to clear Beare's corner and **EVANS** smashed the ball home from point-blank range. Swansea keeper Jock Denoon then made a brave save at the feet of Layton before the Swans drew level. Lloyd's cross was left by Smith to allow **SHELDON** to drive hard and low past the unsighted Jack Kneeshaw.

The home side then stepped up a gear and it seemed as if there was only going to be one winner. Swansea took the lead after 76 minutes when ex-Barry Town favourite David Evans' accurate cross found **SHELDON** who scored his and his side's second goal.

Cardiff made great efforts in the closing stages to get back on level terms but found Jock Denoon in the Swansea goal equal to anything they threw at him! On the final whistle, Brittan's unnecessary foul on Lloyd incited the home fans who were baying for the Cardiff player's dismissal!

SWANSEA TOWN:, J.Denoon, F.Robson, T.Hewitt, J.Collins, W.Y.Brown, J.Durnin, A.Lloyd, F.Sheldon, J.Weir, I.Brown, D.Evans.
CARDIFF CITY: J.Kneeshaw, R.Brittan, A.Layton, H.Harvey, E.Smith, F.Keenor, G.Beare, W.Grimshaw, W.Devlin, K.Bennett,J.Evans.

Venue: Vetch Field
Scorers: Swansea Town (Sheldon 2)
Cardiff City (Evans)
Attendance: 15,500

Weakened Swansea put up good fight

6th October 1919
Friendly

CARDIFF CITY 1 SWANSEA TOWN 1

A crowd of 3,500 were at Ninian Park for the occasion of George Latham's benefit match. Neither team had a representative side out, although Swansea suffered in this respect more than the Bluebirds. Latham himself turned out, captaining the home side.

Play had the usual 'friendly flavour' and there were some exciting incidents at both ends of the pitch. In one of these, Swansea keeper Jock Denoon received a kick to the knee and though he carried on for a little while, he eventually left the field to be replaced by Hewitt the Cardiff reserve goalkeeper.

Cardiff winger George Beare was having a bit of a field day and it was from one of his touch-line runs that, after beating four Swansea defenders, he crossed accurately into the middle for **DEVLIN** to apply the finishing touch.

Swansea then got into the game more and both Spencer and Jones came close, bringing fine saves out of Jack Kneeshaw in the Cardiff goal. The City keeper was at last beaten in the semi-darkness in which the game finished, the ball coming in from the left from Durnin for **SPENCER** to score.

The Bluebirds failed to settle down to their usual game, the Swans fully deserving their draw.

SWANSEA TOWN: J.Denoon, F.Robson, J.McKie, W.Ogley, E.Wordley, J.Durnin, F.Harris, E.Jones, S.Spencer, J.Bradshaw, I.Brown.
CARDIFF CITY: J.Kneeshaw, G.Latham, A.Layton, H.Harvey, E.Smith, K.Bennett, G.Beare, W.Devlin, W.Cox, C.Jones, J.Evans.

Scorers: Swansea Town (Spencer)
Cardiff City (Devlin)
Attendance: 3,500

Largest-ever Southern League crowd

7th February 1920
Southern League Division 1

CARDIFF CITY 1 SWANSEA TOWN 0

A new record was established at Ninian Park when all previous figures for a Southern League game were eclipsed. A crowd of 24,371 witnessed the game between Cardiff and Swansea and £1,402 was taken at the turnstiles. The number of spectators present was the largest seen at any match at the Grangetown enclosure.

The Bluebirds side was completely disorganised owing to injuries and suspensions but, even allowing for this fact, the marksmanship of the forwards was continually ineffective. Both Beare and Cox missed goalscoring chances when faced in a one-to-one situation with Swansea keeper Jack Crumley, whilst Cashmore shot wildly over the bar when placed.

Swansea lost the services of Nicholas, probably the club's best defender, when a leg injury forced him to leave the field just before the interval. The Swans played the whole of the second half with ten men but could still have taken the lead had Spottiswoode and Brown showed a little more composure in front of goal.

West came close for the home side but they had to wait until five minutes from time before a goal from winger George **BEARE**, side-footing home at the far post following good work by Evans, gave them the points.

SWANSEA TOWN: J.Crumley, F.Robson, J.Nicholas, J.Durnin, J.Collins, J.Williams, B.Hole, I.Jones, I.Brown, E.Jones, J.Spottiswoode.
CARDIFF CITY: J.Kneeshaw, R.Brittan, A.Barnett, W.Hardy, P.Cassidy, F.Keenor, G.Beare, W.Cox, A.Cashmore, G.West, J.Evans.

Scorers: Swansea Town (-)
Cardiff City (Beare)
Attendance: 24,371

City too good for ten-man Swansea

24th March 1920
Welsh Cup semi-final

CARDIFF CITY 2 SWANSEA TOWN 1

In what was the fourth meeting between the two sides this season, the Bluebirds ran out winners by 2-1 and in doing so, qualified for the Welsh Cup Final.

Brittan received a nasty cut over the right eye at end of five minutes' play, but the Cardiff captain, after having his injury cleaned and dressed, returned to play an important part in the Bluebirds' victory. It was Brittan who set up West for the best chance of the first half but he shot tamely into the hands of Swansea keeper Crumley.

The second half was only minutes old when the Swans were reduced to ten men, Brown having to retire with a head injury. Though they battled on manfully, they went behind after 58 minutes when **EVANS** scored from the spot following a handball decision against Robson. There is no doubt that Cardiff were superior territorially and but for a string of outstanding saves by Jack Crumley, the margin of their victory would have been much wider. As it was, their second goal came from **WEST** as he headed home Cashmore's pin-point cross.

Five minutes from the end **BENYON** got his head to a centre from Spottiswoode to score for Swansea and, though Ball might have scored in injury-time, it would have been a complete travesty.

SWANSEA TOWN: J.Crumley, F.Robson, J.Walton, J.Durnin, J.Collins, J.Williams, W.Messer, W.Ball, J.Benyon, I.Brown, J.Spottiswoode.
CARDIFF CITY: A.Layton, R.Brittan, A.Barnett, F.Keenor, E.Smith, W.Hardy, G.Beare, W.Cox, A.Cashmore, G.West, J.Evans.

Scorers: Swansea Town (Benyon)
Cardiff City (Evans pen, West)
Attendance: 7,000

Cardiff reach Welsh Cup Final after five-goal thriller

11th April 1923
Welsh Cup semi-final

SWANSEA TOWN 2 CARDIFF CITY 3

This Welsh Cup semi-final produced some of the best football seen in a South Wales derby.

In the first half, there was only one team in it as Cardiff attacked for virtually the entire 45 minutes. Len Davies almost gave the Bluebirds the lead after four minutes but his drive from the edge of the area hit the underside of the bar and bounced to safety. Grimshaw then forced Denoon into making a brave save, the Swansea keeper having to dive at the winger's feet as he seemed certain to score. Clennell then headed inches over the top and Grimshaw saw his first-time shot brilliantly turned over by Denoon. Cardiff took the lead after 31 minutes when Hardy's cross was headed home by Len **DAVIES**. Though the Bluebirds had other chances, there was no further scoring as the referee blew for half-time.

The second half was only three minutes old when the Swans equalised with what was their first real attack of the game. There was a touch of good luck about it as Nelson miskicked and it landed in the path of **SMITH,** who beat Farquharson with ease.

Cardiff set about regaining the lead in workmanlike manner and **CLENNELL** finally beat Denoon after the Swansea keeper had failed to hold Fred Keenor's rasping shot. **CLENNELL** extended the Bluebirds' lead in the 79th minute, cutting inside Bennett and unleashing an unstoppable shot.

The Swans pulled a goal back in the dying minutes of the game through **THOMPSON,** but even then there was time for Grimshaw to race to the other end and smack a shot against Denoon's left-hand upright.

SWANSEA TOWN: J.Denoon, E.Bennett, E.Morley, J.Roulson, J.Harwood, J.Williams, W.Hole, H.Deacon, J.Smith, L.Thompson, J.Spottiswoode.
CARDIFF CITY: T.Farquharson, J.Nelson, J.Page, H.Evans, E.Smith, W.Hardy, W.Grimshaw, F.Keenor, L.Davies, J.Clennell, J.Evans.

Scorers: Swansea Town (Smith, Thompson)
Cardiff City (Davies, Clennell 2)
Attendance: 12,000

Swansea stroll it

2nd March 1925
Welsh Cup 5th Round

SWANSEA TOWN 4 CARDIFF CITY 0

A crowd of 15,000 - considerably more people than watched the weekend's international - were at the Vetch Field to watch this fifth round Welsh Cup tie.

Very little was seen of the Cardiff attack and in practically the first move they made, Jack Evans injured his foot and took no further part in the game. Swansea took the lead after 27 minutes when **THOMPSON** beat the Bluebirds offside-trap to run on and slot the ball past the advancing Farquharson. The Cardiff keeper then saved well from Spottiswoode before **THOMPSON** netted his and Swansea's second goal minutes before the interval, following good work by Sykes and Bellamy.

Early in the second half, **WHITEHEAD** extended the home side's lead when a cross from Hole found the Swans centre-forward completely unmarked and he headed firmly past Farquharson. Ten-men Cardiff were firmly on the defensive and both Deacon and Thompson hit the woodwork before the referee awarded the home side a penalty following a handball decision against Page. Thompson took the kick in the hope of completing his hat-trick but Farquharson turned the ball round the post. Minutes later, **WHITEHEAD** completed the scoring, tapping in a simple chance at the far post.

Cardiff never really looked like scoring and Jock Denoon was practically a spectator in a most one-sided game.

SWANSEA TOWN: J.Denoon, E.Bennett, W.Milne, L.McPherson, J.Sykes, H.Bellamy, W.Hole, H.Deacon, W.Whitehead, L.Thompson, J.Spottiswoode.
CARDIFF CITY: T.Farquharson, J.Nelson, J.Page, H.Wake, E.Whitcombe, T.Sloan, D.Lawson, J.Gill, J.Nicholson, H.Beadles, J.Evans.

Scorers: Swansea Town (Thompson 2, Whitehead 2)
Cardiff City (-)
Attendance: 15,000

Cardiff through despite missed chances

2nd April 1928
Welsh Cup 6th Round

CARDIFF CITY 1 SWANSEA TOWN 0

If Cardiff City had set out upon their sixth round Welsh Cup tie with Swansea Town with the sole intention of demonstrating to their supporters that goalscoring had become a lost art, they could not have done it more thoroughly! The Bluebirds missed at least half a dozen simple opportunities but the goal that they did score was highly controversial!

When Hughie Ferguson swung across a ball from out on the left, it seemed that **SMITH-POTTER** was standing well offside. The referee thought otherwise and the Cardiff forward took the ball to the edge of the six-yard box before unleashing a powerful shot straight at the Swansea keeper, who failed to hold the ball and could only watch as it trickled over the line.

The Swansea goal led a charmed life as the Cardiff forwards failed to make the most of what was virtually one-way traffic. Blackburn intercepted the ball near the halfway line and wormed and swerved his way past at least half a dozen opponents. Left with just Ferguson to beat, he shot tamely wide ! Despite the miss, the Cardiff wing-half was given a great ovation. It was one of the few times during the match that the crowd became really enthusiastic.

For the most part they sent up groans of disappointment and despair because of the utter inaptitude of the forwards in front of goal. Hughie Ferguson was unfortunate on two occasions, once when he struck the crossbar and again when, after being tripped by Collins, he ran through and netted but was recalled for a free-kick against the Swansea defender - the referee failing to exercise his discretion to allow advantage to the home side.

SWANSEA TOWN: A.Ferguson, W.Sampy, W.Milne, J.Collins, J.Sykes, C.Lloyd, G.Thomas, T.Woodward, W.Lewis, L.McPherson, W.Hole.
CARDIFF CITY: T.Farquharson, J.Nelson, J.Jennings, F.Keenor, T.Sloan, G.Blackburn, W.Thirlaway, T.Smith-Potter, H.Ferguson, L.Davies, G.McLachan.

Scorers: Swansea Town (-)
Cardiff City (T.Smith-Potter)
Attendance: 10,000

All-square at Ninian Ark

5th October 1929
Football League Division 2

Cardiff City 0 Swansea Town 0

As the two sets of players disappeared into their changing rooms at the end of this first meeting in the Football League, a spontaneous roar of applause broke from the near 30,000 rain-soaked spectators. This demonstration could only be interpreted as an expression of the satisfaction which the supporters of both clubs felt regarding the displays given by the respective teams.

As is so often the case when rivalry is so keen and partisanship is at a fever pitch, the result was a goalless draw!

Yet there were numerous occasions when goals might have been scored and a few occasions when goals should have been scored.

In the first half the Bluebirds, playing with the wind at their backs were clearly the better side. Matson, Robbins and Keenor all sent in powerful drives in quick succession, bringing three fine saves out of Ferguson. When the Swansea keeper was beaten by a Len Davies header, Milne was on the line to knock the ball clear.

If Cardiff were the better team in the first half, Swansea were superior after the interval. Though the wind played a part in their change of fortune, they also adopted a route-one approach. Both Hole and Glyn Davies provided Deacon with goalscoring opportunities but Farquharson in the Cardiff goal was equal to his efforts. Glyn Davies and Armand should have scored but both shot weakly with just the Cardiff keeper to beat.

SWANSEA TOWN: A.Ferguson, B.Williams, W.Milne, J.Collins, J.Sykes, L.McPherson, W.Hole, H.Deacon, J.Armand, A.Freeman, G.Davies.
CARDIFF CITY: T.Farquharson, J.Jennings, W.Roberts, H.Wake, F.Keenor, G.Blackburn, F.Matson, F.Harris, L.Davies, W.Robbins, F.Warren.

Scorers: Swansea Town (-)
Cardiff City (-)
Attendance: 29,093

Lindsay goal separates sides

8th February 1930
Football League Division 2

SWANSEA TOWN 1 CARDIFF CITY 0

Just before the game started, a policeman walked across the ground and placed a chair near one of the goalposts. A wag in the crowd shouted that it was for one of the goalkeepers to sit on - he didn't say which one!

In fact, armchairs could have been provided for both goalkeepers as both Ferguson and Farquharson had a leisurely afternoon and except when Lindsay scored the all-important goal, neither were seriously troubled.

Though the Swans occupied the lowest rung of the League table, they played well enough to make Cardiff City look a bad side. Wingers Handley and Thomas had the beating of the Cardiff full-backs and if Armand and Easton had taken the chances created for them, then Swansea's winning margin would have been far greater. Swansea's goal came midway through the second half and was the result of some fine approach play from Armand and Handley. The Swansea winger cut inside Nelson and crossed to the far post where **LINDSAY** outjumped a static Bluebirds defence to head in just under the bar.

In the last ten minutes, the visitors showed more urgency with 17-year-old Leslie Jones and Robinson both going close with long range shots. When Ferguson was beaten in the last minute of the game, former Wolves defender Len Williams was on hand to clear the danger.

SWANSEA TOWN: A.Ferguson, L.Williams, W.Milne, H.Deacon, J.Sykes, A.Freeman, G.Thomas, J.Lindsay, J.Armand, W.Easton, C.Handley.
CARDIFF CITY: T.Farquharson, J.Nelson, W.Roberts, H.Wake, F.Keenor, G.Blackburn, W.Thirlaway, L.Davies, R.S.Williams, L.Jones, M.Robinson.

Scorers: Swansea Town (Lindsay)
Cardiff City (-)
Attendance: 22,121

Cardiff run out four-goal winners

2nd April 1930
Welsh Cup 6th Round

CARDIFF CITY 4 SWANSEA TOWN 0

After failing to find the net in both of this season's League encounters with the Swans, Cardiff City made amends in this sixth round Welsh Cup tie.

Yet the Swans could have been two goals up inside the opening quarter of an hour as first Ranson and then Lindsay brought fine saves out of Farquharson. Wake, Keenor and Blackburn formed a powerful half-back line which dominated the game and consequently the Cardiff forwards were able to make for themselves at least three scoring chances for every one that fell to the visitors.

The game was still goalless when Deacon dribbled through the Bluebirds defence before putting the ball into the side-netting from an acute angle.

The Bluebirds took the lead after 35 minutes when Ferguson, under pressure from Miles, failed to hold Leslie Jones' shot and in nipped **THIRLAWAY** to force the ball home. Leslie **JONES,** who was the best forward on view, scored the second, shooting through a crowded penalty area to beat the unsighted Ferguson. The Swansea keeper's most glaring mistake came on the stroke of half-time when he failed to get down to Len **DAVIES'** long shot which put Cardiff 3-0 up.

The second half was rather uneventful except for a tremendous shot by Robbins which Ferguson turned round the post. However, the Swansea keeper could do nothing to prevent **NELSON** scoring direct from a free-kick on the edge of the area in the final minute of the game.

SWANSEA TOWN: A.Ferguson, L.Williams, W.Milne, H.Deacon, H.Hanford, W.Tabram, W.Hole, J.Lindsay, R.Williams, J.Ranson, C.Handley.

Cardiff City: T.Farquharson, J.Nelson, W.Roberts, H.Wake, F.Keenor, G.Blackburn, W.Thirlaway, L.Davies, A.Miles L.Jones, W.Robbins.

Scorers: Swansea Town (-)
Cardiff City (Thirlaway, Jones, Davies, Nelson)
Attendance: 8,000

Five goals for Ron Williams as Swans win "Benefit" match

**28th April 1930
Friendly**

SWANSEA TOWN 6 CARDIFF CITY 2

Some interesting football was served up in this game, arranged for the benefit of a number of the Swansea players. Both sides set out to play football and both succeeded.

The Bluebirds were clearly on top in the early stages and they took the lead after just five minutes when **JONES** rose to head home Bill Hardy's corner-kick. They could have extended their lead shortly afterwards but Jones shot tamely into the side-netting. As it was, it was Swansea who scored the game's next goal on 26 minutes, Ron **WILLIAMS** equalising with a left-foot shot from just outside the area. Four minutes later, **WILLIAMS** netted his and Swansea's second goal though the referee and linesman were the only ones in the Vetch who didn't think he was offside!

On the stroke of half-time the Bluebirds drew level when Hanford, under pressure from Harris, handled and **JONES** made the score 2-2 from the penalty spot.

There was only one team in it in the second half as Swansea attacked from virtually start to finish. Former Leeds United forward Jack **ARMAND** put the Swans ahead before Ron **WILLIAMS** completed his hat-trick, heading home a deep cross from Deacon.

This was definitely Ron **WILLIAMS**' day. He netted his fourth goal after 82 minutes, fastening on to a through ball from Milne and then, in the closing stages of the game, **WILLIAMS** completed a personal triumph by netting his fifth goal as the Swans ran out 6-2 winners.

Scorers: Swansea Town (R.Williams 5, Armand)
Cardiff City (Jones 2)
Attendance: 10,000

Swansea hold on in rousing derby

30th August 1930
Football League Division 2

SWANSEA TOWN 3 CARDIFF CITY 2

This game, played on the opening day of the season and in tremendous heat, produced one of the most entertaining of South Wales derbies.

Though Swansea secured the points, they were not the better team, luck at critical moments of the game favouring them just a little. Two of Swansea's goals were more than a shade lucky and Cardiff had a goal disallowed after the referee had been prevailed upon to consult a linesman.

The best goal of the match was the first scored by Cardiff after 15 minutes. Good approach play by Wake, Jones and Robbins bewildered the Swansea defence, allowing **RALPH WILLIAMS** to fire home from an acute angle.

Swansea drew level midway through the first half when Armand outpaced McJennett before crossing into the Cardiff box. The ball found its way to the opposite wing where Thomas returned it first time into the middle, for **EASTON** to beat Keenor to the ball and shoot past Farquharson. The home side took the lead just before half-time when Cardiff's defence failed to clear Hole's cross and **RON WILLIAMS**' shot was too strong for the Bluebirds keeper to hold. Swansea's third goal also came from **RON WILLIAMS**, who appeared to impede Farquharson as the two jumped for Thomas' cross. If the Cardiff keeper had attempted to punch the cross away instead of trying to catch the ball, Williams might still have fouled him but the ball would have been safely away.

Cardiff reduced the arrears late in the game when **RALPH WILLIAMS** crowned a clever right-wing move by Harris and Emmerson by forcing both Ferguson and the ball over the line.

SWANSEA TOWN: A.Ferguson, L.Williams, W.Milne, H.Deacon, H.Hanford, J.Sykes, G.Thomas, W.Easton, R.Williams, J.Armand, W.Hole.
CARDIFF CITY: T.Farquharson, G.McJennett, W.Roberts, H.Wake, F.Keenor, G.Blackburn, G.Emmerson, F.Harris, R.S.Williams, L.Jones, W.Robbins.

Scorers: Swansea Town (R.Williams 2, Easton)
Cardiff City (R.S.Williams 2)
Attendance: 20,368

Jones scores only goal in disappointing derby

27th December 1930
Football League Division 2

CARDIFF CITY 1 SWANSEA TOWN 0

As a spectacle this South Wales derby at Ninian Park was a huge disappointment. It lacked colour and interest for long periods and fell a long way below the traditional Bluebirds-Swans standard. Yet if Swansea had been as alert in front of goal in the first half as they were dominant in midfield, the game might have taken a different course.

It was not until they forged ahead through Leslie **JONES** in the 53rd minute that Cardiff began to inspire confidence and for the rest of the game they were clearly the more dangerous side. It was only the stubborn work of Milne and Les Williams plus the goalkeeping of Ferguson that prevented Cardiff from scoring further goals.

Swansea, who were playing their third game in successive days, were probably feeling more leg-weary than Cardiff. They were also disorganised through an injury sustained by Ron

Williams before the game had been in progress half an hour. Even so, by then the Swans could have been 2-0 up. Cardiff keeper Tom Farquharson turned aside a pile-driver from Lindsay and then bravely dived at Gunn's feet when he seemed certain to score.

At the other end the home side came close to extending their lead in the dying moments of the game, but Ferguson produced an outstanding save to thwart Emmerson and Joe Sykes cleared Valentine's header off the line with the Swansea keeper beaten.

SWANSEA CITY: A.Ferguson, L.Williams, W.Milne, J.Sykes, H.Hanford, J.Miller, J.Lindsay, W.Easton, R.Williams, K.Gunn, G.Bell.
CARDIFF CITY: T.Farquharson, J.Smith, T.Ware, T.Helsby, F.Keenor, G.Blackburn, G.Emmerson, A.Valentine, R.S.Williams, L.Jones, W.Robbins.

Scorers: Swansea Town (-)
Cardiff City (L.Jones)
Attendance: 24,232

Walton save takes tie to replay

9th March 1933
Welsh Cup 8th Round

SWANSEA TOWN 1 CARDIFF CITY 1

Despite the disparity between the success which the clubs enjoyed this season, Cardiff City fully deserved the right of a replay which they forced with the holders Swansea Town in this eighth round Welsh Cup tie.

Though the standard of play was not particularly high, this was more than made up for by the lively nature of the exchanges and the many exciting incidents.

Cardiff had the better of the early exchanges with Leslie Jones hitting the underside of the bar following good work by Maidment. Emmerson cut inside Milne before firing across the face of the goal and Cribb shot tamely over the bar with only Walton to beat. The Bluebirds eventually took the lead on the half-hour mark when **MAIDMENT**, easily the best forward on view, beat Milne and Walton with some deft footwork before rifling his shot into the roof of the net. Cardiff almost extended their lead when Maidment's shot was pushed out to Emmerson but the Bluebirds forward screwed his shot wide.

The Swans drew level midway through the second half when the industrious **BLAIR** beat Russell with ease before firing past Farquharson. Moments later, a reckless back-pass by Russell almost gifted Swansea the lead but the ball rolled inches wide of the target with Farquharson out of position.

In the last minute of the game, Cardiff almost snatched a winner when Emmerson raced clear of the Swansea defence, only to see Walton first parry and then clear in a remarkable fashion at the second attempt.

SWANSEA TOWN: J.Walton, S.Lawrence, W.Milne, F.Jones, H.Hanford, J.Miller, H.Blair, W.Molloy, T.Martin, K.Gunn, T.Olsen.
CARDIFF CITY: T.Farquharson, R.Pollard, G.Russell, F.Harris, J.Galbraith, A.Keating, G.Emmerson, T.Maidment, J.McCambridge, L.Jones, S.Cribb.

Scorers: Swansea Town (Blair)
Cardiff City (Maidment)
Attendance: 3,000

Welsh Cup replay goes to extra time

15th March 1933
Welsh Cup 8th Round Replay

CARDIFF CITY 2 SWANSEA TOWN 1

It was a fine performance on the part of Cardiff City to beat Swansea in this Welsh Cup 8th round replay but the Bluebirds cut things fine in allowing the game to go into extra-time.

THE SOUTH WALES DERBIES

For half an hour, the home side played some beautiful football and if they had built a lead of three goals instead of the one they got, Swansea could not have complained.

Cardiff took the lead after 11 minutes when Emmerson's free-kick was met by the head of **MAIDMENT** who beat Walton from the edge of the six-yard box. The Bluebirds continued to press forward and Walton saved well from both Cribb and Pollard. McCambridge then rattled the crossbar from close range but Hanford was the first to react, clearing the ball well upfield to Blair. He was fouled and from the resultant free-kick **MARTIN** rose highest, his header taking a slight deflection to deceive Farquharson.

Midway through the second period, Cardiff were awarded a penalty when McCambridge was hauled down just inside the area. The referee had no hesitation in pointing to the spot but was immediately surrounded by angry Swansea players protesting about his decision. Cribb took the kick and though he sent Walton the wrong way, he also placed the ball well wide! At the other end, Swansea almost took the lead when a long punt upfield by Lawrence deceived Farquharson and after bouncing over his head, hit the crossbar!

Five minutes into extra-time, Cardiff scored what proved to be the winning goal, Leslie **JONES**' first-time shot with his left foot simply flying into the net. The Swansea defence came under further heavy pressure but Emmerson and McCambridge failed to make the most of two scoring opportunities.

SWANSEA TOWN: J.Walton, S.Lawrence, W.Milne, J.Sykes, H.Hanford, J.Miller, H.Blair, E.Reid, T.Martin, H.Scot, E.Rees.
CARDIFF CITY: T.Farquharson, R.Pollard, G.Russell, F.Harris, J.Galbraith, A.Keating, G.Emmerson, T.Maidment, J.McCambridge, L.Jones, S.Cribb.

Scorers: Swansea Town (Martin)
Cardiff City (Maidment, L.Jones)
Attendance: 5,000

Little better than a trial in disguise

20 August 1938
Jubilee Benevolent Fund

SWANSEA TOWN 3 CARDIFF CITY 3

Beyond providing something like £450 towards the FA Jubilee Benevolent Fund, the keenly-awaited South Wales derby was little more than a useful pre-season work out.

With five new players in their side, Swansea soon fell behind when, with just 11 minutes played, **SIMONS** put through his own goal. The Swans centre-half, under pressure from Collins, attempted a back-pass to his keeper but placed the ball wide of John and into the empty net. **BRUCE** equalised after 23 minutes, cutting inside Kelso and drilling the ball past the advancing Jones in the Cardiff goal.

A neat move involving Chedgzoy and Lewis almost gave Swansea the lead but Granville was quick to clear the impending danger.

COLLINS gave the Bluebirds the lead again shortly after the resumption with a fine drive from an oblique angle but it was short-lived for first **MILLINGTON** with a powerful header and then **BRUCE** with a shot from the edge of the area scored for Swansea.

Cardiff threw caution to the wind as they went in search of an equaliser. After coming close on a couple of occasions, they drew level four minutes from time when **COLLINS** forced the ball over the line following a goalmouth scramble.

SWANSEA TOWN: R.John, S.Lawrence, T.Emmanuel, R.Rhodes, R.Simons, W.Imrie, S.Chedgzoy, J.Lewis, J.Connor, W.Bruce, J.Millington.
CARDIFF CITY: B.Jones, J.Kelso, A.Granville, C.McCaughey, B.Bassett, W.Corkhill, R.Pugh, G.Walton, J.Collins, L.Talbot, A.Turner.

Scorers: Swansea Town (Bruce 2, Millington)
Cardiff City (Collins 2, Simons og)
Attendance: 10,000

Last kick levels scores in Welsh Cup thriller

8th February 1939
Welsh Cup 5th Round

CARDIFF CITY 2 SWANSEA TOWN 2

When McCaughey the Cardiff wing-half equalised with the last kick of the game, it meant that the clubs would have to replay this Welsh Cup tie on a Sunday - it was the last thing the clubs wanted!

Swansea had taken the lead after 20 minutes when Bamford outjumped Cardiff's reserve centre-half Tommy Williams to set up **OLSEN,** who coolly slipped the ball past the advancing Fielding. There was no further scoring in the first half although Collins missed a golden opportunity to level the scores just after the half-hour mark when, with only Swansea keeper Moore to beat, he put his shot into the side-netting.

The Bluebirds finally equalised early in the second half when Ballsom, running through a wide open space on the right, switched the ball into the Swansea goal area where Egan laid the ball back for **McKENZIE** to score with a low shot.

A little later, a badly directed pass by McCaughey enabled Rhodes to swing the ball into the middle and **BAMFORD** outjumped Williams to give the Swans the lead. The visitors almost added a third minutes later, but Lewis saw his shot hit the inside of the post before being cleared by Kelso.

There were just seconds remaining when Swansea conceded a free-kick out on the left. The ball was swung into the goalmouth and with the defence only partially clearing, **McCAUGHEY** from fully 35 yards out fired in a brilliant shot that beat Moore all ends up - there wasn't even time to replace the ball in the centre!

CARDIFF CITY: W.Fielding, W.G.Ballsom, J.Kelso, W.Corkhill, T.Williams, C.McCaughey, E.Walton, T.Rickards, J.Collins, H.Egan, J.McKenzie.

SWANSEA TOWN: S.Moore, S.Lawrence, A.Roberts, R.Rhodes, P.Tabram, J.Lloyd, S.Chedgzoy, I.Lewis, T.Bamford, T.Olsen, J.Millington.

Scorers: Swansea Town (Olsen, Bamford)
Cardiff City (McKenzie, McCaughey)
Attendance: 4,000

Bluebirds run out easy winners

23rd February 1939
Welsh Cup 5th Round Replay

SWANSEA TOWN 1 CARDIFF CITY 4

Playing football that completely puzzled their Second Division opponents, Cardiff City deservedly beat Swansea 4-1 in this Welsh Cup fifth round replay.

Both sides fielded experimental teams but the Bluebirds would have been pleased with their experiment of playing Egan at centre-forward with Ballsom behind him.

Yet it was Swansea who had the better of the opening exchanges in which outside-right Williams missed a golden opportunity to open the scoring. Cardiff were the first to score when **EGAN** netted. He broke through on his own, fell down in front of Moore and then, calmly rising, walked the ball round the goalkeeper.

Ten minutes into the second half, **IMRIE** equalised for Swansea with a terrific shot from a free-kick on the edge of the penalty area. It would be no exaggeration to say that very few spectators saw the ball enter the net and Fielding knew nothing about it until he picked it out of the net!

On the hour mark, Cardiff went ahead when **EGAN** netted his and the Bluebirds' second goal, placing the ball well out of Moore's reach. Then, a quarter of an hour from the end, **RICKARDS** netted from close range to put the game out of Swansea's reach. **RICKARDS** completed the rout five minutes from time, shooting high into the roof of the net from fully 30 yards out.

SWANSEA TOWN: S.Moore, R.Davies, D.Emmanuel, P.Tabram, J.Imrie, R.Rhodes, R.Williams, W.Burns, T.Bamford, T.Olsen, J.Millington.
CARDIFF CITY: W.Fielding, A.Granville, J.Kelso, W.Corkhill, W.G.Ballsom, C.McCaughey, W.Baker, T.Rickards, H.Egan, L.Talbot, R.Smith.

Scorers: Swansea Town (Imrie)
Cardiff City (Egan 2, Rickards 2)
Attendance: 1,500

Midnight capture saves game for City

19th August 1939
Jubilee Benevolent Fund

CARDIFF CITY 1 SWANSEA TOWN 1

On 7th May 1939, Cardiff City manager Cyril Spiers patiently awaited the arrival of midnight when Sheffield United forward Ernest Marshall's contract expired. Though competition for the Bramall Lane player was intense, he duly signed for the Bluebirds, albeit whilst in his pyjamas!

The Cardiff manager's nocturnal vigil had a happy sequel in this Jubilee Benevolent Fund match when with just five minutes to go, the former Blades player netted the equaliser.

Up to that point, the Swans seemed well set for victory. Twice in the first half, Meek, who was one of the most industrious players on the pitch, broke through only to finish weakly. Early in the second half Fielding dived at full length to save a hard shot from Bamford when the Swansea leader seemed to have the Cardiff goal at his mercy.

The Bluebirds only clear cut chance came shortly afterwards when Myers rounded Swansea keeper Moore but saw his shot cleared off the line by Davies.

Swansea took the lead after 65 minutes when **ROGERS** fastened on to Coulter's pin-point cross to beat Fielding all ends up. The Swans almost extended their lead moments later but Tommy

Bamford's header landed on the roof of the net with Fielding beaten.

Cardiff's equaliser in the 85th minute came courtesy of **MARSHALL**, who followed up a Collins free-kick that Moore was unable to hold.

SWANSEA TOWN: T.Moore, W.Davies, L.Emmanuel, S.Briddon, P.Tabram, W.Sneddon, E.Rogers, J.Meek, T.Bamford, J.Gallon, J.Coulter.
CARDIFF CITY: W.Fielding, E.Sykes, J.Kelso, W.Corkhill, W.Booth, J.Cringan, R.Pugh, E.Marshall, J.Collins, H.Egan, J.Myers.

Scorers: Swansea Town (Rogers)
Cardiff City (Marshall)
Attendance: 10,000

Cardiff miss hatful of chances

23rd September 1939
Friendly

CARDIFF CITY 1 SWANSEA TOWN 1

With the competitive instinct missing from this game it encouraged a cultured conception of the finer phases, but there was too much finesse in this game for both sets of supporters. If either side had been so generous in a League game, there would have been an uproar!

Though the match ended in a 1-1 draw, the Bluebirds had sufficient chances in the last quarter of an hour to have won comfortably. During this period their attack swept through the Swansea defence with ease, but there were some amazing misses when Moore was the only barrier, notably by Court and Collins.

The only incident of note in a goalless first half came when Swansea centre-forward Bamford took exception to a challenge by Kelso, the referee having to speak sternly to both players.

Swansea keeper Stan Moore had a good match but he should have been beaten more than once, although even then he was unlucky. Cardiff's goal came in the 83rd minute - Moore went down at full length to parry aside a low shot by Pugh, but he only pushed the ball out to **COLLINS** who promptly banged it into the net.

Only a minute remained when Swansea Town equalised. There was a misunderstanding between Kelso and Cardiff keeper Fielding and **BAMFORD** nipped in to obtain a gift goal. The visitors could have snatched a dramatic victory but Squires held on to the ball too long when Allen was handily placed.

Scorers: Swansea Town (Bamford)
Cardiff City (Collins)
Attendance: 5,000

Bamford double shatters Bluebirds

30th September 1939
Friendly

SWANSEA TOWN 4 CARDIFF CITY 1

The Swans had little difficulty in beating Cardiff in a game which was in keeping with its label 'friendly'. Although the clubs had met twice previously this season and drawn on each occasion, there was never any doubt as to which side was the better in this encounter.

Swansea's key man was Bryn Allen, who scored one of their goals and had a hand in the other three. The 19-year-old inside-forward exploited to the full Sneddon's classy through-balls and had the Cardiff defenders continually guessing.

Swansea took the lead in the 11th minute when Edwards and Allen worked an opening on the left for the latter to cross to the far post, where Tommy **BAMFORD** headed past Fielding. Cardiff came close to drawing level minutes later but Court's shot struck the crossbar. Moore in the Swansea goal saved well from Egan before **COLLINS** levelled the scores with a snap-shot from the edge of the area.

Just before half-time, Sneddon's diagonal long ball found **ALLEN** and he rounded Kelso before chipping the ball out of Fielding's reach and into the far corner of the net.

Collins was having a fine game for the Bluebirds but he generally had to play a lone hand. At the other end, Allen hit the woodwork before **BAMFORD** forced the ball and the Cardiff keeper Fielding over the line! Just seconds remained when **SQUIRES** scored with a delightfully struck free-kick after a foul on Allen.

Scorers: Swansea Town (Bamford 2, Allen, Squires)
Cardiff City (Collins)
Attendance: 3,000

Game of two halves

28th October 1939
South-West Wartime League

CARDIFF CITY 2 SWANSEA TOWN 2

This was a game of two distinct phases and fittingly ended in a 2-2 draw. In the first half, Cardiff City were the better side and at one stage led by two goals but, after the interval, Swansea Town made most of the running.

Cardiff's goals came within a minute midway through the opening half. First **COURT** broke through the Swansea defence and shot past John from an oblique angle. Then brilliant inter-passing between Bryn Jones and Marshall gave **SABIN** a clear opening and although John tried to narrow the angle, the diminutive winger scored with a low shot.

A minute before the interval, **SQUIRES** reduced the Bluebirds' lead with a magnificent shot from fully 25 yards.

The Swans equalised in the opening minute of the second half when a back-pass by Williams put **HAINES** on-side and the Swansea No.9, who played well throughout the game, took his chance well.

Subsequently, Cardiff might have taken the lead but Court failed from close range and when Collins was on the mark, John in the Swans goal made a spectacular save. The Welsh international keeper later made good saves from Pugh and Bryn Jones as the Bluebirds went in search of the winning goal.

Scorers: Swansea Town (Squires, Haines)
Cardiff City (Court, Sabin)
Attendance: 5,000

Ten minutes of madness

16th December 1939
South-West Wartime League

SWANSEA TOWN 4 CARDIFF CITY 0

One of the most spectacular individual goals ever seen in a South Wales derby outweighed some disagreeable incidents which occurred later in the game.

ALLEN had given the Swans an early lead, cutting inside Ballsom and rifling an unstoppable shot past Reid. Midway through the first half, the home side extended their lead when Ballsom's back-pass was woefully underhit. This allowed **EDWARDS** to use his speed and, after beating Reid to the ball, he rolled it into the empty net.

The Bluebirds could have reduced the arrears just before half-time when the referee awarded the visitors a penalty following a handball decision against Emmanuel. Granville sent John the wrong way but missed the target!

Swansea went further ahead early in the second half when the raven-haired **SQUIRES** picked up a pass just inside his own half and went on to beat five Cardiff players in a mazy run before shooting home a powerful shot from the edge of the box! It was a classic goal but was immediately followed by a most unpleasant ten-minute spell. Provoked by a partisan crowd, some of the Swansea players resorted to tactics which were not in accordance with the rules and City's Arthur Granville, who was nowhere near the ball was so badly fouled that he was carried off with broken ribs.

Jimmy Collins then dropped back into Granville's position but the Bluebirds, who had been disorganised at the back after the late arrival of centre-half Gunn, fell further behind when **PAYNE** fired home through a crowd of players.

Scorers: Swansea Town (Allen, Edwards, Squires, Payne)
Cardiff City (-)
Attendance: 2,500

Swans deserve narrow win

23rd March 1940
South-West Wartime League

SWANSEA TOWN 1 CARDIFF CITY 0

Perhaps the Swans deserved their narrow one-goal win because of their second half superiority but the Bluebirds in the closing minutes should have equalised.

The last ten minutes saw them sweep through the Swansea defence in continuous waves and from one of these, Pugh, from a few yards out, shot across the face of the goal. The ball was slightly diverted to Marshall who only had to tap it over the line, but he slammed the ball into the side-netting. Then Harris cleared courageously with a couple of forwards on top of him and Cardiff's whirlwind finish was in vain.

The only goal of the game came after 55 minutes. Pugh was harshly penalised and Emmanuel swung the free-kick into the goalmouth. There was a partial clearance but **SQUIRES** darted in and scored with a low shot. Subsequently, Wilkinson in the Cardiff goal made some tremendous saves, notably from Bamford and Allen before he was beaten by Payne, only for the ball to strike his right-hand upright.

In a game where conditions were all against accurate football, both sides contrived to give the somewhat partisan crowd plenty of action.

Scorers: Swansea Town (Squires)
Cardiff City (-)
Attendance: 3,000

Bluebirds retain unbeaten home record

18th May 1940
South-West Wartime League

CARDIFF CITY 2 SWANSEA TOWN 2

Cardiff City had gone through a topsy-turvy season of Regional League football without being beaten at Ninian Park.

This was their last home game of the season and though they retained their record by drawing 2-2 against Swansea, it was a close-run thing. A few minutes from the end the Swans claimed they scored the winning goal, but after consulting a linesman the referee changed his decision and gave a goal-kick on the linesman's word that Squires had carried the ball over the line.

Cardiff had the better of the early exchanges but Parker wasted the best of a number of goalscoring opportunities, heading over the bar from just six yards out. Marshall's pass split the Swansea defence wide open but Tobin took the ball too close to Harris, allowing the Swansea keeper to pluck the ball off his toes.

Swansea took the lead after 35 minutes through a penalty by **DAVIES**, after Booth had handled the ball on the line with Wilkinson out of position. The Bluebirds drew level early in the second half when **JAMES** hooked Baker's cross into the roof of the net from close range. Minutes later, Cardiff went ahead following a sweeping movement which ended with **TOBIN** shooting past Harris from just inside the penalty area.

Then with time running out, Cardiff keeper Wilkinson again showed bad judgement in coming out for a cross and **SQUIRES** was able to equalise.

It was an entertaining game, contested in the best sporting spirit throughout.

Scorers: Swansea Town (Davies pen, Squires)
Cardiff City (James, Tobin)
Attendance: 2,000

James and Moore net hat-tricks in Cardiff's record win

26th October 1940
South Wartime League

CARDIFF CITY 8 SWANSEA TOWN 0

Cardiff City's eight-goal win over the Swans has not been surpassed in the series of games between the clubs. Swansea were completely outplayed and only Davies in the visitors' goal prevented the rout from being more severe!

True, in the second half they were handicapped by the absence of Thomas, their centre-forward, but the game had been won and lost long before that.

The Bluebirds "blitzkrieg" started quite early and within 10 minutes they were two goals up. **JAMES** fastened onto Pugh's through ball and placed his shot wide of Davies before **MOORE** was on hand to force the ball over the line after the Swansea keeper had failed to hold James' header. Midway through the half **PARKER** controlled Tobin's pass before curling his shot wide of Davies and, moments later, the same player saw his shot cleared off the line by Francis. Davies saved well from Tobin but could do little about **JAMES**' powerful drive after he had been set up by Wood.

Early in the second half, **MOORE** headed home Pugh's pin-point cross, the ball entering the net off the inside of the post. **JAMES** completed his hat-trick on the hour mark, side-footing home from Tobin's pass. **MOORE** too netted a hat-trick, his third goal being the pick of the bunch as he beat three players before hitting an unstoppable shot past Davies. The Swansea keeper was beaten for an eighth time when **PARKER** scored from a free-kick whilst the nearest Swansea came to scoring was when Squires struck the upright and Payne saw his header pushed onto the crossbar.

Scorers: Swansea Town (-)
Cardiff City (James 3, Moore 3, Parker 2)
Attendance: 4,000

Bluebirds deserve Christmas win

25th December 1940
South Wartime League

SWANSEA TOWN 1 CARDIFF CITY 3

Cardiff City celebrated Christmas with a well-merited victory over Swansea Town at the Vetch Field. They played by far the more effective football after having taken the lead as early as the third minute.

A long ball out of defence by Granville found **MOORE** and he brought it down instantly before shooting past Davies in the Swansea goal. The home side pressed hard for the equaliser with both Squires and Comley going close. They eventually drew level on 25 minutes when Payne and Squires combined to set up **COMLEY** whose shot entered the net off the underside of the bar.

The Bluebirds went ahead just after the half-hour mark when Davies was drawn from his goal and **JAMES** netted with ease.

For a time in the second half, Swansea dominated the proceedings and on several occasions should have scored. Payne shot high and wide when well placed, Squires hit the post with only the keeper to beat and Comley shot into the side-netting when it seemed easier to score.

As it was, Cardiff went down the other end and scored a third goal through **JAMES**, the Bluebirds forward outjumping a static Swansea defence to head past Davies.

Scorers: Swansea Town (Comley)
Cardiff City (Moore, James 2)
Attendance: 3,000

Sides prepare for future

25th January 1941
South Wartime League

CARDIFF CITY 3 SWANSEA TOWN 2

Both teams were composed of a number of young players but they showed all the craft and intelligence of experience and the game, which the Bluebirds won 3-2, was enlivened by some excellent football.

Baker almost opened the scoring for the home side after just five minutes when he cut in from the wing and unleashed a powerful drive which scraped the outside of Davies' right-hand post. The opening quarter of an hour was all Cardiff and it came as no surprise when shortly after this period had elapsed, they took the lead through **MOORE**.

Only moments later, the Swans were on level terms in what was their first attack of the match. Squires beat three Cardiff defenders before laying the ball into the path of **ALLEN** who made no mistake from about twelve yards out.

Cardiff regained the lead in the final minute of the first half when clever play by Baker set up **MOORE** for his second goal of the game.

Early in the second half, James was injured in a harmless looking challenge and spent the majority of the last forty-five minutes hobbling on the wing.

Swansea drew level after 54 minutes when **SQUIRES**, who was having a fine game, scored an outstanding individual goal. The Swans inside-forward again rounded three Cardiff defenders before chipping the ball over the Bluebirds keeper and into the roof of the net.

Ten minutes from time, the Bluebirds scored what proved to be the winning goal when the injured **JAMES** managed to force Baker's cross over the line.

Scorers: Swansea Town (Allen, Squires)
Cardiff City (Moore 2, James)
Attendance: 1,500

Swansea leave comeback too late

15th February 1941
League War Cup 1st Round 1st Leg

CARDIFF CITY 3 SWANSEA TOWN 2

Many of the wartime cup games were thrilling to watch and this game was certainly one of them. Goals counted and football assumed a new and more exciting character - the Bluebirds, after leading 3-0 at the interval, beat Swansea 3-2 but were desperately hanging on at the final whistle.

Cardiff went ahead when **MOORE** volleyed home a cross from James, his shot entering the net off the underside of the bar. On 28 minutes, **PARKER** extended the Bluebirds lead, heading past Davies from six yards out. The home side were well on top and five minutes later went 3-0 up when a pin-point cross from Pugh found **JAMES** completely unmarked and he was left with a simple tap-in. Cardiff could have gone in at half-time 4-0 up but Reggie Pugh of all people missed a penalty after the referee had spotted a handball infringement in the area.

After the interval Swansea, with Fisher taking over the centre-forward position, put more thrust into their football and on the hour mark **EDWARDS** pulled a goal back, side-footing home from close range. Minutes later, **FISHER** reduced the lead even further when he powered a header past the Cardiff keeper.

A minute later, Swansea thought they had drawn level but Fisher's 'goal' was disallowed for offside - a decision that angered the visiting supporters who felt he was clearly on-side.

Scorers: Swansea Town (Edwards, Fisher)
Cardiff City (Moore, Parker, James)
Attendance: 4,000

Moore hat-trick as Cardiff give object lesson in finishing

29th February 1941
League War Cup 1st Round 2nd Leg

CARDIFF CITY 6 SWANSEA TOWN 2

Cardiff City qualified to meet Reading in the next round of the Football League War Cup competition by defeating Swansea Town 6-2 in the second leg. The return match should have been played at the Vetch Field but circumstances dictated otherwise and the Bluebirds, seizing their chance, made the aggregate score for the two games 9-4 in their favour.

Swansea were neat and clever but too orthodox with many of their moves lacking initiative. On the other hand, Cardiff used the open spaces with greater intelligence and were also quicker on the ball.

The Bluebirds took the lead after 13 minutes when **MOORE** side-footed home from close range after good work by James. **MOORE** netted his and Cardiff's second goal on the half-hour mark before **FISHER,** the Swans centre-forward, reduced the arrears with a powerful downward header. Minutes before the interval, **PARKER** made it 3-1 to Cardiff with a first-time shot on the turn.

Early in the second half Cardiff extended their lead when **PARKER** lobbed the Swansea keeper Davies from fully 30 yards, the ball entering the net off the inside of the keeper's left-hand post. Swansea came back strongly and their best player, **SQUIRES,** scored probably the game's best goal with a speculative shot from distance. **JAMES** headed home a Parker cross to restore Cardiff's three-goal advantage and then, in the last minute, **MOORE** completed his hat-trick with a fine opportunist goal after Davies had only been able to parry Parker's powerful shot.

Scorers: Swansea Town (Fisher, Squires)
Cardiff City (Moore 3, Parker 2, James)
Attendance; 4,000

Mistakes galore mar derby

22nd November 1941
South Wartime League

CARDIFF CITY 1 SWANSEA TOWN 0

Though the Bluebirds were without two of their liveliest forwards in James and Tobin, they still dominated the early proceedings and both Parker and Weir went close with first-time efforts.

Davies the Swansea goalkeeper kept out a piledriver from Hollyman whilst Parker's long-range effort came back off Davies' right-hand upright. Swansea's only chance of the first half fell to Fisher but his effort was well saved by the Bluebirds keeper.

Cardiff deservedly took the lead after 40 minutes when the Bluebirds' new outside-right, Weir, made an opening for **PARKER** who flicked the ball over the line from close quarters. In the minutes that remained before half-time, Weir almost netted a second but Davies narrowed the angle and the winger's shot hit the side-netting.

The second half was marred by too much careless passing by both sides and the open spaces were not exploited as they should have been.

Swansea had the chances to draw level, with Squires most prominent, but they lacked a spearhead. When Squires did get the ball past the Cardiff keeper, Hollyman was on hand to race back and clear the danger. Swansea keeper Davies, who had a fine game, produced the save of the match in the last minute to keep out Parker's powerful header.

Scorers: Swansea Town (-)
Cardiff City (Parker)
Attendance: 2,000

First league win of season for Swans

29th November 1941
South Wartime League

SWANSEA TOWN 4 CARDIFF CITY 1

Swansea Town gained their first league win of the season at the expense of Cardiff City in a game played at St Helens.

The Bluebirds took the lead on the half-hour mark when, following good approach work by Tobin and James, **PARKER** snapped up a pass close-in and netted with a low drive. The visitors could have extended their lead minutes later, but snatched at a chance created by Moore and Emmanuel was able to clear the danger.

Swansea equalised just before the interval, Roy **PAUL** steering the ball past Pritchard from the edge of the area.

Immediately on the resumption, Swansea scored twice in as many minutes. The first of these goals was scored by **EMMANUEL** whose long-range shot took a deflection on its way past Pritchard. **SQUIRES** netted the other goal, curling a superb free-kick round Cardiff's defensive wall and into the net off the underside of the bar.

The Bluebirds mounted attack after attack in an attempt to get back into the game but were unable to break down the Swansea back line. In the dying moments, the Swans scored a fourth goal when a long ball out of defence found **COMLEY**.He outpaced the Cardiff defence before slotting the ball past the advancing Evans.

Venue: St Helens
Scorers: Swansea Town (Paul, Emmanuel, Squires, Comley)
Cardiff City (Parker)
Attendance: 3,000

Deserved win for Bluebirds

25th December 1941
South Wartime League

CARDIFF CITY 2 SWANSEA TOWN 1

Cardiff had the better of this Christmas Day fixture, though they could have fallen behind as early as the third minute when Houston fastened on to an underhit back-pass by Steggles and rounded Griffiths in the Cardiff goal, but then placed his shot inches wide of the open goal.

Little was seen of Swansea as an attacking force for much of the first half and Parker, who was causing untold trouble for the visitors' defence, hit the side-netting when it seemed easier to score. The first half remained goalless though Steggles too could have given the Bluebirds the lead but he ballooned the ball high over the bar.

After the interval, Cardiff went ahead through **MOORE** following a free-kick well placed by Wood. The home side continued to dominate the opening period of the second half and it came as no surprise when **PARKER** scored a second goal just after the hour mark. Moore almost added a third ten minutes from time but Evans in the Swansea goal saved well.

From his long kick downfield, **HOUSTON** brought the ball under control and lobbed the Cardiff keeper from 30 yards. It was a goal out of the blue but it inspired the visitors and in the final minutes of the game, Comley almost scored an undeserved equaliser.

Scorers: Swansea Town (Houston)
Cardiff City (Moore, Parker)
Attendance: 5,500

Weak finishing means points are shared

January 1942
League War Cup Qualifying Competition

SWANSEA TOWN 1 CARDIFF CITY 1

In a game played at the St Helens ground, both sides created a number of goalscoring opportunities but marksmanship was poor.

As early as the eighth minute, Comley was clean through for the home side but failed to hit the target with only Griffiths to beat. Squires was the only Swansea forward likely to score and his fierce shot was beaten away by Griffiths. As it was, it was the visitors who took the lead on the half-hour mark, Beriah **MOORE** cutting in from the left and curling the ball into the far corner past the outstretched arms of Swansea keeper Wilf Davies. Parker and Moore played a neat one-two before the Bluebirds centre-forward screwed his shot wide.

After the interval, **SQUIRES** put the Swans on level terms with a well-taken penalty awarded for handball against Jones.

Midway through the second half, after a number of chances had gone begging, Parker thought he had given Cardiff the lead but the 'goal' was disallowed after the referee had consulted a linesman.

The Bluebirds dominated the final stages of the game and though the Swans struggled to get the ball out of their own half, the home forwards failed to make full use of some accurate crosses from the wings.

Venue: St Helens
Scorers: Swansea Town (Squires)
Cardiff City (Moore)
Attendance: 2,500

Swans unlucky!

17th January 1942
League War Cup Qualifying Competition

CARDIFF CITY 1 SWANSEA TOWN 1

Despite producing a number of goalmouth thrills, this League Cup match produced just two goals.

It was the visitors who had the better of the early exchanges and Lowery's header almost gave the Swans a ninth-minute lead, landing on the roof of the net with Griffiths out of his goal. In fact, the Cardiff keeper did well moments later when a powerful drive by Thomas was turned round the post after the ball had taken a deflection. Cardiff too came close when Moore's shot hit the outside of Evans' right-hand post with the Swansea keeper beaten.

Swansea took the lead after 42 minutes when a fine through-ball by Payne found **LOWERY**. His shot hit Wright but looped up in the air for the Swans forward to head past Griffiths.

Early in the second half, Swansea had the misfortune to lose Arthur Granville, the Cardiff City full-back who was assisting them. He received a nasty leg injury and was forced to leave the field. The 10 men of Swansea battled on gamely but with just four minutes to play, having missed a number of goalscoring opportunities, **PARKER** forced the ball over the line from close range for the equalising goal.

Scorers: Swansea Town (Lowery)
Cardiff City (Parker)
Attendance: 4,000

Three for Wright in Cardiff romp

21st February 1942
League War Cup Qualifying Competition

SWANSEA TOWN 1 CARDIFF CITY 5

Though the Bluebirds had a convincing victory, Swansea had a fair share of the game and with better finishing the scoreline would have been much closer.

George **WRIGHT** gave Cardiff the lead in the sixth minute in what was the visitors' first attack of the game, turning in Parker's pass from the edge of the six-yard box. The goal which came against the run of play inspired the Bluebirds and after 13 minutes **PARKER** added a second. Swansea tried to hit back and Squires was unlucky when his delicate lob from the edge of the area beat the Cardiff keeper but landed on the roof of the net.

Both sides had chances as the first half drew to a close - Beriah Moore shooting straight into the hands of Swansea keeper Wilf Davies and Squires heading inches wide from a Thomas cross.

After the interval, Swansea threw caution to the wind and **SQUIRES** reduced the arrears with a well-struck shot. The Swans rallied for a period but subsequently Cardiff's left-winger **MOORE** dribbled through a virtually non-existent Swansea defence to score. The Swans could have been back in the game a minute later but Briddon missed a penalty awarded to the home side.

Swansea continued to attack but on 72 minutes **WRIGHT** broke free from his marker, drew Davies and coolly lobbed the ball into the empty net. Cardiff put the result beyond doubt two minutes from time when **WRIGHT** completed his hat-trick, heading home a Moore corner.

Venue: St Helens
Scorers: Swansea Town (Squires)
Cardiff City (Wright 3, Parker, Moore)
Attendance: 3,000

Four goals in ten minutes as Bluebirds run riot

28th February 1942
League War Cup Qualifying Competition

CARDIFF CITY 8   SWANSEA TOWN 1

Anyone at half-time tipping Cardiff City to beat Swansea Town 8-1 would have been football's biggest optimist. At that stage, the Bluebirds led by a goal and Swansea had played just as well. In fact, the Swans took the lead after four minutes when **COMLEY**'s speculative shot from just inside the Cardiff half caught the wind and carried over Griffiths' head.

Cardiff levelled after 21 minutes when **WEIR** latched on to a fine through-ball by Moore, drew Swansea keeper Wilf Davies and slipped the ball under his body and into the far corner. The home side took the lead just before the interval with a fine individual goal, **WOOD** outpacing the Swans defence to shoot past the advancing Davies.

A number of chances fell to the Swansea forwards during the early stages of the second half but their finishing was poor.

However, it was a lack of understanding in defence which became more accentuated when they changed their first half tactics that led to Cardiff extending their lead. Goals from **PARKER** and then **WEIR** in the 62nd and 63rd minutes gave the Bluebirds a 4-1 lead before the Swans defence collapsed completely and, in the last ten minutes, Cardiff added four more goals.

WOOD fired home from close-range following a goalmouth scramble and then **MOORE** got on the scoresheet with a well-taken free-kick curled round the Swansea wall. **PARKER** then headed home Wood's cross before **WEIR** completed the scoring with his third goal of the game.

It has to be said that though Cardiff had scored 19 goals in their last three games, they were flattered by this result!

Scorers: Swansea Town (Comley)
Cardiff City (Weir 3, Parker 2, Wood 2, Moore)
Attendance: 5,000

Cardiff made to fight all the way

21st March 1942
Wartime League

CARDIFF CITY 4 SWANSEA TOWN 1

Though the scoreline makes the game look a little one-sided, Cardiff City had to fight every inch of the way to secure the points in this Football League (South) game at Ninian Park.

The Swans made all the early running with Evans and Edwards both going close with headers and it was no more than the visitors deserved when **EDWARDS**, receiving the ball from Fisher, beat Cardiff keeper Griffiths from an awkward angle. The visitors were unlucky not to score again minutes later but Fisher's long-range shot struck the bar with Griffiths well beaten.

Cardiff drew level on 38 minutes when **WRIGHT** tried his luck from just inside the Swansea half. The wind carried the ball over Davies in the Swansea goal for a freak equaliser. There was nothing lucky about the Bluebirds' second goal five minutes later when, following a tussle in the Swansea goalmouth, the ball came out to **LEWIS** who drilled his shot into Davies' top left-hand corner of the net.

The second half was only minutes old when Weir's shot-cum-cross landed on the roof of Davies' net and then Moore saw his goalbound shot deflected onto the post with Davies stranded. Cardiff extended their lead midway through the half when left-winger Beriah **MOORE** headed home Weir's corner at the near post. **MOORE** then made the issue safe with virtually the last kick of the game after Davies had only been able to parry a hard shot from Weir.

Scorers: Swansea Town (Edwards)
Cardiff City (Moore 2, Wright, Lewis)
Attendance: 4,500

Moore treble as youngsters shine

25th May 1942
Wartime League

CARDIFF CITY 4 SWANSEA TOWN 1

Two young sides contested this local derby with Cardiff including two youngsters in Griffiths and Stitfall, who were playing in schoolboy football at the outbreak of the war.

The Cardiff side was one of the youngest that the League has seen and they proceeded to play some very good football. Swansea joined in the spirit of the game and were often constructive, but there was more speed and 'punch' in the Bluebirds attack and more decisive tackling in their defence.

Cardiff took the lead after 13 minutes when Phillips' long ball out of defence found **MOORE** and he coolly lobbed the Swansea keeper from fully 30 yards. The home side went further ahead on 27 minutes and again the scorer was **MOORE**, who held off the challenge of two Swansea defenders before slotting the ball past the advancing Wilf Davies.

Swansea got back in the game on the stroke of half-time when their best player **PAYNE** cut in from the right wing and curled a lovely left-foot shot past Griffiths in the Cardiff goal.

Ken **GRIFFITHS** restored Cardiff's two-goal lead after a mix-up in the heart of the Swansea defence before **MOORE** completed his hat-trick with a shot that the visitors' keeper should really have saved. The Cardiff winger could have had a fourth goal but his snap shot hit the underside of the bar before being cleared.

Scorers: Swansea Town (Payne)
Cardiff City (Moore 3, K.Griffiths)
Attendance: 4,000

Lively game at the Vetch

10th October 1942
West Wartime League

SWANSEA TOWN 2 CARDIFF CITY 4

Though the Bluebirds were worthy of their 2-1 lead at half-time, the Swans showed considerable improvement in attack after the break and on balance did not deserve to lose.

The Cardiff forwards, ably led by Macauley, caused untold problems for the Swansea defence in the opening quarter of the game, yet for all their pressure they had just one goal to show for their endeavours when **CLARKE** forced the ball home from close range after Herdman had failed to hold Moore's shot.

The Swans drew level on 32 minutes when Lyn **THOMAS** headed home Payne's accurate cross. It was the home side's first attack of the half! Cardiff regained the lead just before the interval when **K. GRIFFITHS** curled a superb free-kick round the Swansea wall and into Herdman's net off the inside of the post.

Roy **CLARKE** extended the visitors lead early in the second half, cutting in from the left and firing past the outstretched arms of Swansea keeper Herdman. The play was now end to end and on 64 minutes Lyn **THOMAS** netted his and Swansea's second goal with a well-taken header.

Swansea went in search of an equaliser and came close on a number of occasions - the nearest being a Thomas header which landed on top of the bar, which would have given him his hat-trick.

As it was, the Bluebirds broke away in injury time and Ken **GRIFFITHS** latched on to Macauley's astute pass to shoot home.

Scorers: Swansea Town (Thomas 2)
Cardiff City (Clarke 2, K.Griffiths 2)
Attendance: 3,500

Swansea lose keeper as Cardiff go nap

17th October 1942
West Wartime League

CARDIFF CITY 5 SWANSEA TOWN 0

Four goals down, Swansea Town had the misfortune of losing their goalkeeper just before the interval and seemed beyond recovery, but such was their spirit that they played better in the second half than the first!

It was all one-way traffic in the opening quarter of an hour and both Clarke and Moore hit the Swansea woodwork before the home side were awarded a rather dubious penalty - the ball hitting Richards on his shoulder! Nevertheless, the impressive George **WRIGHT** tucked the ball past Herdman. The Bluebirds almost went 2-0 up moments later but Parker's shot hit the underside of the bar and was then rather hastily cleared upfield by Rogers. Cardiff eventually extended their lead on 27 minutes when **CLARKE** shot home from the edge of the area following good work by Moore. It was **MOORE** who put the home side 3-0 up on the half-hour mark, heading past Herdman as the Swansea defence appealed in vain for offside. **PARKER** netted a fourth in the 38th minute after playing a neat one-two with Moore, but then Cliff Herdman in the Swansea goal was accidentally caught by Wright as the Cardiff wing-half challenged for a high ball and was stretchered off.

In the second half, ten-men Swansea employed frequent use of the offside trap. This infuriated both the Cardiff players and the home fans who saw Roy **CLARKE** net his second and the Bluebirds' fifth goal near the end.

Scorers: Swansea Town (-)
Cardiff City (Clarke 2, Wright pen, Moore, Parker)
Attendance: 5,000

Bluebirds dominate but Swans win

25th December 1942
West Wartime League

SWANSEA TOWN 3 CARDIFF CITY 1

Though it was a match the Bluebirds dominated from the kick-off, Swansea ran out 3-1 winners, scoring in each of their only attacks of the game!

Cardiff almost went ahead in the fourth minute when Clarke outpaced the Swansea defence before crossing for Ken Griffiths to fire against Herdman's right-hand upright. Minutes later, Parker forced the Swansea keeper into making a good save at the foot of the post before a long-range shot from full-back Jones rattled the crossbar. Midway through the first half, Swansea, completely against the run of play, scored through **THOMAS** who fastened onto Payne's through-ball, drew McLoughlin and placed his shot low into the bottom right-hand corner of the Cardiff keeper's net.

The Bluebirds continued to create chances and from one of these just before half-time, Roy **CLARKE** cut inside his full-back and curled a shot into the top right-hand corner of Herdman's net.

The second half saw Cardiff hit the woodwork twice in the opening ten minutes through Parker and Wright before **READSHAW** gave the Swans the lead with a first-time shot from distance. With Cardiff going all out for the equaliser Lyn **THOMAS** netted his second goal of the game to put the Swans 3-1 up.

The Bluebirds almost pulled a goal back on the stroke of full time but Herdman saved well from Moore's header.

Scorers: Swansea Town (Thomas 2, Readshaw)
Cardiff City (Clarke)
Attendance: 2,500

Honours even in Boxing Day thriller

26th December 1942
League North Cup Qualifying Competition

CARDIFF CITY 2 SWANSEA TOWN 2

Cardiff had the better of the opening exchanges and both Parker and Wright went close with glancing headers from crosses by Griffiths. The Bluebirds were far more aggressive than the visitors and it seemed only a matter of time before they scored the game's opening goal.

However, midway through the first half, the Swans broke away to score in what was their first attack of the game. Readshaw's effort was kicked off the line by Sherwood but the ball fell to the unmarked **RICHARDS** who smashed it high into the roof of the net.

The goal, which was completely against the run of play stirred Cardiff and both Moore and Louie Ford forced the Swansea keeper into making good saves.

The Bluebirds levelled the scores in the 49th minute when Ken Griffiths made a run into the middle and passed to **PARKER**, who, taking the ball in his stride, scored a well-taken goal. A minute later, Griffiths had a goal disallowed for an infringement off the ball but shortly afterwards **WRIGHT** gave Cardiff the lead from a free-kick just outside the Swansea box.

Swansea pushed forward in search of an equaliser and, after coming close on a couple of occasions, **READSHAW** put the Swans on terms near the end.

Scorers: Swansea Town (Richards, Readshaw)
Cardiff City (Parker, Wright)
Attendance: 4,500

Missed penalty gifts Bluebirds victory

20th February 1943
League North Cup Qualifying Competition

SWANSEA TOWN 1 CARDIFF CITY 2

Both teams were strong in defence with Swansea's Tommy G. Jones at centre-half in outstanding form. The Everton and Wales defender, who was 'guesting' for the Swans, made two goal-line clearances in the opening quarter of an hour as Cardiff went in search of the game's first goal. Parker almost put the Bluebirds ahead in the 21st minute but his goalbound header was inadvertently diverted the wrong side of the post by Turner.

Cardiff took a deserved lead on the half-hour mark when a long ball out of defence by Bird found the unmarked **CLARKE** and he placed his shot wide of Herdman in the Swansea goal. On the stroke of half-time, the visitors went 2-0 up when full-back Jones, up for a corner, flicked the ball on for inside-left **DALY** to turn it into the net from close range.

The second half was only four minutes old when Payne and Lyn Thomas combined to set up Rogers, but he shot wide of the target when well placed. The Swans did pull a goal back after 58 minutes when **THOMAS** beat three Cardiff defenders in a mazy dribble before drilling the ball past McLoughlin. Payne too was causing the Cardiff defence problems and looked poised to level the scores when he had his feet pulled from under him. Rogers missed the resultant spot-kick and though, the home side continued to press forward in search of an equaliser, their forwards lacked cohesion and passes were apt to go astray.

Scorers: Swansea Town (Thomas)
Cardiff City (Clarke, Daly)
Attendance: 3,000

Sparshott double gives Bluebirds victory

6th March 1943
West Wartime League

CARDIFF CITY 2 SWANSEA TOWN 0

With both clubs unsuccessful in their qualifying League Cup games, the Bluebirds and the Swans met at Ninian Park to resume their League West games.Cardiff were the worthy winners and were on the offensive throughout, almost from the kick-off.

Hollyman was outstanding at half-back and his fine passes to the forwards were the beginning of many splendid movements. Clarke and Parker were unfortunate with early attempts and a little more steadiness in front of goal after their other efforts would have brought certain goals.

The Swansea goal had a charmed life under the heavy attacks and only hard work by Fisher and the alertness of Herdman in goal sent the Swans in at half-time on level terms.

Cardiff's heavy pressure was bound to tell on the hard-worked Swansea defence and, after coming close twice in the opening minutes of the second period through Clarke and Parker, **SPARSHOTT**, a newcomer to the City side, scored with a powerful header. **SPARSHOTT** netted his and Cardiff's second goal on the hour mark, cutting inside from the left and unleashing a tremendous drive that went in off Herdman's left-hand upright.

This was a very one-sided game and resulted in Cardiff's first home win of the year!

Scorers: Swansea Town (-)
Cardiff City (Sparshott 2)
Attendance: 4,500

Draw is fitting result

13th March 1943
West Wartime League

SWANSEA TOWN 1 CARDIFF CITY 1

A draw was a fitting result to this South Wales derby - the teams were evenly matched, both defences proving sound under pressure.

The home side had the better of the early exchanges and Fisher ought to have done better when put through by Lowrey. Having beaten the Cardiff offside trap, he only had Griffiths to beat but pulled his shot wide of the target. At the other end, a long range effort from Sergeant caught Herdman unawares, the ball bouncing free from his grasp to Moore, who shot into the side-netting. Chances were few and far between for the remainder of the first half but within two minutes of the restart, **LOWREY** had given Swansea the lead, heading home Wheatman's deep cross to the far post.

A fine movement involving Fisher and Lowrey ended with the latter's shot being headed off the line by Jones. As the second half wore on, Cardiff's half-backs began to link up with their forwards more effectively with the result that the visitors began to create more chances.

The equaliser, which was thoroughly deserved, came courtesy of Beriah **MOORE** who evaded Fisher's desperate lunge to shoot past Herdman. The Bluebirds could have sneaked it at the death but Sergeant miskicked with only Herdman to beat.

Scorers: Swansea Town (Lowrey)
Cardiff City (Moore)
Attendance: 3,000

Swansea reach final

24th April 1943
League Cup West

CARDIFF CITY 2 SWANSEA TOWN 5

By their surprise victory over Cardiff City at Ninian Park, Swansea Town qualified for the League (West) Cup Final to meet Lovells over two legs.

An amazing second half rally by the Swans, in which they netted five times after being two goals down, was the remarkable feature of this game.

The Swans did have a number of early chances but both Rogers and Comley wasted good opportunities. City then dominated the remainder of the first half and **MURPHY** gave them the lead on 18 minutes, cutting in from the right to score with a fine left-foot shot. The home side created opening after opening but due to the forwards' erratic shooting there was no further scoring in the first period.

Beriah **MOORE** extended Cardiff's lead soon after the interval with a downward header from Clarke's cross before **FORD** immediately reduced the deficit. After **ROGERS** had raced through to equalise, **COMLEY** gave Swansea the lead with a terrific drive from the edge of the box. It was now all Swansea and Evans cracked a shot against the crossbar from distance before **COMLEY** netted again, this time from close range. Cardiff's defence was now virtually non-existent and after the woodwork had come to their rescue on two occasions, **LOWREY** added a fifth goal just before the end.

Scorers: Swansea Town (Comley 2, Ford, Rogers, Lowrey)
Cardiff City (Murphy, Moore)
Attendance: 6,000

Williams treble in easy win

23rd October 1943
West Wartime League

CARDIFF CITY 5 SWANSEA TOWN 0

Cardiff continued on their winning path with a fine win over Swansea who - with the exception of their 'guest' player Dave McCulloch, the Derby County and Scottish international - were completely outplayed.

Having said that, the first chance of the game fell to the Swans but Comley completely mishit his shot after being put through by Jones.

The Bluebirds took the lead on 27 minutes when a pass from Wood paved the way for **WILLIAMS** to open the scoring. Five minutes later, Cardiff went 2-0 up when **MOORE** headed home Alf Sherwood's cross. **WILLIAMS** soon put the home side further ahead after the resumption before both Clarke and Moore missed golden opportunities to put the matter beyond doubt. As it was, on 72 minutes Clarke beat the Swansea full-back for pace and crossed to the far post where **WILLIAMS**, racing in on the blind side of the Swansea defence, completed his hat-trick.

Cardiff continued to press forward and looked likely to score every time they attacked. In one goalmouth scramble, Raybould was badly injured when diving to head Moore's cross and had to be stretchered off.

Just before the final whistle, **CLARKE** controlled Fred Stansfield's long upfield ball, beat two defenders and coolly slid the ball past the advancing Gow to complete the rout.

Scorers: Swansea Town (-)
Cardiff City (Williams 3, Moore, Clarke)
Attendance: 5,000

Action reminiscent of pre-war Cup-tie

30th October 1943
West Wartime League

SWANSEA TOWN 1 CARDIFF CITY 3

In a game that was always lively and interesting, the issue was in doubt until the closing stages when Cardiff scored twice within the last minute.

The Swans had a chance to take the lead before a minute had been played - Alf Sherwood's back-pass to goalkeeper Griffiths was underhit and, though Scrines beat Griffiths to the ball, he rolled his shot wide of the target.

Cardiff went ahead on 14 minutes when **MOORE** brought Sherwood's high ball into the area under control and hit a fantastic first time shot past Jack Parry. The Swansea keeper then saved well from Raybould before needing treatment after diving at the feet of winger Moore. The Bluebirds almost extended their lead on 43 minutes when Clarke's cross found the unmarked Moore but his header thudded against the bar.

Within minutes of the restart, Griffiths was beaten by **SCRINES**' dipping volley, hit with the outside of his left-foot from 30 yards - it was a wonderful goal.

The visitors rallied and Parry in the Swansea goal received lengthy treatment on the pitch after taking a kick in the head as he dived at the feet of the onrushing Moore.

It was **MOORE** who put Cardiff 2-1 up in the 89th minute with a well-taken free-kick. The Cardiff winger was eager to complete his hat-trick but unselfishly set up **RAYBOULD** for Cardiff's third goal when he so easily could have scored himself.

Scorers: Swansea Town (Scrines)
Cardiff City (Moore 2, Raybould)
Attendance: 3,000

Roy Clarke goal separates the teams

4th December 1943
West Wartime League

CARDIFF CITY 1 SWANSEA TOWN 0

A late goal secured a victory for Cardiff City and this did Swansea a little injustice, for the visitors were by far the better side.

Cardiff fielded a young side and it was they who had the better of the opening exchanges with both Clarke and Williams missing good chances. In fact, City's young forwards were inclined to crowd each other out in their eagerness to get on the scoresheet.

Swansea were most unfortunate not to take the lead on 32 minutes when, following a good move involving Davies and Rogers, Comley's shot struck the upright with Griffiths the Cardiff keeper rooted to the spot. Rogers too was unlucky to see his header beat Griffiths, but the ball landed on top of the bar before going behind for a goal-kick. Minutes before half-time, Stansfield cleared off the line from Davies and then the impressive Cardiff defender took the ball off Comley's toes as he shaped to shoot.

Early in the second half the Bluebirds were awarded a rather dubious penalty but Alf Sherwood drove his spot-kick well wide of the target.

Swansea came back strongly but their attack lacked punch in front of goal. A goalless draw seemed on the cards when with virtually the last kick of the game, **CLARKE**'s shot took a deflection off Davies to give the Bluebirds the most unlikeliest of victories.

Scorers: Swansea Town (-)
Cardiff City (Clarke)
Attendance: 4,500

Result in doubt in six-goal thriller

11th December 1943
West Wartime League

SWANSEA TOWN 2 CARDIFF CITY 4

Thanks to Swansea keeper Jack Parry, the result of this South Wales derby was in doubt until the last ten minutes.

Cardiff took the lead after nine minutes when **RAYBOULD** latched on to a loose ball on the edge of the area and beat Parry with a ground shot, which the Swansea keeper got his hands to but couldn't prevent crossing the line. The Bluebirds were on top for whole of the opening half an hour and only Parry prevented them from extending their lead. He beat out Stansfield's long-range shot and tipped a Williams' header over the bar.

Yet on 33 minutes, the Swans were level. **SCRINES** scored with a terrific cross-shot and only Griffiths in the Cardiff goal prevented them going in ahead at the interval when he bravely dived at the feet of Taylor as he shaped to shoot.

Swansea lost the services of J. Jones early in the second half with a badly gashed head and, though down to 10-men, they battled gamely until the 70th minute when **WILLIAMS** gave Cardiff the lead. **TAYLOR** equalised for Swansea within a minute and a draw looked the likeliest outcome until Cardiff scored a freak goal on 84 minutes.

Moore's corner-kick hit **RAYBOULD** on the back before entering the net! Swansea's defence then went to pieces in the few minutes that remained and **MOORE** snapped up Cardiff's fourth goal in the last minute following a brilliant save by Parry who could not hold a drive from Williams.

Scorers: Swansea Town (Scrines, Taylor)
Cardiff City (Raybould 2, Williams, Moore)
Attendance: 4,000

Moore hat-trick in Cardiff's biggest win of season

8th January 1944
League North Cup Qualifying Competition

CARDIFF CITY 7 SWANSEA TOWN 1

Cardiff gained their biggest win of the season against Swansea and, though their display on the whole did not merit the high scoring, they were a far more speedier and thrustful side than Swansea.

Cardiff took the lead after 22 minutes when, following some fine interpassing by Carless and Williams, **MOORE** curled his shot wide of Jack Parry's despairing dive and into the net off the far post. Three minutes later, Cardiff were 2-0 up when **WOOD** gained possession of a loose ball and ran through to beat Parry. The home side piled on the pressure and both Moore and Rees hit the woodwork before Sherwood's long-range shot was turned round the post by Parry.

Soon after the start of the second half, **SHERWOOD** put Cardiff further ahead from the penalty spot after Carless had been bowled over when clean through. The Bluebirds looked like scoring every time they attacked and though their approach play lacked skill, they scored four goals in the space of a quarter of an hour.

WOOD headed home an Alf Sherwood free-kick in the 73rd minute, whilst a minute later **REES** found himself unmarked at the far post to side-foot Moore's deep cross past Parry. There were just ten minutes remaining when **MOORE** chipped Parry from 30 yards and then after 88 minutes **CARLESS** dribbled through the non-existent Swansea defence for Cardiff's seventh goal.

Swansea's consolation goal came in the final minute when the unmarked **COMLEY** lobbed the ball over the on-rushing McLoughlin.

Scorers: Swansea Town (Comley)
Cardiff City (Moore 3, Wood, Sherwood pen, Rees, Carless)
Attendance: 6,000

Pitch invasion mars game

15th January 1944
League North Cup Qualifying Competition

SWANSEA TOWN 1 CARDIFF CITY 2

Though there has always been football of high tension between the two South Wales clubs, it has been a long time since there was such unruly football as this wartime meeting brought.

Quite early in the game, players on both sides were apt to be reckless in their tackling and too often played the man rather than the ball. Perhaps they were incited by the behaviour of the crowd, a small section of which at one period invaded the pitch, while at another time one of the Swansea supporters ran on to challenge Cardiff defender Fred Stansfield. Thankfully, the storm which always threatened to break was fortunately averted.

Swansea took the lead as early as the fifth minute when **CORBETT** scored with a rising shot from the edge of the area. The home side wasted a couple of goalscoring opportunities before **REES** equalised for Cardiff just before the interval, heading home a Carless cross.

The game was scrappy but what football was played in the second half came from Cardiff, who controlled the second forty-five minutes from start to finish. Only four minutes of the second half had been played when **WOOD** put the Bluebirds ahead with an angled shot.

After this, except for occasional Swansea raids, it was nearly all Cardiff with Carless making many good openings which Rees, Williams and Wood all wasted with the goal at their mercy.

Scorers: Swansea Town (Corbett)
Cardiff City (Rees, Wood)
Attendance: 3,500

Gibson hat-trick gives Bluebirds comfortable win

22nd April 1944
League North Second Competition

SWANSEA TOWN 2 CARDIFF CITY 4

Superior in speed, stamina and skill, Cardiff City were comfortable winners of their game with Swansea Town at the Vetch Field.

GIBSON opened the scoring for the visitors after nine minutes when he headed Lester's cross into the roof of the net. After that, the much-changed Swansea team never at any moment suggested that they could match the Bluebirds.

Yet despite attacking non-stop for the remainder of the first half there was no further scoring when the half-time whistle sounded. This was down to the hard work of goalkeeper Gow and centre-half Corbett and a fantastic goal-line clearance by Tabram.

Nothing had been seen of Swansea's attack in the first half yet within five minutes of the restart, they were 2-1 ahead. **PASSMORE** pounced on a handling error by Cardiff goalkeeper Griffiths before the referee awarded the Swans a direct free-kick on the corner of the box. **PASSMORE's** kick hit the wall and looped over Griffiths' head for the home side's second goal.

GIBSON the Cardiff right-winger then levelled the scores with a fine individual goal, beating three defenders before shooting past Gow. A minute later **GIBSON**, in giving Cardiff the lead, completed his hat-trick with a fine shot from an acute angle. He had been a persistent worry to Swansea's hard-worked defence and in the closing stages it was he who was brought down just outside the area, allowing **LESTER** to score Cardiff's fourth goal from the resultant free-kick.

Gibson almost had a fourth goal in injury-time when his free-kick, awarded against Gow for handling outside the area, hit the bar.

Scorers: Swansea Town (Passmore 2)
Cardiff City (Gibson 3, Lester)
Attendance: 3,500

Theatrical referee provides chief entertainment

29th April 1944
League North Second Competition

CARDIFF CITY 3 SWANSEA TOWN 1

A rather theatrical but otherwise efficient referee provided the chief entertainment at Ninian Park as a mediocre Cardiff City beat a poor Swansea side.

There was certainly an end-of-season flavour about the match, but there was compensation for the Bluebirds and their supporters by their win as Cardiff qualified to meet Bath City in the final of the West Cup over two legs.

Cardiff did most of the attacking in the opening stages of the game and came close on a number of occasions to opening the scoring. As it was, they had to wait until the 37th minute before **REES** gave them the lead, fastening on to Gibson's measured pass and shooting hard and low past the advancing Gow.

The home side extended their lead midway through the second half when Fred Stansfield's long shot came back off the post and **REES** pounced for his and Cardiff's second goal. Gibson, who netted a hat-trick at the Vetch in the last meeting between the clubs, shot into the side-netting before **CARLESS** put the result beyond doubt with a well-placed shot from just inside the area.

Little had been seen of Swansea as an attacking force but they did net a consolation goal a minute from time. The referee adjudged that Jones had handled in the area and **PASSMORE** stepped up to send Griffiths the wrong way.

Scorers: Swansea Town (Passmore pen)
Cardiff City (Rees 2, Carless)
Attendance: 5,500

Jepson's heroics can't stop Cardiff

21st October 1944
West Wartime League

CARDIFF CITY 3 SWANSEA TOWN 2

Cardiff attacked from the off and for the first ten minutes they began a barrage of assaults on the Swansea goal. Chance after chance went begging as poor finishing let them down.

However, on 16 minutes **WOOD** opened the scoring for the Bluebirds with a fine shot into the far corner and, two minutes later, **CLARKE** headed home Fred Stansfield's cross. The Swansea defence was at sixes and sevens and on 23 minutes, Beriah **MOORE** outpaced Fisher to shoot past Jepson and put the Bluebirds 3-0 up.

Cardiff looked like scoring on a number of other occasions in a one-sided first half but Arthur Jepson in the Swansea goal made a string of fine saves. The best of them saw the Nottinghamshire cricketer twist in mid-air to turn Terry Wood's deflected shot over the bar.

The second half was a complete contrast to the first as Swansea came out fighting. A reckless challenge on Daniels as he burst through the Cardiff defence resulted in the Swans being awarded a penalty which Roy **PAUL** put away. The second half was barely five minutes old when the visitors netted a second. **BURNS** outpaced Lester and lifted the ball over the advancing Smith. Swansea then went in search of an equaliser and should have drawn level when Fisher found himself completely unmarked with just Smith to beat but he delayed his shot, allowing the Cardiff keeper to smother his effort. With the full-time whistle looming, Paul's free-kick from distance struck the foot of the post.

Scorers: Swansea Town (Paul pen, Burns)
Cardiff City (Wood, Clarke, Moore)
Attendance: 5,000

Ragged Swans well beaten

28th October 1944
West Wartime League

SWANSEA TOWN 0 CARDIFF CITY 4

Cardiff's superior marksmanship made all the difference in their game with Swansea at the Vetch Field. Play was at times fast and furious with both sides bringing off some excellent moves, but Swansea's finishing was ragged and uncertain whereas Cardiff's forwards certainly knew where the goal was.

The Bluebirds front-line combined well from the word 'go' with Rees, Gibson and Wood all having goalscoring opportunities in the opening quarter of an hour. Cardiff eventually took the lead in the 20th minute when **CLARKE**, receiving the ball from Lester, cut inside Fisher before unleashing a powerful left-foot drive past Jepson.

Just before the interval, Cardiff doubled their lead when Terry **WOOD** headed home a Lewis cross, the ball entering the net off the underside of the bar. Swansea's best chance of the first half fell to Burns but he blazed wide from just six yards out.

Early in the second half, **CLARKE** was on the end of Rees' delicately-placed through-ball and steered it wide of Jepson. **REES** then made it 4-0 with a fine individual goal, beating three Swansea defenders before rounding the keeper and sliding the ball into an empty net.

The Swans did have a couple of chances to reduce the arrears but both Phillips and Allen wasted the opportunities.

Scorers: Swansea Town (-)
Cardiff City (Clarke 2, Wood, Rees)
Attendance: 4,000

Well-deserved victory for Bluebirds

2nd December 1944
West Wartime League

SWANSEA TOWN 1 CARDIFF CITY 3

Cardiff City's pace, teamwork and stamina gave them a well-deserved victory in a game which contained more vigour than finesse, particularly in the second half when play deteriorated into a display of shirt pulling and over-the-top tackling!

Swansea had the encouragement of an early goal when **ALLEN** scored a well-worked goal after good play by Jones and Fisher. Although Cardiff's Terry **WOOD** took advantage of a defensive mistake to equalise in the fifth minute, the Swans remained the more impressive side in midfield but lacked the subtlety to outwit the Cardiff defence in which Stansfield and Lever were outstanding.

The home side's first half promise was not maintained after the interval when Cardiff, playing with the confidence of league leaders, frequently had Swansea's defence all at sea.

Beriah **MOORE** gave Cardiff the lead in the 57th minute, heading home Lever's cross and, ten minutes later, **R. MOORE** made the issue certain by scoring direct from a corner-kick.

Swansea staged a late recovery, during which Cardiff keeper Smith made a couple of good saves from Jones and Fisher. Dimond also went close for the home side but his header landed on the roof of the net. Yet in the last minute, Wood almost netted a fourth for Cardiff - only a brave save by Swansea's debutant goalkeeper Tom Gilchrist prevented him from doing so.

Scorers: Swansea Town (Allen)
Cardiff City (Wood, B.Moore, R.Moore)
Attendance: 3,500

Gilchrist prevents rout

9th December 1944
West Wartime League

CARDIFF CITY 3 SWANSEA TOWN 1

Swansea gave Cardiff quite a shock in this Ninian Park encounter when they took the lead a minute before the interval. Prior to that, the visitors had played much the better football and created a number of goalscoring opportunities which Jones and Eastman in particular had wasted. However, it was these two Swansea forwards who created the goal - Jones, cutting in from the left, beat two Cardiff defenders before laying the ball into the path of **EASTMAN** and his first time shot rocketed past Smith.

Gilchrist in the Swansea goal had a fine game. Early in the second half he saved shots from all angles and always came out on top in goalmouth action. At one time it looked as if he was going to win the match single-handedly for the Swans but in the 76th minute Roy **CLARKE** beat him with a header from Gibson's corner.

Then Cardiff were awarded a penalty for what appeared to be a fair tackle - the referee adjudged otherwise and **WOOD** gave them the lead from the spot. In Cardiff's next attack, **REES** scrambled the ball over the line after Gilchrist appeared to be held down by a Bluebirds forward.

Cardiff were now rampant and only Gilchrist with a fine reflex save from a Wood header prevented them from extending their lead.

Scorers: Swansea Town (Eastman)
Cardiff City (Clarke, Wood pen, Rees)
Attendance: 5,000

Cardiff City crowned champions

25th December 1944
North Cup Qualifying Competition

CARDIFF CITY 3 SWANSEA TOWN 1

On Christmas Eve, Cardiff City, despite losing at home to Lovells, won the League West Championship on goal average from Bristol City. This Christmas Day fixture against Swansea was a Cup game and though the Bluebirds were firm favourites, they only won after a hard struggle.

Cardiff had plenty of the early play and Gibson's fine run and cross led to Clarke firing into the side-netting. Both Clarke and Wood went close with headers before Gilchrist saved well from Gibson. The Bluebirds took the lead on 31 minutes when **WOOD** hooked his shot wide of Gilchrist after being set up by Lever. The home side continued to dominate proceedings and extended their lead just before half time with a quite remarkable goal. They were awarded a free-kick fully 40 yards from the Swansea goal. Arthur **LEVER** shot hard, the ball still rising as it passed Tom Gilchrist's despairing dive.

Swansea pulled a goal back just after the interval when **ALLEN**, the visitors' most impressive forward, scored from an acute angle.

Cardiff though came back well and both Rees and Clarke had shots charged down before Gilchrist saved well from Gibson. Swansea were always dangerous on the break but with just four minutes remaining, **CLARKE** scored a third for Cardiff and so sealed their victory.

Scorers: Swansea Town (Allen)
Cardiff City (Wood, Lever, Clarke)
Attendance: 8,000

Bluebirds are worthy winners

30th December 1944
North Cup Qualifying Competition

SWANSEA TOWN 1 CARDIFF CITY 3

The Vetch Field was more like a skating rink than a football field for this Cup match but despite the slippery conditions, both sides created a host of chances.

Trevor Ford had an early opportunity to open the scoring for the Swans, but Stansfield's interception as the Swansea centre-forward shaped to shoot saved the day. Allen too came close for the home side but his shot skidded inches past Smith's right-hand post. At the other end, Clarke was well tackled by Briddon when it seemed he would score and Corbett headed Wood's shot off the line with Gilchrist beaten. Cardiff went ahead after 36 minutes when **REES** played a neat one-two with Moore before placing the ball wide of the advancing Swansea keeper.

ALLEN was Swansea's most dangerous forward and it was he who levelled the scores five minutes later. He met Trevor Ford's cushioned header with a powerful right-foot volley that flew past Smith.

Moore and Clarke had shots well saved by Gilchrist before **CLARKE** beat Briddon to Stansfield's through ball to fire the Bluebirds ahead. There were just five minutes remaining when Terry **WOOD** ran through unchallenged to complete the scoring and, though at the other end Ford went down in the box after a clumsy challenge by Lever, the referee deemed it a fair one.

Scorers: Swansea Town (Allen)
Cardiff City (Rees, Clarke, Wood)
Attendance: 4,000

Last minute winner for Swansea

10th March 1945
League West Cup

SWANSEA TOWN 1 CARDIFF CITY 0

A last minute goal gave Swansea Town victory in this first round match in the League West Cup competition after a game in which there was plenty of action and thrills.

The Swans had a shock prior to the kick-off when their goalkeeper Tom Gilchrist was forced to withdraw because of injury. He was replaced by Billy Corbett, the Swansea defender who had been outstanding in recent meetings between the two clubs.

Cardiff hit the woodwork twice in the opening exchanges as first Lester and then Phillips beat Corbett with shots from the edge of the area. It seemed only a matter of time before the visitors opened the scoring, but the Swansea defence in which Lewis and Fisher were having good games held firm.

Swansea winger Jones was beginning to cause the Bluebirds defence all sorts of problems and from one of his pin-point crosses, Comley fired inches over the bar. The home side were now coming into the game more and only a last-ditch tackle by Arthur Lever prevented Burns from giving them the lead.

Though Cardiff had been more thrustful in attack, their finishing was poor and they were made to pay in the 90th minute when Frank **BURNS**, who for most of the match had been well-shackled by Stansfield, fastened on to Comley's pass and shot past Smith to give the Swans a dramatic win.

Scorers: Swansea Town (Burns)
Cardiff City (-)
Attendance: 3,500

'Youth Day' at Ninian Park

17th March 1945
League West Cup

CARDIFF CITY 6 SWANSEA TOWN 2

It was 'Youth Day' and Mrs Winston Churchill, in her capacity as wartime president of the YWCA, graced the game with her presence and appealed to Cardiff's sportsmen to join in the city's £10,000 fund for the YWCA.

Cardiff City and Swansea Town each fielded a side dominated by youth for this League West Cup second-leg tie.

The Bluebirds took the lead after nine minutes when **LESTER** surprised everyone - friend and foe alike - with a perfectly judged free-kick, a yard outside the box. Then **REES**, the home side's strong and speedy centre-forward, extended Cardiff's lead with a close-range header. Midway through the first half, **REES** just beat Corbett to Gibson's through-ball and toe-poked the ball into the empty net. A minute later, Corbett was hurt in a challenge with the Cardiff No.9 and had to leave the field for treatment. His replacement, Norman, was soon called into action to save from Gibson but just before half time, **REES** completed his hat-trick to give the Bluebirds a 4-0 lead at the interval.

Corbett returned for the second half with his thigh heavily strapped but it was his opposite number Smith who was first in action. He brought down Allen as he ran through on goal and from the resultant spot-kick, **BURNS** reduced the arrears. Then **REES** scored his fourth goal of the game. He brought the ball under control and shot in one movement to restore Cardiff's four-goal lead. The Bluebirds scored a sixth after 84 minutes when Colin **GIBSON** cut in from the right and shot under Corbett's body. Still, Swansea were not finished and **BURNS** added a consolation goal with a well-hit shot from 25 yards.

Scorers: Swansea Town (Burns 2 - 1 pen)
Cardiff City (Rees 4, Lester, Gibson)
Attendance: 7,000

Cardiff hold on in seven-goal thriller

16th August 1945
Friendly

CARDIFF CITY 4 SWANSEA TOWN 3

Both teams entered into the 'VJ' spirit by throwing caution to the wind in one of the most entertaining games between these two South Wales rivals.

Cardiff came close to scoring in the opening minute of the game but Lester's shot rattled the bar with Norman well beaten. It didn't take long for the home side to open the scoring for, four minutes later, **CARLESS** headed home Clarke's pin-point cross. The Bluebirds attacked incessantly throughout the first period but their second goal didn't arrive until the 40th minute when **REES** latched on to a fine through-ball by Lester and chipped it over the advancing Swansea keeper. **REES** netted his second goal on the stroke of half-time, steering Gibson's pass wide of Norman to give the Bluebirds a 3-0 lead at half-time.

The second half was only minutes old when **CARLESS** scored the home side's fourth goal. There seemed no way back for the Swans but, midway through the half, they scored three goals in quick succession. Trevor **FORD** headed the first off the underside of the bar in the 63rd minute and then, seconds later, **FORD** bundled the ball over the line in a goalmouth scramble. There were still twenty minutes to play when Swansea pressure forced **WOOD** to inadvertently steer a back pass wide of his keeper for the visitors' third goal.

The Swans went in search of a fourth goal that would have given them a share of the spoils, but Ford was denied a hat-trick by an outstanding save from Cardiff keeper Smith in the last minute of the game.

Scorers: Swansea Town (Ford 2, Wood og)
Cardiff City (Carless 2, Rees 2)
Attendance: 6,000

Bluebirds scrape Home

27th August 1949
Football League Division 2

CARDIFF CITY 1 SWANSEA TOWN 0

The visit of Swansea Town attracted a record crowd of 57,510 to Ninian Park, The Swans, under the guidance of Billy McCandless, had been promoted as champions of the Third Division (South).

For the second time within a week the Bluebirds scraped home by the only goal of the match and, while their play against Swansea did not come up to the standard of that displayed against Sheffield Wednesday, they still deserved their victory.

Swansea had the better of the early play, their football being much more methodical and attractive than that of the home side. Indeed, the Swansea attacks in the first half always threatened to bring a goal and the genius of Lucas was much in evidence. Quick recoveries by Montgomery and Lever in particular got City out of many an awkward predicament. Sadly for Swansea, they lost Rory Keane with a knee injury and once down to 10-men, they faded from the game.

The Bluebirds attacked at will after the break with Stevenson hitting an upright and Blair the side-netting before Canning saved well from Edwards. The goal that Cardiff had been threatening to score since the second-half got underway came on 74 minutes when Tommy **BEST** headed Edward's corner into the roof of the net. It was thought this would open the floodgates but that wasn't so and Swansea came close to snatching a point in the closing stages when O'Driscoll outjumped both Sherwood and Lever to send a header inches over the bar.

SWANSEA TOWN: L.Canning, J.Feaney, R.Keane, R.Paul, R.Weston, F.Burns, J.O'Driscoll, S.McCrory, S.Richards, W.Lucas, F.Scrine.
CARDIFF CITY: P.Joslin, A.Lever, A.Sherwood, G.Williams, S.Montgomery, W.Baker, K.Hollyman, D.Blair, T.Best, E.Stevenson, G.Edwards.

Scorers: Swansea Town (-)
Cardiff City (Best)
Attendance: 57,510

Paul inspires Swans to record League win

24th December 1949
Football League Division 2

SWANSEA TOWN 5 CARDIFF CITY 1

Swansea's record crowd for a league meeting with rivals Cardiff City on Christmas Eve saw a game that will be remembered for a very long time. The Bluebirds, with several injured players, switched their attack to include the two Stitfalls at outside-right and centre-forward whilst Swansea made one change, Elwell replacing the unwell Feeney.

Both sides attacked vigorously in the first few minutes and Swansea forced the first corner, which was cleared by Montgomery and Sherwood. Roy Paul's brilliance led to Swansea's opening goal after six minutes. He centred accurately to Joslin who failed to hold the ball. **LUCAS,** following up, put it in the net. Swansea's second goal came in the 20th minute. Keane put in a long shot which appeared to be going wide, but Richards diverted the ball to **McCRORY** who drove it into the corner of the net, giving Joslin no chance. Cardiff pulled a goal back on 31 minutes but it was a 'gift'. Canning had done the hard work by saving Stevenson's shot but he then dropped the ball at the feet of Ron **STITFALL**, who calmly side-footed it into the empty net. The robust and energetic leader, whose determination worried Weston, thoroughly deserved his goal.

The second half was only six minutes old when Irish international winger John **O'DRISCOLL** cut in from the right and curled a left-foot shot into Joslin's top right-hand corner of the net. The Swans went further ahead after 70 minutes when Billy **LUCAS** scored his second goal of the match following good approach play by Beech and McCrory. Roy Paul was having an outstanding game and he came close to scoring five minutes later, but his powerful drive was held at the second attempt by Joslin.

Cardiff had no answer to the repeated onslaughts of the Swans and with just four minutes remaining, **O'DRISCOLL** completed the scoring from close range.

This meeting of the Welsh rivals brought into opposition several Welsh internationals but none stood out like Swansea wing-half Roy Paul, who had a brilliant game.

SWANSEA TOWN: L.Canning, T.Elwell, R.Keane, R.Paul ,R.Weston, F.Burns, J.O'Driscoll, S.McCrory, S.Richards, W.Lucas, C.Beech.
CARDIFF CITY: P.Joslin, A.Lever, A.Sherwood, W.Baker, S.Montgomery, D.Blair, A.Stitfall, R.Williams, R.Stitfall, E.Stevenson, G.Edwards.

Scorers: Swansea Town (Lucas 2, McCrory 2, O'Driscoll)
Cardiff City (R.Stitfall)
Attendance: 27,264

City's errors gift
Swans three goals

23rd February 1950
Welsh Cup 7th Round

SWANSEA TOWN 3 CARDIFF CITY 0

In a match which reached a remarkably high standard considering the appalling conditions, Swansea thoroughly deserved to make further progress in the Welsh Cup competition, for they adapted to the difficult going far better than Cardiff.

Oddly enough, the best Swansea movements did not produce goals and it was defensive errors by the Bluebirds defence which let Swansea through on three occasions.

The Swans took the lead in the 14th minute when **RICHARDS** got possession in what looked like an offside position and his shot entered the net off Joslin's right-hand post. Shortly before half-time **SCRINE,** left completely unmarked at the far post, headed home Swansea's second goal. Swansea could have had a third on the stroke of half-time but Cardiff keeper Joslin turned Sam McCrory's header over the bar.

There is no doubt that Cardiff were missing Alf Sherwood, though his replacement Ken Devonshire was playing well. Swansea extended their lead even further on 61 minutes when **SCRINE** fired home from the edge of the box. Stan Richards almost netted a fourth a minute later but Joslin dived low to his right to turn the ball round the post.

By now the pitch was a quagmire and this played a part in Stevenson not getting on the scoresheet in the final minute. His shot beat Canning but stuck in the mud on the goal-line, so allowing the Swansea keeper to recover!

SWANSEA TOWN: L.Canning, J.Feeney, R.Keane, R.Paul, R.Weston, F.Burns, J.O'Driscoll, S.McCrory, S.Richards, W.Lucas, F.Scrine.
CARDIFF CITY: P.Joslin, R.Stitfall, K.Devonshire, K.Hollyman, S.Montgomery, W.Baker, A.Lever, E.Evans, D.Blair, E.Stevenson, G.Edwards.

Scorers: Swansea Town (Richards, Scrine 2)
Cardiff City (-)
Attendance: 10,000

Disputed penalty gifts Swansea the point

4th November 1950
Football League Division 2

SWANSEA TOWN 1 CARDIFF CITY 0

While Swansea Town certainly deserved the two points, they were decidedly lucky to have been awarded the penalty which brought the vital goal. It was not surprising that Cardiff City centre-half Stan Montgomery protested strongly when the referee pointed to the spot!

Cardiff's first attack of the game after six minutes saw Edwards outpace Roberts and cross to the near post where Grant beat Weston to the ball, his header grazing the bar. The Bluebirds were on top and both Hollyman and Blair came close with first-time shots before Jack Parry in the Swansea goal saved Edwards' free-kick.

The penalty awarded to Swansea came midway through the first half. Montgomery emerged from a goalmouth melee with the ball when it popped up suddenly to strike his hand. It was most certainly a harsh decision but **LUCAS** put the ball into the bottom right-hand corner of Morris' goal as the Cardiff keeper went the other way.

After this, the home side gradually got on top although they rarely looked like scoring further goals. Ivor Allchurch, who was due to make his international debut the following week, was having a fine game. The future 'Golden Boy' of Welsh soccer was clean through on goal after 70 minutes but Morris dived bravely at his feet. As a result of this, the Cardiff keeper had to receive lengthy treatment before he could continue.

He was obviously in a lot of pain but the Swansea forwards failed to put him under any pressure and, as a result, a dubious penalty separated the teams.

SWANSEA TOWN: J.Parry, J.Roberts, G.Beech, W.Lucas, R.Weston, D.Williams, J.O'Driscoll, D.Thomas, S.Howarth, I.Allchurch, C.Beech.
CARDIFF CITY: E.Morris, R.Stitfall, A.Sherwood, R.McLaughlin, S.Montgomery, K.Hollyman, R.Williams, W.Grant, G.Williams, D.Blair, G.Edwards.

Scorers: Swansea Town (Lucas pen)
Cardiff City (-)
Attendance: 26,224

City hold Swans Rally

24th March 1951
Football League Division 2

CARDIFF CITY 1 SWANSEA TOWN 0

Cardiff City were certainly made to fight hard for their solitary-goal victory over Swansea and as a result, the Bluebirds occupied second place in Division Two.

The home side had by far the better of the opening half when they had the wind in their favour but after the interval, the Swans fought back well and only two outstanding saves by Joslin in the last ten minutes prevented them sharing the points.

A high wind interfered with play to a great extent and as a result, the game wasn't the spectacle the 41,074 crowd hoped for.

With the Bluebirds on the fringe of promotion they went all out for an early goal and McLaughlin and Grant both saw their efforts turned away by King. Swansea's only threat in the opening quarter of an hour came when Howarth tried his luck from distance, the ball bouncing over both Joslin and the crossbar!

The all-important goal came after 16 minutes when **MARCHANT** hit the ball home from close range following a cross from the left by George Edwards. Cardiff could have doubled their lead on 27 minutes when Tiddy's cross held up in the wind, allowing Grant to outjump both Lucas and Weston, but his header passed inches outside King's left-hand post.

In the second half Swansea were more of an attacking force and Allchurch and Turnbull almost levelled the scores, but their efforts were well held by Joslin. The Swans played far better than their lowly league position but just couldn't quite do enough to share the points.

SWANSEA TOWN: J.King, I.Symmons, G.Beech, W.Lucas, R.Weston, D.Williams, S.Howarth, D.Thomas, R.Turnbull, I.Allchurch, C.Beech.
CARDIFF CITY: P.Joslin, G.Williams, A.Sherwood, K.Hollyman, S.Montgomery, W.Baker, M.Tiddy ,M.Marchant, W.Grant, R.McLaughlin, G.Edwards.

Scorers: Swansea Town (-)
Cardiff City (Marchant)
Attendance: 41,074

Dramatic own goal earns Swans a point

25th December 1951
Football League Division 2

SWANSEA TOWN 1 CARDIFF CITY 1

This Christmas Day encounter at the Vetch, the first meeting between the clubs in a season which saw Cardiff win promotion to the First Division, ended all-square thanks to a Billy Baker own goal in the closing stages of the game.

The high-flying Bluebirds began brightly, winning a corner in the first minute but the Swans cleared without any difficulty. Weston then conceded a free-kick a few yards outside the penalty area to stop Grant but as the ball was floated over the Swansea 'wall', Williams was flagged offside.

Swansea' first real attack came down the left but Hughes comfortably saved Allchurch's shot. Turnbull looked dangerous for the Swans and he hit a low drive which the Cardiff keeper had to push round the post.

At the other end, Blair, taking possession just inside the Swansea half, played a quick one-two with Tiddy, the winger crossing the ball for Blair to head narrowly wide. Cardiff took the lead after 19 minutes when Blair returned the earlier favour, crossing for Mike **TIDDY** to head the ball into the top right-hand corner of King's goal.

Williams was unlucky not to get a penalty, being brought down a yard outside the box by Keane, who received a caution from the referee. Cardiff continued to dominate the first half and Edwards was only inches away with a powerfully struck free-kick.

Early in the second half, Cardiff keeper Iorwerth Hughes was injured when diving at the feet of Bellis and had to receive lengthy treatment. He was obviously in some distress and both Sherwood and Montgomery came to his rescue as the Swans went in search of an equaliser. The Bluebirds were now up against it as the Swans attacked at will. Despite all their pressure, it seemed as though Cardiff would hold out for two vital points until Billy **BAKER** misplaced a back-pass to the hobbling Hughes to 'gift' the home side a deserved equaliser.

SWANSEA TOWN: J.King, R.Keane, G.Beech, W.Lucas, R.Weston, D.Williams, C.Beech, F.Scrine, R.Turnbull ,I.Allchurch, A.Bellis.
CARDIFF CITY: I.Hughes, G.Williams, A.Sherwood ,W.Baker, S.Montgomery, R.McLaughlin, M.Tiddy, D.Blair, W.Grant, R.Williams, G.Edwards.

Scorers: Swansea Town (W.Baker og)
Cardiff City (Tiddy)
Attendance: 19,260

City go top!

26th December 1951
Football League Division 2

CARDIFF CITY 3 SWANSEA TOWN 0

With four goals from their two holiday games with Swansea Town, Cardiff City collected three points and went to the top of the Second Division.

In keeping with the Boxing Day opening of pantomime, the Bluebirds produced a star performer in 24-year-old goalkeeper Ron Howells, who made a great impression on the 46,000 crowd at Ninian Park. Deputising for Welsh international Iorwerth Hughes, who failed to recover from the Christmas Day injury at the Vetch Field, Howells filled the spotlight at this second holiday derby.

Howells, who had an outstanding game in keeping Swansea's forwards at bay, joined Cardiff from Barry Town, though three years earlier he was on Swansea's books before being given a free transfer!

Cardiff's Billy **BAKER** fully atoned for his Christmas Day own goal when he opened the scoring after nine minutes, with a magnificent 25-yard drive. The home side continued to dominate the game up to half-time and both Tiddy and Blair went close before **GRANT** extended the Bluebirds lead on the stroke of half-time with a well-placed header.

Howell made a couple of acrobatic saves early in the second half before saving point-blank shots from Turnbull and Allchurch. Blair and Sullivan then combined to send Mike **TIDDY** away and he drew King before slipping the ball under his body and into the net off the far post.

SWANSEA TOWN: J.King, R.Keane, G.Beech, W.Lucas, R.Weston, D.Williams, C.Beech, F.Scrine, R.Turnbull, I.Allchurch, A.Bellis, **CARDIFF CITY:** R.Howells, C.Rutter, G.Williams, W.Baker ,S.Montgomery, R.McLaughlin, M.Tiddy, D.Blair, W.Grant, D.Sullivan, G.Edwards

Scorers: Swansea Town (-)
Cardiff City (Baker, Grant, Tiddy)
Attendance: 46,003

Ten-man Bluebirds hang on in grandstand finish

30th April 1956
Welsh Cup Final

CARDIFF CITY 3 SWANSEA TOWN 2

Cardiff and Swansea met in the Welsh Cup Final at Ninian Park where a crowd of 37,500 - the biggest in the history of the competition - saw the Bluebirds win 3-2. Tragedy struck City inside-forward Hitchens in the first-half when he was stretchered off with a broken leg.

At the time of the accident, Cardiff were leading through a 13th minute goal by winger Brian **WALSH** who cut in from the right and curled in a left-foot shot well out of the reach of the diving Johnny King.

In the 39th minute, a full ten minutes after being reduced to ten men, Cardiff went 2-0 up when Walsh's pin-point cross was headed home by John **McSEVENEY**. The Bluebirds were fighting heroically and were unlucky not to extend their lead on the stroke of half-time when Trevor Ford's shot hit the foot of the post before being cleared upfield.

Two minutes after the restart, **WALSH** did net a third for Cardiff though there were suspicions of offside.

Swansea then began to take control and reduced the arrears after 78 minutes through a powerful header from centre-half Tom **KILEY**. The Swans fought desperately to make good the two-goal deficit. Mel Charles and Cliff Jones hit the woodwork whilst Des Palmer and Ivor Allchurch shot straight into goalkeeper Graham Vearncombe's waiting arms.

The Swans did score a second goal during injury-time when centre-forward Des **PALMER** headed Cliff Jones' cross into the net off the underside of the bar.

There had been numerous stoppages for injury in this fiery battle and though almost seven minutes extra-time was played, Cardiff held on to record their first Welsh Cup triumph for 26 years.

SWANSEA TOWN: J.King, A.Willis, D.Thomas, M.Charles, T.Kiley, B.Jones, L.Allchurch, H.Griffiths, D.Palmer, I.Allchurch, C.Jones.
CARDIFF CITY: G.Vearncombe, R.Stitfall, D.Sullivan, A.Harrington, D.Malloy, C.Baker, B.Walsh, H.Kirtley, T.Ford, G.Hitchens, J.McSeveney.

Scorers: Swansea Town (Kiley, Palmer)
Cardiff City (Walsh 2, McSeveney)
Attendance: 37,500

Opening day derby ends goalless

24th August 1957
Football League Division 2

CARDIFF CITY 0 SWANSEA TOWN 0

Swansea visited Ninian Park for the opening game of the 1957-58 season with a side full of Welsh internationals - yet a crowd of over 42,000 sun-soaked spectators saw the teams play out a goalless draw.

The Swans were seeking their first Ninian Park victory over the Bluebirds and their first Football League goal in six visits to the ground - and for the first twenty minutes or so they looked like clinching both ambitions with a runaway win.

Then, after there had been misses by twinkle-toed winger Cliff Jones, the hue and cry gave way to a tit-for-tat attitude, which would have cost them the game had Hitchens, Tucker and Hewitt been luckier with first-rate shots.

Man-for-man the Swansea attack was probably the best in the Second Division but on this occasion they lost the poise of their approach the moment the target was in sight. Ivor Allchurch had the best chance of the first half but, with only Vearncombe to beat, the ankle he damaged last season buckled beneath him and the chance had gone.

In the second half, Swansea had far more scoring opportunities - Allchurch had a header tipped over the bar by Vearncombe, Harry Griffiths had a shot cleared off the line by Rutter and Mel Charles outjumped Malloy to head against the bar. Graham Vearncombe in the Cardiff goal had an outstanding game, though he was beaten by an 85th minute shot from Cliff Jones which the wind carried on to the roof of the net!

This historic wind-affected renewal of Division Two strife wasn't the flying start both teams had hoped for, but at least neither side had been beaten yet!

SWANSEA TOWN: J.King, D.Thomas, B.Jones, M.Charles, D.Peake, T.Brown, L.Allchurch, H.Griffiths ,D.Palmer, I.Allchurch, C.Jones.
CARDIFF CITY: G.Vearncombe, C.Rutter, R.Stitfall, A.Harrington, D.Malloy, D.Sullivan, C.Hudson, R.Hewitt, G.Hitchens, J.Nichols, K.Tucker.

Scorers: Swansea Town (-)
Cardiff City (-)
Attendance: 42,482

Historic win for the Bluebirds

21st December 1957
Football League Division 2

SWANSEA TOWN 0 CARDIFF CITY 1

Cardiff secured their first-ever League win at the Vetch Field when Colin Hudson scored the only goal of a largely undistinguished yet historic game.

After giving the Bluebirds a Christmas gift of two points they could ill-afford, the Swans found themselves at the foot of the Second Division table, two points behind Lincoln and Bristol City, both of whom had a match in hand.

Despite a team studded with such stars as Cliff Jones, the Allchurch brothers and Mel Charles, Swansea, after an initial flurry, were never in the game. They had a couple of chances early on, both created by Jones whose speed left a number of Cardiff defenders in his wake, yet both Ivor Allchurch and Mel Charles were guilty of missing chances they would normally have tucked away.

Cardiff took the lead after 34 minutes when winger Brian Walsh's cross found its way through a packed Swansea goalmouth to the unmarked **HUDSON** who coolly lobbed the ball into the net. It was a well-taken goal and encouraged City to go in search of a second. With just a minute to play before the half-time whistle, Hudson almost netted another goal but his well-struck shot was well saved by King.

The second half saw Cardiff emerge as the more compact and workmanlike side with both Joe Bonson and Ron Hewitt going close to extending their side's lead.

SWANSEA TOWN: J.King, H.Griffiths, G.Beech, M.Charles, D.Peake, M.Nurse, L.Allchurch, D.Lewis ,D.Price, I.Allchurch, C.Jones.
CARDIFF CITY: K.Jones, R.Stitfall, A.Milne, A.Harrington, D.Malloy, C.Baker, B.Walsh, R.Hewitt, J.Bonson, C.Nugent, C.Hudson.

Scorers: Swansea Town (-)
Cardiff City (Hudson)
Attendance: 19,483

Nurse penalty helps Swans lay bogey

7th March 1959
Football League Division 2

CARDIFF CITY 0 SWANSEA TOWN 1

Swansea Town needed no longer to consider Ninian Park their bogey ground as they scored their first-ever League goal there and in the process gained their first victory as well.

The Bluebirds were unlucky not to have at least taken a point as the first half belonged entirely to Cardiff for whom Joe Bonson headed narrowly wide when he ought to have done better. Derek Tapscott found himself in a one-to-one with Swansea keeper King, but he was forced wide and when he shot it hit the side-netting. The Bluebirds had a number of shots charged down in the closing stages of the first half as both Nurse and Griffiths threw themselves at powerfully struck shots from the boot of Colin Hudson.

Early in the second half, the home side were unlucky not to be awarded a penalty when Knowles was the victim of a reckless challenge by Griffiths.

Yet minutes later came the incident which gifted Swansea victory. Sullivan tackled Allchurch, who fell heavily and the referee had no hesitation in awarding the visitors a penalty. Up stepped Mel **NURSE** to send Ron Nichols the wrong way.

Swansea could have scored again on the hour mark but debutant left-back Roy Saunders delayed his shot, allowing Malloy to get back and clear the danger.

The latter stages of the game saw Tapscott go close with a powerful header that King tipped on to the bar, and Walsh cut inside Nurse but fired across the face of goal.

SWANSEA TOWN: J.King, R.Daniel, H.Griffiths, B.Hughes, M.Nurse, R.Saunders, L.Allchurch, C.Webster, M.Charles, R.Davies, G.Williams.
CARDIFF CITY: R.Nichols, A.Harrington, A.Milne, C.Baker, D.Malloy, D.Sullivan, B.Walsh, D.Tapscott, H.Knowles, J.Bonson, C.Hudson.

Scorers: Swansea Town (Nurse pen)
Cardiff City (-)
Attendance: 24,450

Bluebirds victorious in Vetch Field mudbath

15th April 1959
Football League Division 2

SWANSEA TOWN 1 CARDIFF CITY 3

In the opening twenty minutes, Swansea looked so superior that every one of the near 15,000 rain-braving crowd must have been expecting them to complete a first historic 'double' over their neighbours.

Then Cardiff centre-forward Derek Tapscott was carried off the field after a rash tackle by left-half Roy Saunders and although the Bluebirds were without him until half-time, they rallied heroically to keep the score at 1-1 and in the second half seized full command.

Cardiff's George Kelly, the tall and swarthy Scot signed from Stoke City last year for £5,000 celebrated his first league match for seven months with two goals which, simple as they were, crowned a display which must have left many wondering why he was on the open-to-offers list!

Colin **WEBSTER** put Swansea ahead in the 10th minute with a well-place shot after two Len Allchurch efforts had rebounded from the legs of desperate defenders. Webster could well have scored a first half hat-trick - his worst miss in that period being when he hit a post in front of an open target - and then he did the same thing again when Swansea missed their only chance in the second half!

Early in the second half, Tapscott thought he had scored with a diving header from Walsh's cross but the linesman had flagged for offside. George **KELLY** was then left with the simple task of converting Walsh's cross from close range and a few minutes later,

KELLY headed into an empty net when Johnny King was caught out of position. With just minutes remaining, Swansea's Mel **NURSE** put through his own goal when under no pressure whatsoever.

It was a thrilling match played in atrocious conditions underfoot and kept firmly under control by London referee Jack Husband despite the ever-present threat of a rough house!

SWANSEA TOWN: J.King, B.Hughes, H.Griffiths, P.Davies, M.Nurse, R.Saunders, L.Allchurch, R.Davies, C.Webster, H.Williams, G.Williams.
CARDIFF CITY: R.Nichols, A.Milne, R.Stitfall, A.Harrington, D.Malloy, C.Baker, B.Walsh, G.Kelly, D.Tapscott, D.Sullivan, C.Hudson.

Scorers: Swansea Town (Webster)
Cardiff City (Kelly 2, Nurse og)
Attendance: 14,893

Recalled Bonson nets winner

7th November 1959
Football League Division 2

CARDIFF CITY 2 SWANSEA TOWN 1

Following this 2-1 defeat of Swansea, Cardiff City shared the top spot of Division Two with Aston Villa. Although Villa led the table on goal average, the Bluebirds had a game in hand over them and enjoyed the distinction of having won more games than any other club in the top two divisions.

With Welsh international wing-half Colin Baker injured, Derrick Sullivan dropped back to replace him and Joe Bonson, a former Wolves centre-forward, replaced Sullivan at inside-forward.

Cardiff had the better of the early exchanges with both Moore and Tapscott going close before Walsh's cross-cum-shot curled onto the crossbar with Reid beaten. The Bluebirds' pressure eventually told when **SULLIVAN** met Watkins' corner with a powerful header that rocketed into the roof of the net. It seemed nothing could knock Sullivan off the goal trail - it was his eighth goal in the last ten games and he headed the Bluebirds scoring charts.

Little had been seen of Swansea as an attacking force but in what was the first attack of the game they drew level when **WEBSTER'S** mishit shot completely deceived Vearncombe.

Joe Bonson was having a fine game. He had created a couple of openings for Tapscott and Moore and forced Reid into making a fine reflex save. It was **BONSON** who scored the game's next goal, meeting Brian Walsh's pin-point cross with a firm header that beat Reid all ends up. The Barnsley-born forward almost netted a second goal in the closing stages of the game but was denied by a last ditch tackle by Harry Griffiths.

SWANSEA TOWN: R.Reid, A.Sanders, H.Griffiths, B.Hughes, M.Nurse, D.Hale, L.Allchurch, R.Davies, B.Reynolds, C.Webster, D.Dodson.
CARDIFF CITY: G.Vearncombe, A.Harrington, R.Stitfall, S.Gammon, D.Malloy, D.Sullivan, B.Walsh, G.Moore, D.Tapscott, J.Bonson, J.Watkins.

Scorers: Swansea Town (Webster)
Cardiff City (Sullivan, Bonson)
Attendance: 34,881

Cardiff come out on top in controversial Welsh Cup-tie

2nd February 1960
Welsh Cup 6th Round

SWANSEA TOWN 1 CARDIFF CITY 2

The sixth round of the Welsh Cup produced one of the most bitter and controversial ties in the history of the competition. Cardiff tried to have the date of the tie changed due to their important League fixture at Leyton Orient two days later. The Welsh FA refused their request and so Bluebirds manager Bill Jones fielded his reserve team, which drew the wrath of the governing body.

Bitterness showed itself on the field as Swansea fielded their full strength Second Division team. In very heavy conditions, Cardiff's reserve XI took the lead midway through the first half when Steve

Mokone's shot took a deflection off Alan **WOODS** to send Johnny King in the Swansea goal the wrong way. As tempers flared, so the tackles became more reckless and there was more embarrassment for the Swans when the Bluebirds doubled their lead through Harry **KNOWLES** with just a quarter of an hour remaining.

The Swans put in a grandstand finish and Ron Nichols was finally beaten when former Bluebird Brayley **REYNOLDS** pulled a goal back with a downward header from a Jones cross.

In the final ten minutes, Colin Hudson was sent off after committing an unnecessary foul. Within minutes of his departure a bout of wrestling between Cardiff's Mokone and Harry Griffiths of Swansea ended with the two players flinging mud at each other. This incident resulted in the pair receiving their marching orders as well.

The only redeeming feature of this game was that a replay was avoided! Following an inquiry by the Welsh FA, Cardiff were fined £350 and ordered to field their strongest available XI in all future Welsh Cup games.

SWANSEA TOWN: J.King, A.Sanders, H.Griffiths, A.Woods, M.Nurse, R.Saunders, B.Jones, H.Williams, B.Reynolds, C.Webster, G.Williams.
CARDIFF CITY: R.Nichols, A.Milne, A.Harrington, S.Gammon, T.Peck, B.Hole, C.Hudson, M.Hughes, H.Knowles, S.Mokone, B.Jenkins.

Scorers: Swansea Town (Reynolds)
Cardiff City (Woods og, Knowles)
Attendance: 11,000

Bluebirds 3-0 up but Swans fight back to earn point

26th March 1960
Football League Division 2

SWANSEA TOWN 3 CARDIFF CITY 3

After drawing at Swansea, Cardiff City needed only four points from their remaining six games to make sure of returning to Division One.

The Bluebirds missed a great chance of recovering the Division Two leadership in this Vetch Field thriller. They showed Championship form in building up a 3-0 advantage with Joe **BONSON** opening the scoring for the visitors after 13 minutes when he rose highest to head home a Watkins cross. They could have gone further ahead seven minutes later when King failed to hold Barrie Hole's long range shot and Tapscott, following up, crashed his shot against the post. Cardiff went 2-0 up on 27 minutes when Graham **MOORE** beat three Swansea defenders in a mazy dribble before firing high into the roof of the net. The visitors netted a third goal five minutes later when Brian **WALSH** smashed a free-kick through the Swansea 'wall' and past an unsighted Johnny King.

As the second half got underway, the Bluebirds seemed content to sit back in the knowledge that their three first half goals would bring them victory.

But this complacency allowed the Swans to get back in the game and in a fantastic six-minute spell midway through the second period, the home side drew level. Brayley **REYNOLDS** played a neat one-two with Herbie Williams before sliding the ball under the body of the advancing Graham Vearncombe and then Dixie **HALE** side-footed home Barrie Jones' cross from close range. **REYNOLDS** then netted his second goal of the game to level the scores, racing on to a fine through ball by Johnson and curling the ball into the top left-hand corner of Vearncombe's goal.

With time running out, Graham Moore almost won it for the Bluebirds but his well-taken free-kick passed inches outside the post with King rooted to the spot!

SWANSEA TOWN: J.King, D.Thomas, H.Griffiths, M.Johnson, M.Nurse, D.Hale, L.Allchurch, H.Williams, B.Reynolds, C.Webster, B.Jones.
CARDIFF CITY: G.Vearncombe, A.Milne, R.Stitfall, B.Hole, D.Malloy, C.Baker, B.Walsh, G.Moore, D.Tapscott, J.Bonson, J.Watkins.

Scorers: Swansea Town (Reynolds 2, Hale)
Cardiff City (Bonson, Moore, Walsh)
Attendance: 24,004

Swans on top but City live to fight again

22nd March 1961
Welsh Cup semi-final

CARDIFF CITY 1 SWANSEA TOWN 1

First Division Cardiff City's hopes of a place in the money-spinning European Cup Winners' Cup next season lived on in this sometimes thrilling but mostly disappointing Welsh Cup semi-final at Somerton Park, the home of Newport County.

On the night, Swansea looked much the better side and were unlucky not to come away with a victory. Cardiff were a huge disappointment - their 11-day 'break' from soccer action since their 3-2 defeat of 'double' chasing Spurs had sapped the drive and pace-control which had marked their recent First Division successes.

The Bluebirds started off the game well enough and when Mel Nurse made a fatal mistake in the seventh minute, **TAPSCOTT** was through in a flash to put City 1-0 up and looking comfortable.

Cardiff centre-half Danny Malloy made his only mistake of the game after 15 minutes when he miscontrolled a pass, allowing Brayley **REYNOLDS** to run on and hammer the equaliser past Nichols.

There could have been several more goals - the chances were there for both sides to win the match, although Swansea in the shape of Reynolds and Webster created the better openings.

However, for what was supposed to be a showpiece of Welsh soccer, there was far too much spoiling tactics and poor play.

SWANSEA TOWN: N.Dwyer, A.Sanders, H.Griffiths, P.Davies, M.Nurse, B.Hughes, B.Jones, R.Davies, B.Reynolds, C.Webster, G.Williams.
CARDIFF CITY: R.Nichols, A.Harrington, R.Stitfall, B.Hole, D.Malloy, C.Baker, B.Walsh, A.Pickrell, D.Tapscott, P.Donnelly, D.Hogg.

Venue: Somerton Park
Scorers: Swansea Town (Reynolds)
Cardiff City (Tapscott)
Attendance; 10,470

Quickfire own goal starts City's downfall

28th March 1961
Welsh Cup semi-final replay

SWANSEA TOWN 2 CARDIFF CITY 1

The replay at Steboneath, Llanelli had a sensational start as Swansea took the lead after just 35 seconds and then netted another some two minutes later!

The two goals were scored by Brayley Reynolds, the quickfire opener coming as **REYNOLDS** was challenged by Cardiff skipper Danny Malloy, but he could do little to prevent the Swansea centre-forward lifting the ball over Bluebirds keeper Graham Vearncombe.

Swansea's second goal came in the third minute after Ron Stitfall had given away a free-kick on the right flank. Barrie Jones floated over an inviting cross which was spectacularly headed home by the diving **REYNOLDS**. This was another goal that should never have been - the Swansea forward was given far too much room and was allowed to score completely unchallenged.

The Bluebirds did reduce the arrears after 18 minutes when Derek **TAPSCOTT**, chasing a Donnelly cross, barged Dwyer who had dropped the ball over the line!

This goal gave Cardiff a boost and they dominated the rest of the first half with both Tapscott and Pickrell going close.

Early after the restart, Derek Tapscott had the chance to level matters when he dashed through the Swans defence but, after beating the advancing Dwyer with a low shot, cried in anguish as his drive thumped against an upright. Donnelly too smashed a shot against the woodwork while City could also have been awarded two penalties when first Hogg and then Pickrell were brought down in the box.

Though by no means a classic game, Llanelli's biggest-ever crowd of mainly Swansea supporters went home happy!

SWANSEA TOWN: N.Dwyer, A.Sanders, H.Griffiths, P.Davies, M.Nurse, R.Saunders, B.Jones, R.Davies, B.Reynolds, C.Webster, G.Williams.

CARDIFF CITY: R.Nichols, A.Harrington, R.Stitfall, B.Hole, D.Malloy, C.Baker, B.Walsh, A.Pickrell, D.Tapscott, P.Donnelly, D.Hogg.

Venue: Steboneath, Llanelli
Scorers: Swansea Town (Reynolds 2)
Cardiff City (Tapscott)
Attendance: 11,965

Disallowed 'goal' robs City

4th September 1962
Football League Division 2

SWANSEA TOWN 2 CARDIFF CITY 1

Swansea Town fully deserved their victory over the Bluebirds, though the final result swung on a vital five-minute spell early in the second half when the Swans scored their two goals and Cardiff had one disallowed.

The first half was fairly nondescript except for the last ten minutes or so, when both Tapscott and Mel Charles brought fine saves out of Swansea keeper Noel Dwyer and Ivor Allchurch rolled the ball wide of a gaping goal after Dwyer had committed himself.

In the 48th minute Herbie **WILLIAMS** beat off a tackle from Hooper, chased the loose ball past Allchurch and Baker and from around 20 yards out scored with a terrific shot.

Two minutes later the ball was in the Swansea net, put there by Tapscott, who hooked the ball past Saunders and lobbed over Dwyer's head. The 'goal' was disallowed for an off-the-ball incident involving the Cardiff No.9.

The fact that Swansea scored again almost immediately was a further frustration for Cardiff. Alan McIntosh made the error that led to the goal by dwelling on the ball too long. He was tackled by Morgans who crossed to the far post where Eddie **THOMAS** headed home.

The Bluebirds had every chance to reduce the arrears thereafter but they showed more desperation than control. It wasn't until the closing minutes that they scored, Mel **CHARLES** back-heading a Tapscott lob over Noel Dwyer's outstretched arms.

SWANSEA TOWN: N.Dwyer, B.Hughes, H.Griffiths, P.Davies, B.Purcell, R.Saunders, B.Jones, E.Thomas, C.Webster, H.Williams, K.Morgans.
CARDIFF CITY: M.Swan, A.Harrington, R.Stitfall, B.Hole, F.Rankmore, C.Baker, A.McIntosh, D.Tapscott, M.Charles, I.Allchurch, P.Hooper.

Scorers: Swansea Town (Williams, Thomas)
Cardiff City (Charles)
Attendance: 24,687

Bluebirds goal blitz demolishes Swans

15th September 1962
Football League Division 2

CARDIFF CITY 5 SWANSEA TOWN 2

The Bluebirds powered their way to one of the most convincing South Wales derby victories.

Swansea's defeat was their third in a row, though at half-time Cardiff led 3-2 and there was very little in it. But after McIntosh had made it four two minutes after the interval, it seemed that the Swans just folded up.

Cardiff were helped to victory by a **DAVIES** own goal after just four minutes, whilst on 10 minutes Mel **CHARLES** squeezed between two Swansea men to head an Alec Milne centre well out of Noel Dwyer's reach.

Swansea struck almost immediately when a mistake by Dilwyn John allowed Thomas to flick the ball back to **WILLIAMS** who forced the ball home from close range. Then on 27 minutes **WILLIAMS** netted his and Swansea's second goal, following up a Webster shot which Cardiff keeper John failed to hold.

Then came one of the finest solo goals in the history of the South Wales derbies scored by Cardiff's Mel **CHARLES**. Controlling a bouncing ball and beating three men at the same time, he moved fully sixty yards with the ball before stroking a calculated shot past Dwyer.

In the second half, **McINTOSH** hammered a 47th minute drive just inside the far post and five minutes later, Peter

HOOPER made his usual contribution with a fine angled drive. The Bluebirds then had a ten-minute spell when they could quite easily have doubled their total. The woodwork came to Swansea's rescue on a couple of occasions, whilst Dwyer produced three outstanding saves from Mel Charles, Hooper and Harrington.

The last twenty minutes were unusually tame but the game had been won and lost by then.

SWANSEA TOWN: N.Dwyer, B.Hughes, H.Griffiths, P.Davies, B.Purcell, R.Saunders, B.Jones, E.Thomas, C.Webster, H.Williams, K.Morgans.
CARDIFF CITY: D.John, A.Milne, R.Stitfall, A.Harrington, F.Rankmore, C.Baker, A.McIntosh, D.Tapscott, M.Charles, I.Allchurch, P.Hooper.

Scorers: Swansea Town (Williams 2)
Cardiff City (Charles 2, McIntosh, Hooper, Davies og)
Attendance: 23,454

Allchurch injury hampers Bluebirds

11th April 1963
Welsh Cup 6th Round

SWANSEA TOWN 2 CARDIFF CITY 0

Cardiff City captain Ivor Allchurch injured his thigh in the early minutes of this Welsh Cup tie at the Vetch Field, which threatened to keep him out for the rest of the season. After only 12 minutes, he appeared to pull a thigh muscle and played with it heavily strapped throughout the second half.

That the Swans deserved their victory there is not the slightest doubt. Throughout the ninety minutes, they were the more purposeful of two sides whose football rarely reached the standard expected of teams in the Second Division.

Swansea keeper Johnny King made one of his rare first team appearances these days and produced some excellent saves, although good fortune was with him on a couple of occasions!

The first half was a scrappy affair though both goals had some narrow escapes. Cardiff keeper Vearncombe dropped a Barrie Jones cross but Edwards was on hand to hook the ball off the line. At the other end, McIntosh and Tapscott combined well for the latter to shoot against the foot of the post before Evans cleared the ball upfield.

Swansea took the lead after 53 minutes when winger Barrie **JONES** put across a shot-cum-centre which appeared to completely deceive Vearncombe and the ball went into the net via an upright. This was the tonic the Swans needed and for some time they subjected the Bluebirds to some heavy pressure. With just over a quarter of an hour to play, the visitors' fate was sealed when Vearncombe's punch went straight to Eddie **THOMAS** who headed the ball into the empty net.

City subsequently did put some bite into their play but there was little method in their attacks.

SWANSEA TOWN: J.King, R.Evans, H.Griffiths, P.Davies, M.Johnson, R.Saunders, B.Jones, D.Draper, E.Thomas, K.Morgans, K.Todd.
CARDIFF CITY: G.Vearncombe, R.Stitfall, T.Edwards, A.Harrington, F.Rankmore, B.Hole, A.McIntosh, D.Tapscott, M.Charles, I.Allchurch, P.Hooper.

Scorers: Swansea Town (Jones, Thomas)
Cardiff City (-)
Attendance: 11.500

A tale of two penalties

19th October 1963
Football League Division 2

CARDIFF CITY 1 SWANSEA TOWN 1

Cardiff City were lucky to escape defeat at the hands of Swansea Town - apart from the fact that Brayley Reynolds missed a penalty ten minutes from the end, the Swans had so much of the second half play that, if they had scored three goals, there could have been no complaint from the home side.

The Bluebirds' makeshift team - injuries causing a number of the first team regulars to miss the game - did well to salvage a point.

Cardiff nearly went into a shock lead in the first minute when Charles hit the crossbar and Swansea too had their bad luck as a sudden low shot by Barrie Jones nearly caught John napping. Midway through the half a John Charles header caught Dwyer going the wrong way but somehow the keeper contrived to smother the ball. Then Thomas headed against the City crossbar but with five minutes to go before half-time, Davies handled the ball to prevent Halliday's header entering the net. There were some antics by the Swansea keeper before the penalty was taken but he failed to put off the cool **SCOTT** whose shot had him diving the wrong way.

The Swans nearly equalised immediately for John made no effort to stop a Reynolds shot and the ball hit the foot of a post. Reynolds then found himself clean through but shot straight at the advancing John. Swansea deservedly drew level after 65 minutes when Barrie Jones' cross was met by **EVANS** who, with John glued to his line, headed home.

Ten minutes from time, following tremendous Swansea pressure, the visitors were awarded a penalty but Reynolds blasted the ball well over the crossbar and deprived his side of what would have been a fully deserved victory.

SWANSEA TOWN: N.Dwyer, R.Evans, B.Hughes, P.Davies, M.Johnson, H.Williams, B.Jones, D.Draper, B.Reynolds, E.Thomas, B.Evans.
CARDIFF CITY: D.John, C.Baker, R.Stitfall, B.Hole, D.Murray, R.Scott, P.King, T.Halliday, J.Charles, I.Allchurch, D.Mallory.

Scorers: Swansea Town (Evans)
Cardiff City (Scott pen)
Attendance: 21,417

Swansea sharpshooters too good for Bluebirds

28th March 1964
Football League Division 2

SWANSEA TOWN 3 CARDIFF CITY 0

Swansea's victory was all the more commendable in view of the fact that they did not have the services of Keith Todd for most of the first half and that, when he did return for the second, he played at outside-left.

The first Swansea goal after just four minutes will be talked about for a long time. Two Swansea shots were beaten out before John Charles appeared to clear a **DRAPER** effort from under the crossbar. However, the linesman signalled a goal and that was that! This was a sorry blow for Cardiff and they sustained another one when Mel Charles put across what appeared to be a perfectly legitimate header for King to shoot into the net. Yet Charles was penalised for an offence not apparent from the touchline.

After Todd had been carried off injured, there was some sustained Cardiff pressure but despite Mel Charles heading against the bar, it was Swansea who scored the game's next goal just before half-time. John King punted the ball well upfield and John Charles was content to let the ball bounce over his head thinking John would run out to clear. Instead, **REYNOLDS** showed great anticipation in nipping round the City centre-half and neatly lobbing the ball over the slow-to-react Cardiff keeper.

With Todd back for the second half, Cardiff's fate was decisively sealed when **REYNOLDS** shot home from close range in the 78th minute after Hole was unlucky to see the ball rebound off him right to the Swansea centre-forward's feet.

SWANSEA TOWN: J.King, R.Evans, B.Hughes, M.Johnson, B.Purcell, H.Williams, B.Jones, D.Draper, B.Reynolds, K.Todd, B.Evans.
CARDIFF CITY: D.John, T.Peck, P.Rodrigues, R.Scott, J.Charles, B.Hole, B.Lewis, P.King, M.Charles, I.Allchurch, G.Farrell.

Scorers: Swansea Town (Draper, Reynolds 2)
Cardiff City (-)
Attendance: 18,721

Boxing Day pantomime!

26th December 1964
Football League Division 2

SWANSEA TOWN 3 CARDIFF CITY 2

The spectators who turned out in force at the Vetch Field saw a Boxing Day pantomime. The Swans thoroughly deserved their victory because they were by far the more versatile side in appalling conditions.

It would have surprised no-one if referee Clements had called the match off at half-time, so bad was the pitch. Snow and ice in the morning followed by torrential rain made the pitch treacherous and the players of both sides deserve credit for sticking to their tasks so manfully.

It was totally against the run of play when Cardiff went into the lead after only 10 minutes. Farrell crossed the ball from the right, Briggs missed it badly and it struck an upright and rebounded to **ELLIS** who had the easiest task in the world to push it home. Three minutes later Dilwyn John nearly punched the ball into his own net following a corner kick and only the covering of Harrington prevented the equaliser.

But an equaliser there had to be with the Swans piling attack on attack. After 39 minutes, Herbie Williams put in a low shot, John was deceived by the pace of the ball off the surface and it rebounded off his chest for the vigilant **TODD** to slam it home.

Early in the second half, **McLAUGHLIN** put the Swans into a deserved lead with a curling shot from the edge of the area. Then **ELLIS** netted his and Cardiff's second goal to level things up after a fortuitous rebound off a post, but **POUND** netted his first Football League goal in the closing stages with John glued to the ground.

SWANSEA TOWN: R.Briggs, B.Hughes, D.Ward, A.Harley, M.Johnson, H.Williams, B.Evans, D.Draper, K.Todd, J.McLaughlin, K.Pound.
CARDIFF CITY; D.John, A.Harrington, P.Rodrigues, J.Charles, D.Murray, B.Hole, G.Farrell, S.Gammon, K.Ellis, P.King, B.Lewis.

Scorers: Swansea Town (Todd, McLaughlin, Pound)
Cardiff City (Ellis 2)
Attendance: 17,875

Farrell's penalty puts out Swans

10th March 1965
Welsh Cup semi-final

SWANSEA TOWN 0 CARDIFF CITY 1

The holders Cardiff City entered the final of the Welsh Cup again at Newport County's Somerton Park when they beat Swansea Town by the only goal of the match. It was a disappointing game with both sides too tense to produce good football.

In the first minute Davies was penalised for a foul on Allchurch and from the resultant free-kick the Cardiff inside-forward hit the Swansea crossbar.

Half an hour had been played when Cardiff went into the lead in an unusual manner. Farrell did extremely well to make progress down his flank, so much so that he drew Black out of goal. His shot hit a defender's legs and rebounded to Ellis who slammed it home. However, the referee had already blown for handball against Davies and awarded a penalty.

FARRELL made no mistake from the spot with a hard low shot which gave Black no chance.

The Swans made spirited efforts to get the equaliser but could do little against a tightly-knit City defence. The Bluebirds could have gone further ahead during the early part of the second half for Farrell was given a gilt-edged opportunity, but his shot went inches outside Black's left-hand post.

The Swans then held advantage territorially but they rarely looked like breaking down a confident Cardiff rearguard. Indeed, the Bluebirds were putting such an accent on defence that one had the impression they were content with their one-goal lead.

SWANSEA TOWN: J.Black, R.Evans, D.Ward, P.Davies, M.Johnson, H.Williams, B.Evans, J.McLaughlin, G.Kirby, K.Todd, K.Pound.
CARDIFF CITY: R.Wilson, T.Peck, P.Rodrigues, J.Charles, D.Murray, B.Hole, G.Farrell, G.Williams, K.Ellis, I.Allchurch, P.King.

Venue: Somerton Park
Scorers: Swansea Town (-)
Cardiff City (Farrell pen)
Attendance: 7,500

Allchurch hat-trick sees Swans relegated

6th April 1965
Football League Division 2

CARDIFF CITY 5 SWANSEA TOWN 0

In what was one of the most sporting engagements ever between the Welsh neighbours, Cardiff avoided relegation whilst Swansea were doomed to play Third Division football next season. It was a tragedy however that such a game should have such an important bearing on the future status of the teams.

Cardiff took the lead after just six minutes when Johnston's cross to the far post was headed home by **ALLCHURCH**. The Bluebirds continued to play the better football and Allchurch went close to netting a second but his shot scraped the outside of Black's right-hand post. Johnston again crossed well and this time King's first-time shot brought a fine save out of Black. City extended their lead in the 19th minute when **ALLCHURCH's** cross-cum-shot caught in the wind and floated over Black's head.

Swansea never gave up and Humphries put in a sudden shot which Wilson did well to save at full-stretch.

Seven minutes before half-time, Peter King hit his shot against the post and then Johnston shot into the side-netting.

Within seconds of the restart, Gareth Williams went through unchallenged and finished with a shot which went only inches the wrong side of an upright. Then Black saved well at the foot of the

**Ivor Allchurch brings an opposing player
to his hands and knees.**

**Derek Tapscott, scorer of 99 goals in his
seven years at Cardiff City.**

**Colin Baker, who appeared in 11 South Wales derbies,
prepares to strike the ball.**

**Cardiff celebrating at Ninian Park after victory over Swansea
in the Welsh Cup Final, 30th April 1956.**

A local derby to start the new season, with a crowd of nearly 43,000 watching City draw 0-0 with Swansea Town at Ninian Park on August 24th 1957. At the top of the 'Bob Bank' is the hospital broadcast box. Here, Gerry Hitchens gets in a header with the help of Johnny Nicholls, watched by Ron Hewitt (8) and Ken Tucker (far right). Ken is now Chairman of the FA of Wales Senior International Committee.

Leighton James

Rory Keane...
battered but not beaten
at Ninian Park v Cardiff,
August 27th 1949.

Ron Stitfall, who made his Cardiff City debut
at just 14 years old.

**Jimmy Gilligan beats Lee Bracey to make it 2-0 on
December 26th 1988, a game which ended
Cardiff City 2 Swansea 2.**

**Swansea keeper Johnny King, who made 368 league
appearances between 1950-64.**

August 24th 1957, Cardiff City 0 Swansea 0.

John Toshack in his Swansea days before a move to Liverpool brought him six major trophies.

Trevor Ford.

George Edwards and Colin Baker.

LEFT: Clockwise from top right : Alan Harrington, Colin Pascoe, Alan Curtis, Phil Dwyer, Robbie James and Nigel Stevenson.

April 30th 1956, Cardiff City 3 Swansea 2.
Left to right: Herbert Powell (secretary, F.A. of Wales), Milwyn Jenkins (president, F.A. of Wales) and Trevor Ford.

With City's squad needing to be rebuilt, Barrie Hole (left) was
eventually sold to Blackburn at the end of '65-66 for £40,000.
Peter Rodrigues had gone to Leicester City fo £40,000 in late
December, 1965. This is Hole in action against Leyton Orient
at Ninian Park on 13th November 1965, with Bob Wilson on
the right. John Toshack made a scoring debut
as substitute in this 3-1 win.

March 24th 1951, Cardiff 1 Swansea 0;
Deri Thomas, Alf Sherwood and Phil Foslin in action.

Harry Griffiths, Swansea's post-war utility player, who played in almost every position in his many seasons at the Vetch Field.

John Buchanan's 40-yard equaliser for Cardiff beats Dave Stewart in a 3-3 stalemate on December 27th 1980.

Thirty-seven year old Robbie James receives his Man of the Match award from Wales team manager Terry Yorath after the Autoglass Trophy game against Swansea City on January 19th 1993.

Mike Ford, a key figure in recent years for Cardiff before injury forced him into retirement.

Terry Boyle and Bob Real.

**F.A.W. Premier Cup Final at Ninian Park;
Cardiff players celebrate a 1-0 win over Swansea
on May 13th 2002.**

**Jason Price challenges Wayne O'Sullivan;
November 22nd 1998, Cardiff City 1 Swansea 2.**

**Steve Watkin v Mark Bonner;
April 18th 1999, Cardiff City 0 Swansea 0.**

**Keith Walter and Carl Dale in a battle for the ball
on November 16th 1991, a game which ended
Cardiff City 1 Swansea 2.**

post from King before Swansea looked certain to score in a goalmouth melee. Four of their forwards had shots charged down before Cardiff went straight to the other end and **ALLCHURCH** completed his hat-trick to make it 3-0. And what a goal it was - the Welsh Wizard beat three men before rounding keeper Black. With six minutes to go, Cardiff went further ahead when John **CHARLES** headed home Johnston's corner-kick. In the closing minutes, **CHARLES** scored the goal of the match, weaving through a packed Swansea penalty area before unleashing a tremendous shot that almost broke the net!

SWANSEA TOWN: J.Black, R.Evans, B.Hughes, H.Williams, M.Johnson, P.Davies, W.Humphries, K.Todd, G.Kirby, J.McGuigan, J.McLaughlin.
CARDIFF CITY: R.Wilson, P.Rodrigues, G.Harris, G.Williams, D.Murray, B.Hole, G.Johnston, I.Allchurch, J.Charles, P.King, B.Lewis.

Scorers: Swansea Town (-)
Cardiff City (Allchurch 3, Charles 2)
Attendance: 15,896

Disputed late goal gives Swansea second chance

4th January 1966
Welsh Cup 5th round

SWANSEA TOWN 2 CARDIFF CITY 2

This fifth round Welsh Cup tie was played in treacherous conditions on a pitch that resembled a paddy field. Swansea forced a draw after twice being in arrears - a hotly disputed goal from Ivor Allchurch seven minutes from time giving the Vetch Field side another chance in the competition.

Cardiff should have taken the lead in the seventh minute when Hole's defence-splitting pass found Harkin who crossed for Andrews but the centre-forward headed against an upright. Fourteen minutes had gone when Herbie Williams slipped. Harkin was on the ball in a flash and, after making ground, sent in a low centre to **ANDREWS** who beat Heyes with a first-time shot. Andrews had a header that landed on the roof of the net and another shot inches wide of Heyes' right-hand post.

The second half was six minutes old when Swansea equalised. The tenacity of Brian Evans enabled him to make progress along the by-line before putting a very low shot across the goal and with Todd pestering **MURRAY** the City centre-half hooked the ball into his own net.

The Bluebirds regained the lead in the 64th minute when Peter **KING** forced Harkin's cross over the line from close range. Andrews then brought a fine save out of George Heyes before Thomas, under pressure from Andrews, sliced the ball over his own bar.

Then, in the 83rd minute, Swansea equalised for a second time. Davies seemed to have smothered Brian Evans' shot but **ALLCHURCH** forced the ball home - Cardiff protested but after consulting a linesman, the referee allowed the goal to stand.

SWANSEA TOWN: G.Heyes, R.Evans, B.Hughes, H.Williams, M.Johnson, G.Thomas, W.Humphries, J.McLaughlin, K.Todd, I.Allchurch, B.Evans.
CARDIFF CITY: L.Davies, A.Harrington, C.Baker, G.Williams, D.Murray, B.Hole, G.Farrell, G.Johnston, G.Andrews, T.Harkin, P.King.

Scorers: Swansea Town (Murray og, Allchurch)
Cardiff City (Andrews, King)
Attendance: 10,275

Murray off as Swans sink City

8th February 1966
Welsh Cup 5th round replay

CARDIFF CITY 3 SWANSEA TOWN 5 AET

In one of the most sensational games seen at Ninian Park, Swansea Town ousted holders Cardiff City from the Welsh Cup after trailing by three clear goals in this fifth round replay.

The astounding change in the game came after Cardiff's centre-half Don Murray had been ordered off in the 62nd minute - at that time, the Bluebirds appeared set for a comfortable victory.

Cardiff took the lead after 20 minutes against the run of play. King started the movement by cutting across field before transferring to Farrell. He put the ball to Gareth **WILLIAMS** whose shot beat Heyes but, in fairness to the Swansea keeper, the ball was deflected off a defender. Six minutes later, the Swans were almost level but Evans' tremendous shot hit an upright. With 35 minutes played, Cardiff increased their lead thanks to Farrell. The winger outwitted Williams and Ward and laid on a perfect pass for **JOHNSTON** to shoot home. It wasn't Swansea's night as Todd then headed against the Cardiff bar with Davies beaten.

Swansea got four corners in as many minutes at the start of the second half before Cardiff went three up in the 54th minute through **JOHNSTON**.

Eight minutes later an incident affected the whole course of the match. Referee Leo Callaghan sent off Don Murray for an alleged head-butt on Swansea's Jimmy McLaughlin.

Within seconds the Swans had reduced the deficit. Thomas put a long ball to Keith **TODD** whose shot from the edge of the area easily beat Davies. Then with 14 minutes to go, the Swans were in the game with a vengeance, for **TODD** volleyed home Humphries' cross. Cardiff's handicap of only having 10 men saw Swansea produce a tremendous extra effort and, after 83 minutes, they levelled the scores when Herbie **WILLIAMS** got the ball into the net after good work on the wing by Humphries.

Cardiff almost snatched a winner in the dying seconds of normal time but Johnston just failed to connect with a Greg Farrell cross.

Swansea went into the lead for the first time in the eighth minute of extra-time. **McLAUGHLIN** put in a shot which Davies half-covered but the ball spun from his grasp and into the net. Three minutes later, the Swans got a fifth goal as **EVANS** headed home an Allchurch free-kick.

In the second half of extra-time there was an amazing scene in the Swansea goalmouth with both Harkin and Andrews failing to get the ball into the net from close range.

SWANSEA TOWN: G.Heyes, R.Evans, D.Ward, G.Thomas, B.Purcell, H.Williams, W.Humphries, J.McLaughlin, K.Todd, I.Allchurch, B.Evans.
CARDIFF CITY: L.Davies, G.Coldrick, C.Baker, G.Williams, D.Murray, B.Hole, G.Farrell, G.Johnston, G.Andrews, T.Harkin, P.King.

Scorers: Swansea Town (Todd 2, H.Williams, McLaughlin, Evans)
Cardiff City (G.Williams, Johnston 2)
Attendance: 9,836

Welsh Cup holders thrashed by Bluebirds

17th January 1967
Welsh Cup 5th round

SWANSEA TOWN 0 CARDIFF CITY 4

Swansea Town the holders said 'goodbye' to the Welsh Cup and any entry into European soccer next season when they were soundly beaten by Cardiff City in this fifth round match at the Vetch Field.

The return of Gareth Williams to the Cardiff side made a tremendous difference, though he appeared to be limping slightly from the kick-off!

It was all Swansea at the start and in the opening ten minutes the home side won four corners. Yet Cardiff went into the lead with their first real attack of the match after 19 minutes. Farrell went through cleverly and teed the ball up for **LEWIS**, whose shot deceived Heyes. Four minutes later, City were two up. This time Lewis did the spadework before passing to Johnston. He placed the ball into the path of **FARRELL** who made no mistake.

Cardiff were now well on top and in the 21st minute they made it 3-0 - Harris sent a high ball to Brown who headed over Purcell. **JOHNSTON**, seeing a chance, raced ahead and beat Heyes with ease.

Although not showing the pace of the first half, the Bluebirds continued to dominate the second period, though for a while they gave the impression of being content with their lead. However, in the 72nd minute a shot by Brown was only palmed out by Heyes and **JOHNSTON**, running up in support, had no trouble in smashing the ball into the net for Cardiff's fourth goal.

SWANSEA TOWN: G.Heyes, R.Evans, V.Gomersall,
D.Coughlin, B.Purcell, A.Jones, W.Humphries, K.Todd,
J.Roberts, I.Allchurch, B.Evans. Sub: J.McLaughlin.
CARDIFF CITY: R.Wilson, G.Coldrick, R.Ferguson, G.Williams,
D.Murray, B.Harris, B.Lewis, G.Johnston, R.Brown,
P.King, G.Farrell. Sub: C.Bird.

Scorers: Swansea Town (-)
Cardiff City (Lewis, Farrell, Johnston 2)
Attendance: 11,816

Toshack at the 'Double'

22nd April 1969
Welsh Cup Final 1st Leg

CARDIFF CITY 3 SWANSEA TOWN 1

It appears that Cardiff City are virtually back in the European Cup Winners' Cup competition after this Welsh Cup Final first-leg victory at the Vetch Field.

The Bluebirds quickly mastered a pitch covered in mud and pools of water by continuous driving rain.

The visitors showed no mercy from the start: they chased enthusiastically for the goals and provided all the thrills for the rain-soaked crowd.

Big John Toshack was the 'ace' in Cardiff's in-form attack, scoring two of their goals and bringing his total for the season to 30. **TOSHACK** opened the scoring with a 13th minute header. He outjumped the Swansea defence to get to a long cross from Sharp and connected brilliantly, with George Heyes much too late in attempting to save to his right. The Cardiff inside-forward almost added a second moments later as he burst through on goal but was denied by a desperate sliding tackle by Heyes. In the 18th minute the Swansea defenders got themselves into an awful mess as Toshack, King and Clark threatened. The mix-up ended with **NURSE** putting through his own goal!

Just before half-time Cardiff went 3-0 up when **TOSHACK** got his head to a Murray cross and though Heyes got his hands to it, he couldn't prevent it from crossing the line.

Herbie **WILLIAMS** pulled a goal back for Swansea in the 50th minute with a glorious header. This inspired the home side and they came back into the game more. However, the only real anxiety for the Bluebirds was when their defenders passed back to Fred Davies and the ball stuck in the mud. The Cardiff keeper made a great save from Brian Evans and in the dying minutes the Swansea winger rattled the City crossbar.

SWANSEA TOWN: G.Heyes, D.Lawrence, V.Gomersall, C.Slee, M.Nurse, B.Hughes, B.Grey, A.Williams, H.Williams, G.Thomas, B.Evans. Sub: W.Screen.
CARDIFF CITY: F.Davies, S.Derrett, D.Carver, P.King, D.Murray, B.Harris, F.Sharp, B.Clark, L.Lea, J.Toshack, B.Jones. Sub: T.Lewis.

Scorers: Swansea Town (H.Williams)
Cardiff City (Toshack 2, Nurse og)
Attendance: 10,207

Bluebirds win Welsh Cup

29th April 1969
Welsh Cup Final 2nd Leg

Cardiff City 2 Swansea Town 0

Cardiff City ensured their entry into next season's European Cup Winners Cup competition with a comfortable victory over Fourth Division Swansea Town.

Cardiff rocked the Swans with two first half goals in eight minutes and this was sufficient for the Bluebirds to race to their third successive Welsh Cup Final victory and their fifth in six years.

Cardiff almost took the lead after 12 minutes when Clark worked the ball across the goal to King but his shot struck an upright with John beaten. There was a scare for the home side when Billy Screen and Grey both had shots blocked on the line after Davies had failed to clear a Brian Evans cross.

The Bluebirds took the lead on 33 minutes when **TOSHACK** met Murray's beautifully flighted free-kick to head powerfully past Dilwyn John. The second goal came in the 40th minute. A Sharp centre was headed forward by Toshack for Leslie **LEA**, who rounded John before rolling the ball into the empty net.

Evans had one great chance to reduce the arrears when he weaved through to within yards of the Cardiff goal-line, but he fired wide at the crucial moment.

Police were called to the popular bank during the match to break up scuffles between supporters and there was a warning given out over the public address system that other culprits would be ordered out of the ground unless order was restored.

SWANSEA TOWN: D.John, D.Lawrence, V.Gomersall, C.Slee, A.Williams, G.Thomas, B.Grey, H.Williams, D.Gwyther, W.Screen, B.Evans. Sub: B.Hughes.
CARDIFF CITY: F.Davies, S.Derrett, D.Carver, P.King, D.Murray, B.Harris, F.Sharp, B.Clark, L.Lea, J.Toshack, B.Jones. Sub: R.Bird.

Scorers: Swansea Town (-)
Cardiff City (Toshack, Lea)
Attendance: 12,617

Toshack's golden goal earns Cardiff replay

11th March 1970
Welsh Cup semi-final

CARDIFF CITY 2 SWANSEA TOWN 2

Swansea City put up a great fighting performance as they forced the Welsh Cup holders to a semi-final replay.

However, this meant that both sides faced a hectic end-of-season programme that included a busy Easter period that could clinch promotion for the two Welsh clubs.

The Bluebirds raced into the lead after just 75 seconds of the start with a splendidly taken goal. Clark headed on a goal-kick to Toshack, who put Lea clear. The winger centred and there was Bobby **WOODRUFF** up with play to clip the ball home on the turn. A minute later, Toshack grazed the bar after a fine Clark-Sutton move. Then Clark himself was not far off target with a sweeping drive.

But the Swans rocked Cardiff with a 14th minute equaliser. Evans fed Allchurch and the winger outpaced Bell before crossing for **EVANS** to surprise the Bluebirds defence with a smart header. Gwyther netted in the 28th minute but he was adjudged offside.

Toshack then forced Millington into making a fine save before King's header flashed just outside his right-hand upright.

Cardiff continued to create chances galore but weak finishing coupled with some good defensive work kept the scoreline respectable for the Fourth Division promotion hunters. Then against the run of play, **WILLIAMS** sent the Swansea fans wild with delight, heading home Len Allchurch's pin-point cross.

Back came Cardiff and **TOSHACK** nipped in to meet an accurate Sutton cross with a glorious header that gave Millington no chance. This gave the Bluebirds new life and Sutton and Woodruff both went close. There were appeals for a Cardiff penalty late in the game when Lea was brought down but the referee adjudged the foul to have taken place just outside the area.

SWANSEA TOWN: T.Millington, C.Slee, D.Lawrence, A.Williams, M.Nurse, G.Thomas, L.Allchurch, D.Gwyther, H.Williams, W.Screen, B.Evans. Sub: V.Gomersall.
CARDIFF CITY: F.Davies, D.Carver, G.Bell, M.Sutton, D.Murray, R.Woodruff, P.King, B.Clark, B.Harris, J.Toshack, L.Lea. Sub A.Allan.

Scorers: Swansea Town (Evans, H.Williams)
Cardiff City (Woodruff, Toshack)
Attendance: 18,050

Extra-time victory sends Bluebirds into Europe

2nd May 1970
Welsh Cup semi-final replay

Swansea City 0 Cardiff City 2 aet

Cardiff City will represent Wales in next season's European Cup Winners' Cup competition even though they have yet to win the Welsh Cup! Their victory in extra-time over the Swans in the Welsh Cup semi-final replay gave them automatic representation because the other finalists, Chester, were not eligible.

Cardiff created many more chances than Swansea in what was a dreary replay. But weak finishing plus the occasional fine and at times lucky save by Tony Millington prevented goals.

Millington kept out Cardiff for ninety minutes by blocking good goal attempts by Bobby Woodruff, Peter King and Brian Clark. The Welsh international keeper also saved a penalty from Ronnie Bird after Mel Sutton had been upended in the area. The Bluebirds dominated the game for long periods yet rarely looked dangerous in the Swansea goalmouth where Mel Nurse and Alan Williams excelled in front of the full-of-confidence Tony Millington.

BIRD made amends for his penalty miss in extra-time with an extremely well-taken goal following a neat flick on by the hard-working Brian Clark.

Toshack livened up proceedings but it was not until the dying minutes of extra-time that Peter **KING** made the game safe by hitting a glorious second goal from some 25 yards after he had accepted a return pass from Clark.

Swansea had toiled bravely with David Gwyther once hitting the crossbar but Cardiff always had the edge.

SWANSEA CITY: T.Millington, C.Slee, V.Gomersall, A.Williams, M.Nurse, G.Thomas, L.Allchurch, D.Gwyther, H.Williams, W.Screen, B.Evans. Sub: D.Lawrence.
CARDIFF CITY: F.Davies, D.Carver, G.Bell, M.Sutton, D.Murray, B.Harris, P.King, R.Woodruff, L.Lea, B.Clark, R.Bird. Sub: J.Toshack.

Scorers: Swansea City (-)
Cardiff City (Bird, King)
Attendance: 20,400

Clark and Warboys sink Swans

3rd January 1972
Welsh Cup 5th Round

SWANSEA CITY 0 CARDIFF CITY 2

Cardiff City, winners of the Welsh Cup for the past five seasons, were given a 90 second boost when striker Alan **WARBOYS** nipped in to score after hesitancy in the Swansea defence.

The Swans, relying on an unchanged team, responded to this early blow with a spell of pressure that unsettled a nervous-looking Bluebirds defence. With Barrie Hole and Geoff Thomas working hard in midfield, the Swans certainly looked capable of upsetting the visitors.

But as the game wore on, Cardiff's Ian Gibson probed menacingly and created many openings for his front men. Both Warboys and Rees should have done better but there was no further scoring as the first half drew to a close.

In the 65th minute, Swansea manager Roy Bentley sent on Welsh international Brian Evans in place of Glen Davies but Cardiff's tightness at the back kept out the frantic Swans. Millington kept Swansea in the game with a brilliant save. Warboys' header from a Rees centre seemed out of the goalkeeper's reach but Millington somehow pushed the ball up and, diving backwards ,gathered it cleanly at the second attempt.

Cardiff confirmed their entry into the sixth round of the competition when Clark scored in the 83rd minute. Rees won possession just inside the Swans half. He showed great determination in shrugging off two tackles before pushing an accurate pass to Brian **CLARK** who hammered the ball into the far corner.

SWANSEA CITY: T.Millington, P.Jones, T.Screen, A.Williams, H.Williams, B.Hole, P.Holme, G.Thomas, G.Davies, D.Gwyther, A.Beer. Sub: B.Evans.
CARDIFF CITY: W.Irwin, D.Carver, G.Bell, M.Sutton, D.Murray, L.Phillips, I.Gibson, B.Clark, R.Woodruff, A.Warboys, N.Rees. Sub: A.Couch.

Scorers: Swansea City (-)
Cardiff City (Warboys, Clark)
Attendance: 14,319

Bruton 'Double' earns teams replay

17th February 1976
Welsh Cup 6th Round

CARDIFF CITY 1 SWANSEA CITY 1

Swansea City defender Dave Bruton had the scoresheet to himself in this Ninian Park derby. He presented the Bluebirds with a gift own-goal in the first half and then cracked home the equaliser to earn a replay of the two Cities' Welsh Cup quarter-final.

Early in the game, Alan Curtis picked up a loose ball in his own half, ran 20 yards and then played a neat one-two with James before shooting straight into the hands of Ron Healey. Gil Reece was unlucky in the 15th minute when he took a glorious return ball from Livermore and swept in, only to be denied a goal by Potter's outstretched leg.

One of Cardiff's best chances came in the 25th minute when Alston sent a sharp shot less than a foot over the bar to round off a good move initiated by Livermore. Then, four minutes later, Phil Dwyer broke strongly on the right and ran in to hit a powerful shot which diving keeper Steve Potter failed to hold. **BRUTON** rushed back and tried a desperate clearance but he hooked the ball into the far corner of his own net from just a couple of yards out.

Less than a minute later, Buchanan was on hand to keep out a Bray effort from Conway's cross.

In the 57th minute, the Swans drew level when Healey left his line to punch out Wyndham Evan's free-kick, but his clearance lacked power and went straight to **BRUTON** who whipped the ball in from about 12 yards with the Cardiff defence at a standstill.

The Swans were showing plenty of fight and Bray and Curtis both went in close in the final stages of the game. When Clive Thomas blew the final whistle, a number of Cardiff players must have been very relieved!

SWANSEA CITY: S.Potter, W.Evans, G.Thomas, P.Lally, D.Bruton, P.Harris, M.Conway, A.Curtis, R.James, G.Bray, D.Bartley.
Sub: G.Davies.
CARDIFF CITY: R.Healey, P.Dwyer, C.Charles, F.Pethard, R.Morgan, M.England, B.Buchanan, D.Livermore, G.Reece, A.Alston, A.Anderson. Sub: P.Sayer.

Scorers: Swansea City (Bruton)
Cardiff City (Bruton og)
Attendance: 5,812

Alston, Clark put out Swans

2nd March 1976
Welsh Cup 6th Round replay

SWANSEA CITY 0 CARDIFF CITY 3

Adrian Alston hit two second half goals to destroy Swansea City's hopes of European Cup football next season, but the Bluebirds were extremely flattered by the final scoreline, for most of the game they had been on the receiving end of some delightful if unrewarding Swansea attacking play. In fact, if the Swans leading scorer Jeff Bray had scored with two comparatively clear-cut chances midway through the second period, the result might have been different.

Despite the Swans being on top, it was Cardiff who took the lead after 35 minutes. Brian **CLARK** was on hand to profit from Swansea keeper Steve Potter's only mistake, when a corner kick by

Buchanan was fumbled and then dropped. The Swans almost drew level when Danny Bartley's shot beat Ron Healey but Clive Charles was on the line to head clear.

Though the tide eventually turned in a positive direction for the Bluebirds, there were always signs that Swansea could get back into the hunt and it was not until the 72nd minute that Alston made his Australian international presence felt. Accepting a crossfield pass from Livermore, **ALSTON** bent the ball round a packed Swansea goalmouth for it to glide off the far upright and give Cardiff a convincing advantage. Then Swansea substitute Glen Davies slipped and lost possession to **ALSTON**, who coolly slid home the third and clinching goal.

But it was a scoreline that was rather unfair on Swansea, insofar as they took the game to Cardiff and, if they had anybody upfield able to accurately shoot, the result could have been so very different.

SWANSEA CITY: S.Potter, W.Evans, G.Thomas, P.Lally, D.Bruton, P.Harris, M.Conway, A.Curtis, R.James, G.Bray, D.Bartley,
Sub: G.Davies.
CARDIFF CITY: R.Healey, P.Dwyer, C.Charles, F.Pethard, R.Morgan, M.England, B.Buchanan, D.Livermore, G.Reece, A.Alston, B.Clark.
Sub: P.Sayer.

Scorers: Swansea City (-)
Cardiff City (Alston 2, Clark)
Attendance: 10,075

Toshack sets up late win

1st January 1980
Football League Division 2

SWANSEA CITY 2 CARDIFF CITY 1

Cardiff City 'old boys' John Toshack and David Giles brought about the Swans win in the first League clash between the two clubs for 15 years.

Peter Grotier, on loan from Lincoln City, made some excellent early saves from Waddle and Toshack but he was partly to blame for Swansea's first goal in 27 minutes. He seemed slow leaving his line to dispute an in-swinging corner by Giles, which cleared the head of Dwyer for **TOSHACK** to nod home from just a couple of yards.

LEWIS then levelled the scores ten minutes later. His free-kick from 25 yards curved round a line of Swansea defenders, past Letheren and into the far corner of the net.

Bishop's pace posed problems for a suspect Swansea defence. Twice he forced Letheren to make smothering saves on the fringe of his penalty area, the first block rebounding to Ronnie Moore who lifted his shot wastefully over the bar. But in the second half he was twice unfortunate not to get the goal that had eluded him for 12 matches. He also came in for some heavy treatment, one tackle producing a booking for Nigel Stevenson and another challenge by Phillips causing the Cardiff player to angrily show the Swansea full-back studmarks on his ribs.

Cardiff fans thought they had a goal to celebrate in the 87th minute when Lewis' shot from 25 yards hit the junction of the bar and post and rebounded into the welcoming arms of the relieved Letheren.

But then in the second minute of injury-time came Swansea's dramatic winner. Alan Waddle headed on a Leighton Phillips throw-in for Robbie James to push an astute pass to Toshack. The Welsh international shaped to shoot but instead aimed a low centre which **GILES** skilfully controlled before drilling the ball past Grotier - it was Giles' first goal since his £70,000 move from Wrexham the previous month.

SWANSEA CITY: C.Letheren, L.Phillips, D.Rushbury, J.Charles, N.Stevenson, D.Giles, T.Craig, R.James, A.Waddle, J.Toshack, I.Callaghan. Sub: B.Attley.
CARDIFF CITY: P.Grotier, P.Dwyer, C.Sullivan, D.Campbell, K.Pontin, R.Thomas, J.Lewis, R.Bishop, R.Moore, W.Ronson, J.Buchanan. Sub: G.Stevens.

Scorers: Swansea City (Toshack, Giles)
Cardiff City (Lewis)
Attendance: 21,400

Ronson is Bluebirds hero with winning volley

7th April 1980
Football League Division 2

CARDIFF CITY 1 SWANSEA CITY 0

Billy Ronson's goal six minutes from the end settled this absorbing South Wales derby - the first at Ninian Park in the League for 15 years.

After shading a first half in which Buchanan twice blasted wide from reasonable scoring positions, the Bluebirds dominated the second period largely because of the midfield mastery gained by Campbell, Ronson and Grapes. They could have won by three clear goals. Such was Cardiff's defensive domination that Ron Healey's only anxious moment was when he had to stretch to intercept, one-handed, a cunning cross from Neil Robinson.

Buchanan first fired wide in the 15th and 18th minutes, first from a Ronson-inspired attack, then from a Grapes centre won by Pontin.

The Swans' best chance came on the half-hour when Toshack moved into space for a return pass from Giles, only to misconnect when well placed.

Just before half-time, Dave Stewart went full length to turn aside a tremendous cross-shot from Grapes and Buchanan's blast was blocked by Attley on the line.

Despite continuous pressure from the Bluebirds throughout the second half, Swansea's luck seemed to be standing them in good stead for a point, especially when a mistimed Alan Waddle header rebounded to safety off his own upright!

But then on 84 minutes the energetic Ronson exchanged passes with John Lewis, whose double shuffle took him past Wyndham Evans. Lewis's first goal effort was beaten out by Stewart and his second attempt was also blocked, the ball rebounding to John Buchanan. For the second time in the game, Brian Attley checked Buchanan's drive on the goal-line but **RONSON** seized on the second rebound to shoot home from 10 yards.

SWANSEA CITY: D.Stewart, W.Evans, N.Robinson, L.Phillips, N.Stevenson, D.Giles, T.Craig, B.Attley, A.Waddle, J.Toshack, J.Mahoney. Sub: M.Baker.

CARDIFF CITY: R.Healey, P.Dwyer, J.Lewis, D.Campbell, K.Pontin, R.Thomas, J.Buchanan, G.Stevens, R.Moore, W.Ronson, S.Grapes. Sub: C.Sullivan.

Scorers: Swansea City (-)
Cardiff City (Ronson)
Attendance: 14,667

Swans foiled in six-goal thriller

27th December 1980
Football League Division 2

CARDIFF CITY 3 SWANSEA CITY 3

John Buchanan's goal of a lifetime salvaged a point for the Bluebirds when all seemed lost. With just three minutes to play, Wayne Hughes touched a short free-kick fully 35 yards from goal for Buchanan to hit the ball with such power it was in the Swansea net before Scottish international keeper Dave Stewart could move.

The Bluebirds took the lead on 13 minutes when tall striker Gary **STEVENS** kept his composure to convert a perceptive 40-yard pass from Buchanan with a close-range volley.

Despite the Swans having most of the possession in the first half, Cardiff contained them with little discomfort until all their hard work was undone by two glaring mistakes. An atrocious square-pass by Phil Dwyer led to the Swans' first goal after 40 minutes. John Lewis's failure to clear the danger set up the chance for Neil **ROBINSON** to break clear and beat Ron Healey with a splendid shot. Swansea took the lead after 43 minutes when Healey failed to hold a stinging shot from Robbie James. Leighton James was first to the rebound and he crossed for **CURTIS** to net from a few yards.

A recurrence of a thigh injury to Phil Dwyer meant that he did not re-appear for the second half, forcing Cardiff to reorganise.

When the unmarked Leighton **JAMES**, subdued for most of the match, looped a 73rd minute header over Healey after a piece of Curtis magic created the opening, the Bluebirds' cause looked lost. But in the 86th minute a poor clearance by Stewart presented an opportunity which **KITCHEN** ruthlessly exploited. Just 90 seconds later Cardiff were on terms thanks to that monumental goal by **BUCHANAN** and in the last few minutes both sides had chances to win it. Bishop and Buchanan hit shots off target and Bishop fired tamely when Kitchen was better placed. In the last minute, Healey made a great save from Robbie James.

SWANSEA CITY: D.Stewart, B.Attley, D.Hadziabdic, J.Mahoney, N.Stevenson, L.Phillips, A.Curtis, R.James, L.James, J.Charles, N.Robinson.
CARDIFF CITY: R.Healey, L.Jones, J.Lewis, W.Hughes, P.Maddy, P.Dwyer, R.Bishop, P.Kitchen, G.Stevens, W.Ronson, J.Buchanan.
Sub: P.Giles.

Scorers: Swansea City (Robinson, Curtis, L.James)
Cardiff City (Stevens, Kitchen, Buchanan)
Attendance: 21,239

Healey's spot-kick save shatters Swans

18th April 1981
Football League Division 2

SWANSEA CITY 1 CARDIFF CITY 1

A last-minute change of mind helped Cardiff keeper Ron Healey make the breathtaking penalty stop that may save the Bluebirds from relegation and deny the Swans promotion.

Alan Curtis was unlucky not to put Swansea ahead after 21 minutes from an opening created by a typical Leighton James run which took him past Jones, Ronson and Dwyer. The drive by Curtis beat Healey but rebounded off the base of a post.

Jeremy Charles missed an easier headed opportunity from a measured free-kick, again from Leighton James, who showed how chances should be taken two minutes before half-time. **JAMES** rifled the perfect left-footed drive past Healey to punish a poor John Lewis clearance that went straight to Wyndham Evans. Fortune smiled on Ron Healey a minute later when after failing to hold a cross-shot by Swans acting captain Tommy Craig, he saw Yugoslav Ante Rajkovic miss from close range.

Cardiff, who had hardly managed a shot in the first 45 minutes, were much more positive after the break when Lewis began to show his attacking qualities. From his dangerous cross on the hour mark, Gary Stevens headed onto Swansea's crossbar. Steve Grapes fired wide from a cross by Paul Giles before the youngster made way for Tarki Micallef.

Then on 69 minutes the Swans were awarded a penalty for handball by Keith Pontin. Leighton James placed his shot accurately enough with his right-foot and the ball was going just inside the post until Healey hurtled at full stretch to his right to hold it cleanly. The save inspired the Bluebirds to sustain their second half superiority and ten minutes from time they drew level. A fine cross by Lewis was headed home by Peter **KITCHEN** - his 18th goal of the season and this with just four minutes of this full-blooded derby clash to play.

SWANSEA CITY: D.Stewart, W.Evans, D.Hadziabdic, A.Rajkovic, N.Stevenson, D.Lewis, A.Curtis, R.James, L.James, J.Charles, T.Craig.
Sub: B.Attley.
CARDIFF CITY: R.Healey, L.Jones, C.Sullivan, S.Grapes, K.Pontin, P.Dwyer, J.Lewis, P.Kitchen, G.Stevens, W.Ronson, P.Giles.
Sub: C.Micallef.

Scorers: Swansea City (L.James)
Cardiff City (Kitchen)
Attendance: 19,038

Bold Bluebirds bring best out of Davies

12th May 1982
Welsh Cup Final 1st Leg

CARDIFF CITY 0 SWANSEA CITY 0

Cardiff City made the boldest of bids to wrest the Welsh Cup from their greatest rivals, a Swansea side that had maintained a pace in the top six of the First Division all season, in an intriguing first leg of the final at Ninian Park.

The Bluebirds took the game to the Swans and Phil Lythgoe, who until recently was playing Southern League football for Witney, had two reasonable chances to have given Cardiff an interval lead. From a half-cleared corner by Micallef, the winger volleyed over the bar. Then, seven minutes before the break, he was again too high after Dave Bennett had got past Nigel Stevenson to set up the chance.

Cardiff looked the more likely to score, Mick Henderson shaving the bar with a powerful header before Dai Davies produced the first of two second half saves in the 70th minute with a wonderful reflex save from Tarki Micallef. The second came five minutes later when he went full length to turn aside a cross-shot by Gary Bennett.

It was not until the closing minutes that the Swans began to show glimpses of their true form. Ray Kennedy, searching for a Welsh Cup winners' medal to add to his glittering array of trophies, was inches away with a glancing header and a teasing cross by Leighton James almost crept in under the bar. Then with four minutes to play, an incredible save by Andy Dibble prevented Robbie James from breaking the deadlock. The same player thought he had scored a last-minute winner when his header beat 17-year-old Dibble but an upraised linesman's flag ruled out the score.

SWANSEA CITY: D.Davies, C.Marustik, D.Hadziabdic, N.Stevenson, R.Kennedy, A.Rajkovic, A.Curtis, R.James, L.James, M.Thompson,

B.Latchford. Sub: G.Stanley.
CARDIFF CITY: A.Dibble, L.Jones, M.Henderson, K.Pontin, C.Micallef, J.Mullen, G.Lythgoe, T.Gilbert, G.Bennett, D.Bennett, G.Stevens.
Sub: S.McEwan.

Scorers: Swansea City (-)
Cardiff City (-)
Attendance: 11,960

Latchford's 'Double' clinches Welsh Cup

19th May 1982
Welsh Cup Final 2nd Leg

SWANSEA CITY 2 CARDIFF CITY 1

Swansea City retained the Welsh Cup in a pulsating match at the Vetch Field, with former England striker Bob Latchford inflicting the final wound in Cardiff City's season of torment.

In an all-action Cup Final, the most memorable for years and containing even more drama than the first leg, the Swans were a far more potent attacking force than when they were held to a goalless draw at Ninian Park.

Former Blackpool midfielder Stan McEwan produced a goal for Cardiff with his first touch - a probing pass behind Dzemal Hadziabdic that put through Linden Jones. A horrendous mistake by the usually unflappable Rajkovic gifted the goal to the Bluebirds, his sliced clearance spinning up for Gary **BENNETT** to force the ball home off his chest and knee.

Cardiff's lead was short-lived as slack marking allowed **LATCHFORD** to hit an unstoppable volley past Andy Dibble from no more than three yards, after Robbie James had found him with an accurate cross. Dibble had no chance either with **LATCHFORD,s** second goal, driven home emphatically from 12 yards after a misjudgment by Tim Gilbert had allowed him a clear strike at the target. It was also Latchford who popped up to make the goal-line clearance that prevented Gary Bennett scoring the second goal that would have given Cardiff the Cup on the away goal ruling in the event of the scores finishing level.

Though for the most part the game was played in a sporting spirit, it had a 69th minute flashpoint when Ante Rajkovic was sent off.

The Swansea skipper checked a Cardiff counter-attack by blatantly tripping Phil Lythgoe when his break from the halfway line threatened to tear open the home side's flimsy defensive cover. Referee Gwyn Owen of Anglesey, in his final game, had no alternative but to show Rajkovic the red card, having previously cautioned him for a foul on Mick Henderson.

Ironically, Rajkovic returned at the final whistle to receive the trophy that ensured Swansea European competition next season in the Cup Winners' Cup.

Sadly this marvellously entertaining game was marred by the trouble caused by a mindless minority, with at least one policeman being hurt in clashes with the fans.

Swansea City: D.Davies, N.Robinson, D.Hadziabdic, N.Stevenson, R.Kennedy, A.Rajkovic, A.Curtis, R.James, L.James, G.Stanley, B.Latchford. Sub: M.Thompson.
Cardiff City: A.Dibble, L.Jones, M.Henderson, K.Pontin, C.Micallef, J.Mullen, G.Lythgoe, T.Gilbert, G.Bennett, D.Bennett, S.McEwan. Sub: G.Stevens.

Scorers: Swansea City (Latchford 2)
Cardiff City (G.Bennett)
Attendance: 15,858

Lee settles Ninian Park cracker

26th December 1983
Football League Division 2

CARDIFF CITY 3 SWANSEA CITY 2

Trevor Lee celebrated his Cardiff City debut with what proved to be the winning goal to halt a run of three defeats. It made him an instant favourite with Bluebirds fans, in a bumper Boxing Day morning crowd of 14,580, enjoying a five-goal thriller.

Ian Baird, who struck up a promising partnership with Lee - veteran of more than 300 first team games for Millwall, Colchester, Gillingham and Bournemouth - produced a smart save from Chris Sander before Roger **GIBBINS** headed Cardiff into a 24th minute lead from a well-judged cross by Gary Bennett. The teenage Sander whose handling throughout the game was excellent, made a splendid fingertip save to prevent Lee's close-range header increasing the home side's lead four minutes later.

But Swansea got back into the game with a penalty converted by **STANLEY** in the third minute of first half stoppage time. Paul Bodin had conceded the penalty with a clumsy challenge on Colin Pascoe.

Swansea were back on level terms for just three minutes, however, the ever-dangerous Lee nodding down Bodin's cross for Nigel **VAUGHAN** to side foot home in the sixth minute of first half injury-time!

Maddy missed a great chance of a second equaliser within seconds of the restart with the goal at his mercy - a costly miss as **LEE** gave Cardiff a two-goal lead minutes later. The Swans were in need of something special and, ten minutes into the second half, after receiving a crossfield pass from Dudley Lewis, **TOSHACK** set off on a 40 yard run, stepping inside full-back Colin Smith and curving a low right-footed drive round the diving Dibble. It was a superb goal by Swansea's player-manager to mark his first League game for nearly three years.

SWANSEA CITY: C.Sander, W.Evans, G.Stanley, G.Richards, N.Stevenson, D.Lewis, J.Loveridge, C.Marustik, C.Pascoe, J.Toshack, P.Maddy. Sub: I.Walsh.
CARDIFF CITY: A.Dibble, C.Smith, P.Booth, P.Dwyer G.Bennett, D.Tong, G.Owen, R.Gibbins, I.Baird, N.Vaughan, T.Lee. Sub: M.Burke.

Scorers: Swansea City (Stanley pen, Toshack)
Cardiff City (Gibbins, Vaughan, Lee)
Attendance: 14,580

Saunders sparks amazing comeback

21st April 1984
Football League Division 2

SWANSEA CITY 3 CARDIFF CITY 2

Producing one of the South Wales derbies bravest fightbacks, Swansea City overcame a two-goal deficit to avoid the ultimate indignity of being dumped into Division Three by their arch rivals.

The Bluebirds let Swansea off the hook by failing to convert clear cut openings. Roger Gibbins tried to dribble round keeper Mike Hughes, substitute Martin Goldsmith saw his header cleared off the line and Owen ought to have done better from two good opportunities.

Colin **SMITH** gave Cardiff a 15th minute lead, bustling past Colin Pascoe to lift an 18-yard shot past Hughes, stranded yards off his line. And when Gordon **OWEN** fluked his 18th goal of the season with an intended cross that drifted over Hughes when his positional sense again let him down, the result seemed settled.

But the Swans hauled themselves back into the game, Ian Walsh breaking to the by-line to turn back a low centre for Dean **SAUNDERS** to beat Dibble at his near post. Compelling performances by Dudley Lewis and Neil Robinson and a will to win typified by Ante Rajkovic enabled Swansea to dominate the second half.

WALSH levelled the scores in the 72nd minute with a drive that took a wicked deflection off Gary Bennett to spoil his return from a seven-match lay-off. And six minutes later Pascoe, displaying his exciting skills, eluded Bennett's clumsy tackle to supply the pass for **SAUNDERS** to net the winner and complete a remarkable recovery.

SWANSEA CITY: M.Hughes, W.Evans, P.McQuillan, D.Lewis, N.Stevenson, A.Rajkovic, D.Saunders, N.Robinson, I.Walsh, C.Marustik, C.Pascoe. Sub: G.Richards.

CARDIFF CITY: A.Dibble, K.Elsey, D.Grant, P.Dwyer, C.Smith, D.Tong, G.Owen, R.Gibbins, N.Vaughan, G.Bennett, T.Lee. Sub: M.Goldsmith.

Scorers: Swansea City (Saunders 2, Walsh)
Cardiff City (Smith, Owen)
Attendance: 10,275

French nets winner in disappointing friendly

9th August 1985
Friendly

SWANSEA CITY 1 CARDIFF CITY 0

With the big kick-off just over a week away, Cardiff City's attacking limitations were glaringly exposed in their friendly cup-tie at the Vetch Field,

Bluebirds manager Alan Durban left out the tall Graham Withey after a series of punchless performances, but the lightweight strike partnership of Mark Farrington and Tarki Micallef was easily contained by Swansea's Welsh internationals Paul Price and Nigel Stevenson. In fact, Swansea keeper Jimmy Rimmer, his damaged right calf heavily strapped, was so well protected he did not have a telling shot to save!

Cardiff's best efforts came from the industrious Brian Flynn, their most consistent performer in the pre-season games. Allowing for the fact that Swansea were disrupted by injuries to defenders Jake King and John Carver, the Bluebirds ought to have made a much greater impact.

Not that the Swans were much better in front of goal, their match-winner being an untidy affair after 55 minutes.

Nigel French dribbled past Cardiff keeper Chris Sander only to lose possession. But full-back Carlton Leonard failed to clear the ball, nudging it back into the path of the 17-year-old apprentice **FRENCH,** who netted from close in.

In the minutes that remained, scoring chances were few and far between as both sets of defences continued to dominate the game.

Scorers: Swansea City (French)
Cardiff City (-)
Attendance: 5,000

Flynn 'Double' boost Bluebirds

20th August 1985
Football League Cup 1st Round 1st Leg

CARDIFF CITY 2 SWANSEA CITY 1

Brian Flynn's first goal for Cardiff City should have laid the foundation for a conclusive Milk Cup victory at Ninian Park. But after failing to take their chances when they were in control, the Bluebirds allowed Swansea a way back with a soft goal.

The keen rivalry between the sides was reflected by a challenge on Hutchison, for which Ford was sternly lectured by the referee, and by a ninth minute booking of Gibbins for a heavy challenge on French.

Swansea's first counter-attack came after a quarter of an hour, Waddle and French combining to give Turner a chance but he hoisted his drive well wide.

The Bluebirds went ahead three minutes later following an incisive move started and finished by Flynn. From his prompting, Turner, Farrington and Ford were involved in a flowing move and when Vaughan's cross from the left was only partially cleared, **FLYNN** followed up to beat Rimmer with a well-placed drive. Swansea found it hard to break through although Marustik went close with a cross-volley after 28 minutes. Then a superb one-handed save by Rimmer denied Farrington.

The Swans came more into the game and their former keeper Sander made a smart smothering stop from French. On the stroke of half-time however, hesitation by Sander presented Waddle with a headed chance he should have taken.

The second half was only three minutes old when Sander hesitated again, this time in coming for Paul Price's free-kick and

Chris **MARUSTIK** nipped in to nudge the ball past him. Jimmy Rimmer then held onto a close range effort from Farrington, then blocked Vaughan's low drive with his legs. The veteran keeper was finally beaten in the 87th minute when Carver's cross was headed down by Turner and Vaughan rolled the ball back for **FLYNN** to steer another left-footed shot out of Rimmer's reach.

SWANSEA CITY: J.Rimmer, D.Lewis, C.Sullivan, P.Price, N.Stevenson, C.Marustik, T.Hutchison, R.Turner, A.Waddle, R.McHale, N.French.
Sub: K.Andrews.
CARDIFF CITY: C.Sander, J.King, J.Carver, R.Gibbins, M.Ford, J.Mullen, B.Flynn, M.Farrington, R.Turner, N.Vaughan, K.Meacock. Sub: C.Micallef.

Scorers: Swansea City (Marustik)
Cardiff City (Flynn 2)
Attendance: 4,218

Bluebirds crash to Swans 'Quickies'

3rd September 1985
Football League Cup 1st Round 2nd Leg

SWANSEA CITY 3 CARDIFF CITY 1

Swansea City scored three goals in 11 minutes to transform this Milk Cup tie at the Vetch Field, but Cardiff were furious over an extraordinary refereeing decision to award the Swans a goal on the stroke of half-time, which proved to be the turning point.

Swansea almost scored from their first attack, Pascoe taking advantage of an error by Vaughan to break from the halfway line and hit a 20-yard drive which Rees touched onto his crossbar. Kevin Meacock worked tirelessly for openings and, after 21 minutes, Carver forced a diving save from the Swansea keeper with a 25-yard effort from Brian Flynn's short free-kick. As the Bluebirds maintained the pressure, Stevenson almost put through his own goal. Cardiff went ahead after 40 minutes when Mark **FARRINGTON** headed home Vaughan's centre to punish a mistake by Colin Pascoe.

Then, just before half-time, Waddle headed on a long throw by Marustik and Colin **RANDELL** netted from 15 yards. The linesman raised his flag, apparently to signal that a Swansea player directly in front of Mel Rees had strayed into an offside position. However, after consultation, Bristol referee Roger Milford overruled the linesman and allowed the goal to stand.

Within five minutes of the restart, **RANDELL**, making a belated home debut after settling personal differences with John Bond, added his second goal to put the scores level on aggregate. Rees was beaten again in the 55th minute as Waddle nodded down a diagonal cross from Tommy Hutchison for **PASCOE** to force past the keeper from close in.

It put the Swans 4-3 ahead and though Cardiff had several chances to take the game into extra-time, the home side held on to win.

SWANSEA CITY: J.Rimmer, D.Lewis, C.Sullivan, P.Price, N.Stevenson, C.Marustik, T.Hutchison, C.Randell, A.Waddle, R.McHale, C.Pascoe. Sub: N.French.
CARDIFF CITY: M.Rees, C.Leonard, J.Carver, R.Gibbins, M.Ford, J.Mullen, B.Flynn, M.Farrington, N.Vaughan, K.Meacock, P.McLoughlin. Sub: C.Micallef.

Scorers: Swansea City (Randell 2, Pascoe)
Cardiff City (Farrington)
Attendance: 4,621

Vaughan goal gives Cardiff third consecutive win

26th December 1985
Football League Division 3

CARDIFF CITY 1 SWANSEA CITY 0

A crowd of 9,375 - more than double Cardiff's previous best this season - went to Ninian Park to witness the resurrection of Swansea City Football Club.

Spurred on by thousands of fans who had feared they would never see their side play again, the Swans started promisingly, Lee Smelt having to make urgent smothering saves at the feet of Ray McHale and Roger Gibbins. But the Swansea defence was vulnerable to high crosses and the Bluebirds should have taken the lead when Turner nodded Derek Christie's centre back across goal for Farrington - whose header was handled on the line by full-back David Hough. Jimmy Mullen, Cardiff's captain, took the resultant spot-kick but it was close enough to Hughes for the keeper to dive to his right and save comfortably.

McHale then saw his close range attempt touched for a corner and Gibbins hit the side-netting with a diving header.

Early after the restart, Hughes denied Turner with a brilliant reflex save. Finally though, Swans' overworked keeper was punished for his only mistake. Surrey referee Ray Lewis decided to apply the advantage rule when a linesman flagged for a foul on Curtis because the Bluebirds still had possession. And a moment's hesitation by Hughes in reacting to Christie's hanging cross allowed Cardiff's leading scorer Nigel **VAUGHAN** the time to wait for the ball to drop and drive in his ninth goal of the campaign - his fifth in as many matches.

This late goal earned Cardiff their third straight league win and as Swansea's plight obviously aroused far greater public interest, match takings were twice what had been expected.

SWANSEA CITY: M.Hughes, D.Hough, C.Sullivan, P.Price, A.Melville, C.Harrison, R.McHale, T.Hutchison, R.Gibbins, A.Waddle, I.Davies. Sub: S.McCarthy.
CARDIFF CITY: L.Smelt, W.Curtis, D.Giles, M.Ford, N.Stevenson, J.Mullen, D.Christie, N.Vaughan, R.Turner, M.Farrington, C.Micallef. Sub: J.Gummer.

Scorers: Swansea City (-)
Cardiff City (Vaughan)
Attendance: 9,375

McCarthy fires Swans to Last 16

28th January 1986
Freight Rover Trophy

CARDIFF CITY 0 SWANSEA CITY 2

Sean McCarthy fired Swansea into the quarter-finals of the Freight Rover Trophy. The 20-year-old striker, snapped up from Welsh League club Bridgend, scored in each half to earn the Swans a place in the last 16 as winners of their mini-league including Cardiff City and Newport County.

However, it was Tommy Hutchison who left his desk to mastermind this victory. The 38-year-old put himself in the Swans starting line-up for the first time in six matches and emerged as the game's outstanding player.

Cardiff's first genuine attack after 11 minutes forced an urgent save from Hughes. Christie cut in from the right and hit a powerful shot which the keeper could only parry. But when Wheeler followed up with a shot, a team-mate had strayed offside.

Swansea hit back with three quickfire attacks in as many minutes. In the 17th minute, Hutchison's deep cross cleared the Cardiff defence but McCarthy could not control it quickly enough and his drive from a narrow angle hit the side-netting. Hutchison's menacing free-kick a minute later wasn't properly cleared but Price was too high with his effort and, within sixty seconds, Gibbins shot tamely at Smelt after Emmanuel's header had given him the opening.

The Swans' supremacy was rewarded in the 44th minute when **McCARTHY** forced Hutchison's corner home at the far post. Midway through the second half, Waddle and French combined from Price's free-kick and **McCARTHY** was well placed to finish the move off with a firm left-footed drive.

Four minutes from time, keeper Hughes went full length to deny David Giles the goal that would have committed Swansea to a play-off with Newport County.

SWANSEA CITY: M.Hughes, D.Lewis, I.Davies, P.Price, C.Harrison, G.Emmanuel, T.Hutchison, N.French, R.Gibbins, S.McCarthy, D.Hough. Subs: A.Waddle, W.Foley.
CARDIFF CITY: L.Smelt, W.Curtis, D.Giles, C.Marustik, M.Ford, J.Mullen, D.Christie, N.Vaughan, P.Wheeler, P.McLoughlin, C.Micallef. Subs: R.Turner, J.Gummer.

Scorers: Swansea City (McCarthy 2)
Cardiff City (-)
Attendance: 1,006

It's Roger and out for Cardiff

31st March 1986
Football League Division 3

SWANSEA CITY 2 CARDIFF CITY 0

Former Ninian Park forward Roger Gibbins helped drive another nail into Cardiff City's relegation coffin as the Bluebirds slumped to their fourth defeat in 11 days. He was involved in both goals, which rekindled the Swans hopes of staying in the Third Division, although they still faced an uphill task to collect enough points to be safe.

After a scrappy opening, Cardiff ought to have gone into the interval in the lead but Chris Marustik sliced his shot wide from Paul McLoughlin's low centre. On 32 minutes, Wayne Curtis found Phil Brignull but the centre-half headed just over the bar. Moments later, the Swans were caught out again by a quickly taken free-kick involving Curtis and McLoughlin, but this time Mike Ford was unfortunate to see his solid header rebound off the bar with keeper Mike Hughes beaten.

Swansea's best effort of the first half saw Curtis head Colin Randell's effort off the line from Tommy Hutchison's in-swinging corner.

On 52 minutes Chris Sander, the ex-Swansea keeper now with Haverfordwest but deputising for Cardiff's injured Lee Smelt, was at fault for the Swans' first goal. He failed to hold Gibbins' header and David **HOUGH** was on hand to score from close range. The Bluebirds' hopes were dashed by a second Swansea goal on 63 minutes. Gibbins laid the ball into the path of Hutchison, who glided past Curtis and Brignull before crossing for **WILLIAMS** to drive home from 15 yards.

Hughes preserved a clean sheet with the save of the match after 75 minutes, diving to his right to keep out Marustik's power drive.

It was a disappointing display by the Bluebirds, who faced a second successive relegation and Fourth Division football for the first time in their history.

SWANSEA CITY: M.Hughes, D.Hough, C.Sullivan, P.Price, C.Harrison, G.Emmanuel, T.Hutchison, C.Randell, R.Gibbins, S.McCarthy, P.Williams. Sub: C.Pascoe.
CARDIFF CITY: C.Sander, W.Curtis, D.Giles, C.Marustik, P.Brignull, J.Mullen, P.McLoughlin, G.Nardello, R.Turner, C.Micallef, M.Ford. Sub: N.Vaughan.

Scorers: Swansea City (Hough, Williams)
Cardiff City (-)
Attendance: 6,643

Swans denied by McCarthy miss

26th December 1986
Football League Division 4

CARDIFF CITY 0 SWANSEA CITY 0

An extraordinary miss by Sean McCarthy two minutes from time denied Swansea their first Ninian Park win for 27 years.

Sadly the game didn't live up to expectations - the play was often scrappy and the finishing poor.

Nigel Vaughan had a glorious opportunity to give the Bluebirds the lead after just three minutes when a long throw by Chris Marustik was only partially cleared. But Cardiff's leading goalscorer, whose late goal earned his side victory in the corresponding game last season, drove narrowly wide with his right-foot from 20 yards. Marustik went closer against his former club after 22 minutes, his volley skimming the bar after Bartlett had created the opening from a Pike knockdown.

Swansea eventually settled and on 36 minutes they almost broke the deadlock. Cardiff keeper Graham Moseley went full length to keep out Colin Pascoe's well-struck effort from the edge of the penalty area. Moseley was again well positioned minutes later to stop a looping header from Paul Atkinson, who was making his Swansea debut after arriving on loan from Oldham Athletic.

On the hour mark, one of several slips by Cardiff centre-half Phil Brignull let in McCarthy but again Moseley came to his side's rescue with a fine save.

After 88 minutes, Tommy Hutchison's determined challenge on Terry Boyle as they contested a cross by Colin Pascoe won possession for McCarthy. But instead of netting his 14th goal of the season, he somehow managed to steer his right-footed shot wide from inside the six-yard box.

The miss prevented the Swans from reclaiming second spot from Southend United, who went down 4-0 at home to leaders Northampton Town.

SWANSEA CITY: M.Hughes, C.Harrison, T.Phelan, D.Lewis, A.Melville, G.Emmanuel, P.Atkinson, S.McCarthy, I.Love, C.Pascoe, T.Hutchison.
Sub: P.Williams.
CARDIFF CITY: G.Moseley, D.Giles, M.Ford, P.Wimbleton, P.Brignull, T.Boyle, N.Platnauer, K.Bartlett, C.Pike, N.Vaughan, C.Marustik.
Sub: A.Curtis.

Scorers: Swansea City (-)
Cardiff City (-)
Attendance: 11,505

Swans outclass lacklustre Bluebirds

20th April 1987
Football League Division 4

SWANSEA CITY 2 CARDIFF CITY 0

This win, much more emphatic than the 2-0 scoreline suggests, revived the Swan's promotion hopes, though the Vetch Field club were still waiting for the League to hear their appeal against the lost points for failing to play at Rochdale and this outcome could be the decisive factor.

Swansea certainly outclassed a Bluebirds side which never really played well, with the exception of Alan Curtis for whom Swansea had a cash bid rejected on the previous month's transfer deadline.

Cardiff, loaned Swansea's sky blue second strip shorts because their own white ones clashed with the Swans, gave the ball away with monotonous regularity.

Swansea went ahead after 26 minutes when Emmanuel's corner was cleared only as far as **ATKINSON** whose instant 18-yard drive through a crowded goalmouth caught Rees unsighted until it was too late. Swansea's Tommy Hutchison, Paul Atkinson and Gary Emmanuel ran the midfield and when the evergreen Hutchison turned on the style in the second-half, Cardiff only avoided a crushing defeat thanks to keeper Mel Rees who made a string of superb saves.

Yet there was nothing he could do about Swansea's second goal after 77 minutes. Hutchison found space to lift a cross to the far post where McCarthy's downward header was good enough to beat Rees. He would have scored even if Terry **BOYLE** had not put the ball in the net with a despairing attempt to head clear.

The overworked Rees denied McCarthy a hat-trick with breathtaking stops, the best in the final minute when he managed to turn his powerful header onto the post.

SWANSEA CITY: M.Hughes, C.Harrison, T.Phelan, A.Melville, N.Stevenson, G.Emmanuel, P.Atkinson, S.McCarthy, P.Raynor, C.Pascoe, T.Hutchison. Sub: K.Andrews.

CARDIFF CITY: M.Rees, N.Vaughan, M.Ford, P.Wimbleton, P.Brignull, T.Boyle, N.Platnauer, P.Wheeler, S.Mardenborough, A.Curtis, J.Gummer.
Sub: A.Rogers.

Scorers: Swansea City (Atkinson, Boyle og)
Cardiff City (-)
Attendance: 6,653

Gilligan goal gives Bluebirds the edge

29th August 1987
Football League Division 4

CARDIFF CITY 1 SWANSEA CITY 0

Joe Allon's dismissal after 28 minutes undoubtedly wrecked Swansea's chances of winning at Ninian Park for the first time in 28 years. But there was enough quality from both sides to suggest that they can compete among the better Fourth Division clubs this season.

Steve Mardenborough injected genuine pace on the right and almost scored against his old club in the opening minutes from one electrifying run. But Mike Hughes foiled him with an outstanding save. Nicky Platnauer figured in one of the game's most exciting moves, swapping passes with Sanderson during a storming run. But he hit his shot against the bar from less than six yards.

Terry Boyle had to have three stitches put in a gash above his left eye when he was felled by Allon but he returned five minutes later to give a commanding display. Without Allon alongside Colin Pascoe, it was always going to be a struggle for the Swans to take the points but, on 35 minutes, Pascoe took a sharp return from Alan Davies to curl a shot that beat Graham Moseley but rebounded off the post into the keeper's welcoming arms.

The Swans were coping comfortably with ten men until the 53rd minute when Kelly's 25-yard drive was blocked, but the ball fell invitingly for **GILLIGAN** to net with a powerful drive from 12 yards.

Cardiff could have won by at least three goals but for Mardenborough, McDermott and Ford spurning golden opportunities as they over-ran the Swans in the closing stages. All three broke through on the right to attempt shots from narrow angles when, on each occasion, spare man Alan Curtis was unmarked in a central more favourable position waiting for the pass!

SWANSEA CITY: M.Hughes, D.Hough, C.Coleman, A.Melville, A.Knill, A.Davies, P.Williams, J.Allon, P.Raynor, C.Pascoe, K.Andrews.
Sub: S.McCarthy.
CARDIFF CITY: G.Moseley, S.Mardenborough, M.Ford, N.Platnauer, N.Stevenson, T.Boyle, A.Curtis, P.Sanderson, J.Gilligan, B.McDermott, M.Kelly. Sub: J.Perry.

Scorers: Swansea City (-)
Cardiff City (Gilligan)
Attendance: 6,010

Last-gasp goal secures point for Cardiff

1st January 1988
Football League Division 4

SWANSEA CITY 2   CARDIFF CITY 2

The Swans had conceded late equalisers in two of their last three games, while Cardiff had established a reputation as strong finishers. The Bluebirds have come from behind to win or draw games with goals in the closing minutes no fewer than nine times. In this game they forced an 84th minute equaliser, then fell behind again, but salvaged a point in the last minute to delight their large following in a bumper holiday crowd.

Jimmy Gilligan could have given Cardiff a 10th minute lead but for a splendid save by Mike Hughes. Curtis eluded the attention of John Lewis to hit a low left-footer narrowly wide and Gilligan struck the side-netting from a difficult angle.

Swansea's only serious strikes in a barren first half were a tame attempt by Colin Pascoe and a snap shot from Joe Allon.

Within a minute of Kevin Bartlett replacing Wheeler on the hour, Swansea went ahead in spectacular style. The lofty Alan Knill headed on Melville's free-kick and **ALLON** met it with an overhead kick, the ball rocketing past Scott Endersby.

Mark Kelly replaced McDermott after 70 minutes and he was involved in Cardiff's equaliser six minutes from time. Curtis helped Kelly's in-swinging corner on for **FORD** to head home from close range. The Bluebirds were still congratulating themselves when Paul **RAYNOR** punished their lapse of concentration by beating Endersby with a fierce cross-shot from a tight angle.

But the Bluebirds drew level again in the last minute from another set piece in which Curtis was again involved. From the near post free-kick by Phil Bater, Curtis headed into the six-yard box for **GILLIGAN** to claim his 16th goal of the season.

SWANSEA CITY: M.Hughes, C.Harrison, J.Lewis, A.Melville, A.Knill, G.Emmanuel, A.Davies, P.Raynor, J.Allon, C.Pascoe, K.Andrews.
Subs: C.Coleman, P.Williams.
CARDIFF CITY: S.Endersby, P.Bater, N.Platnauer, P.Wimbleton, N.Stevenson, T.Boyle, A.Curtis, M.Ford, J.Gilligan, B.McDermott, P.Wheeler. Subs: M.Kelly, K.Bartlett.

Scorers: Swansea City (Allon, Raynor)
Cardiff City (Ford, Gilligan)
Attendance: 10,360

Bluebirds pay for Boyle blunder

30th August 1988
Football League Cup 1st Round 1st Leg

CARDIFF CITY 0 SWANSEA CITY 1

There is no doubt that the Swans would have taken a bigger lead into the return leg of this Littlewoods Cup tie but for some spectacular saves by Cardiff keeper George Wood - including a penalty.

The Swans were given the controversial chance to capitalise on a good start when Paul Raynor's shot hit Nicky Platnauer. The referee saw nothing wrong with the interception until his attention was drawn to the upraised flag of a linesman. He ruled that Platnauer had deliberately handled the ball and awarded Swansea a penalty. Robbie James struck the spot-kick powerfully towards the left-hand corner of Wood's net but the former Scottish international dived the right way and turned the ball round the post at full stretch.

Terry Yorath's side set about their task with such commitment that Lee Bracey in the Swansea goal wasn't tested until the 37th minute, when he held on to Jimmy Gilligan's low drive despite Kevin Bartlett's attempt to deceive him by stepping over the shot.

The Swans went ahead five minutes later when Steve **THORNBER** ran onto a weak headed backpass from Terry Boyle to chip the ball over Wood as the Cardiff keeper left his line.

Just after the restart, Boyle atoned for his earlier error with a goal-line clearance to deny Wade a second goal for the Swans. Then Wood produced another outstanding save to prevent Love doubling his side's lead with a classic header from a Raynor cross.

Cardiff, though completely outplayed, almost drew level in the closing stages when a curling free-kick from Alan Curtis caught Lee Bracey unawares, but the ball passed inches wide of the target.

SWANSEA CITY: L.Bracey, D.Hough, C.Coleman, A.Melville, A.Knill, A.Davies, S.Thornber, B.Wade, I.Love, R.James, P.Raynor.
Subs: T.Hutchison, D.D'Auria.
CARDIFF CITY: G.Wood, I.Rodgerson, N.Platnauer, J.Gummer, N.Stevenson, T.Boyle, A.Curtis, K.Bartlett, J.Gilligan, B.McDermott, M.Kelly. Subs: I.Walsh, S.Lynex.

Scorers: Swansea City (Thornber)
Cardiff City (-)
Attendance: 6,241

Cardiff's late burst kills off Swans

20th September 1988
Football League Cup 1st Round 2nd Leg

SWANSEA CITY 0 CARDIFF CITY 2

Two goals in the space of three minutes of high drama transformed Cardiff City's fortunes at the Vetch Field to earn them a place in the second round of the Littlewoods Cup against Queens Park Rangers.

Swansea, a goal to the good after the first leg at Ninian Park, did not over-stretch themselves in the first half. They rarely looked like adding to Steve Thornber's goal from the first leg although Swans captain Robbie James slanted a rising shot against the bar when he took a return pass from Paul Raynor in the 37th minute. A minute later, Tommy Hutchison saw his snap-shot glance off Terry Boyle for a corner.

After the break, Cardiff ran the Swans ragged and only several spectacular saves from Lee Bracey prevented Jimmy Gilligan and Paul Wimbleton from getting on the scoresheet. Eventually though, the Swans crumbled and in the 77th minute, just eight minutes after replacing Alan Curtis, Paul Wheeler levelled the scores on aggregate with his first goal of the season. A right flank raid, prompted by Ian Rodgerson's free-kick and carried on by Gilligan and Steve Lynex, presented Wheeler with the chance to shoot low and hard from 15 yards. Bracey blocked the drive but **WHEELER** made no mistake from the rebound.

Bluebirds skipper Terry Boyle made sure of the club's first League and League Cup win at the Vetch for 30 years with the winner 10 minutes from time. An in-swinging corner on the left by Mark Kelly was firmly headed home by **BOYLE** with new Welsh cap Alan Knill and his defenders in disarray.

SWANSEA CITY: L.Bracey, D.Hough, C.Coleman, A.Melville, A.Knill, R.James, S.Thornber, T.Hutchison, I.Love, A.Davies, P.Raynor.
Subs: D.D'Auria, D.Lewis.

CARDIFF CITY: G.Wood, I.Rodgerson, N.Platnauer, P.Wimbleton, N.Stevenson, T.Boyle, S.Lynex, A.Curtis, J.Gilligan, J.Gummer, M.Kelly. Subs: P.Wheeler, P.Bater.

Scorers: Swansea City (-)
Cardiff City (Wheeler, Boyle)
Attendance: 6,987

Curtis outguns old club

6th December 1988
Sherpa Van Trophy

CARDIFF CITY 2 SWANSEA CITY 0

The Swans needed only to draw to get through this preliminary round tie in the Sherpa Van Trophy and, after safely negotiating the first half in which Alan Curtis posed the only threat, it seemed as if they would do.

Curtis had forced Swansea keeper Lee Bracey into a couple of urgent saves in the first half, the first forcing the former West Ham keeper to dive to his left to push out a swerving drive in the 28th minute and then five minutes later to turn a rasping drive by the Welsh international over the bar.

Apart from a 20-yard drive from captain Robbie James which forced a diving save from George Wood, the Swans found it difficult to break down a Cardiff defence that had gone six previous home games without conceding a goal.

Swansea had made several abortive attempts to sign Curtis for a third spell and just two minutes after the restart he put the skids under his old club. Moving on to a return pass from Bartlett, **CURTIS** stroked a right-footed drive wide of the Swansea keeper from 20 yards. He then went close with a volley from a half-clearance and Phil Bater shot over within a minute of replacing Jason Gummer on 54 minutes. The Bluebirds would have won by a much bigger margin but for a bad miss by Paul Wimbleton.

Swansea's best reply came from Dave Puckett, the on-loan forward from Bournemouth who forced the 36-year-old Wood into making a fine save with a close-range header.

The Bluebirds then clinched victory with a spectacular second goal in the 71st minute. Bartlett wrong-footed the visitors' defence by jumping over the ball, allowing Cardiff's leading scorer Jimmy **GILLIGAN** to dart in and crash home his 11th goal of the season from the edge of the six-yard box.

SWANSEA CITY: L.Bracey, D.Lewis, I.Marsh, D.Hough, A.Knill, R.James, S.Thornber, B.Wade, T.Hutchison, A.Davies, D.Puckett. Subs: I.Love, P.Bodak.

CARDIFF CITY: G.Wood, I.Rodgerson, N.Platnauer, P.Wimbleton, G.Abraham, T.Boyle, A.Curtis, K.Bartlett, J.Gilligan, J.Gummer, S.Lynex. Subs: P.Bater, P.Wheeler,

Scorers: Swansea City (-)
Cardiff City (Curtis, Gilligan)
Attendance; 2,986

Gilligan 'Double' then Swans fightback

26th December 1988
Football League Division 3

CARDIFF CITY 2 SWANSEA CITY 2

When Jimmy Gilligan scored twice in the opening six minutes, the Swans seemed destined for their customary defeat at Ninian Park, a ground where they had won just once in 18 league visits.

The fans were still pouring into the ground for this high noon showdown when the Bluebirds took the lead. Alan Knill fouled Kevin Bartlett on the edge of the penalty area and Jimmy **GILLIGAN** escaped the attentions of the centre-half to score with a splendid diving header. The Cardiff striker caused more misery for Knill on six minutes. This time **GILLIGAN** eluded the out-of-form defender to beat Lee Bracey to Paul Wimbleton's cross and so punish the Swansea defence for not coming out quickly enough at a half-cleared corner.

Only ten minutes had been played when Gilligan had the chance to complete his hat-trick, but his chipped effort as he lost his footing flew narrowly wide.

But as it was two minutes later, the Swans pulled a goal back. Alan Davies flicked on Tommy Hutchison's near-post corner and **PUCKETT** hit a low drive which Steve Lynex on the goal-line couldn't keep out. Then George Wood had to dive full length to keep out a 25-yard drive from Robbie James that took a deflection before on 32 minutes, the Swans drew level in controversial fashion.

The referee penalised Nigel Stevenson for a clumsy challenge on Andy Melville as they disputed Hutchison's high cross and awarded the Swans a free-kick. Steve Thornber ran over the ball and Alan **DAVIES** drilled the ball into the top right-hand corner of George Wood's net with the outside of his right foot.

Though the second half brought an anti-climax for the holiday crowd, either side could have won the game in its final stages. Alan Curtis glided effortlessly past three men to set up a chance wasted by Wimbleton shooting over, whilst at the other end Wood was at full stretch to save from James.

SWANSEA CITY: L.Bracey, A.Melville, C.Coleman, D.Hough, A.Knill, A.Davies, S.Thornber, R.James, T.Hutchison, D.Puckett, D.Lewis. Subs: I.Love, D.D'Auria.
CARDIFF CITY: G.Wood, I.Rodgerson, N.Stevenson, P.Wimbleton, G.Abraham, T.Boyle, A.Curtis, K.Bartlett, J.Gilligan, J.Gummer, S.Lynex. Subs: M.Kelly, P.Wheeler.

Scorers: Swansea City (Puckett, Davies)
Cardiff City (Gilligan 2)
Attendance: 10,675

Boyle sent off but Bluebirds deny Swans winner

27th March 1989
Football League Division 3

SWANSEA CITY 1 CARDIFF CITY 1

Cardiff City captain Terry Boyle's dismissal after 26 minutes left the Bluebirds with a backs-to-the-wall battle to preserve their early lead.

The visitors took the lead after just six minutes and inevitably the scorer was Jimmy Gilligan, who had scored six times in seven appearances against them. Alan Knill failed to cut out Phil Bater's cross and **GILLIGAN** scored with an emphatic downward header. Apart from a hastily punched clearance from Tommy Hutchison's cross in the first minute, Cardiff keeper George Wood was a virtual spectator in the first half. During that period, the Swans forced six corners without reply but failed to press home their territorial advantage.

Cardiff were much more dangerous and only an excellent block tackle by Andy Melville denied Lynex a goal in the 12th minute. Another fluent Cardiff move gave Wheeler a clear-cut chance but he drove wide from 18 yards.

Then on 26 minutes, Raynor was felled by an unfair tackle by Boyle for which he was penalised. The Swansea striker lashed out with his feet at the Bluebirds defender and Boyle foolishly retaliated by appearing to stamp on Raynor while he was on the ground. Referee Paul Durkin was close to the incident and immediately showed Boyle the red card.

Cardiff should have extended their lead after 39 minutes when Wheeler set up a great opportunity for Wimbleton but he pulled his drive wide of the target.

Swansea drew level on 51 minutes when Woods' punched clearance fell at the feet of **RAYNOR**, who netted with a glorious left-foot drive from 15 yards. Swansea continued to press forward in search of a winner and Wood made a full-length save to deny man-of-the-match Robbie James. Then in the last minute, West's clever flick-on provided David Hough with the chance to win the game but he shot straight at Wood.

SWANSEA CITY: L.Bracey, A.Melville, C.Coleman, D.Lewis, A.Knill, R.James, D.Hough, A.Davies, P.Raynor, C.West, T.Hutchison. Subs: S.Thornber, B.Wade.
CARDIFF CITY: G.Wood, I.Rodgerson, N.Platnauer, P.Wimbleton, T.Boyle, N.Stevenson, A.Curtis, P.Bater, J.Gilligan, P.Wheeler, S.Lynex. Subs: I.Walsh, M.Holmes.

Scorers: Swansea City (Raynor)
Cardiff City (Gilligan)
Attendance: 9,201

Barnard's quickfire strike settles derby

26th December 1989
Football League Division 3

SWANSEA CITY 0 CARDIFF CITY 1

A goal after just 45 seconds of this South Wales derby by Leigh Barnard earned the Bluebirds their first Vetch Field League win for 30 years in this Boxing Morning battle. The kick-off was delayed by a quarter of an hour as Swansea fans queued to claim vouchers for the all-ticket FA Cup tie with Liverpool!

New signing Keith Walker, an £80,000 purchase from St Mirren committed an unnecessary foul on Steve Lynex which earned the free-kick from which Cardiff scored the vital goal. Chris Pike flicked on the kick hoisted by former Swans player Roger Gibbins and **BARNARD** was the first to the ball, stretching to force in a shot that went in off a post.

Cardiff almost doubled their lead after four minutes but Freestone turned Pike's smart effort round the post.

It then took a quality save by Roger Hansbury to prevent the Swans drawing level five minutes before the break. Neat footwork by Raynor set up Trick and new signing Walker met his early cross with a header that produced a full-length diving save by Hansbury. That triggered off a spell of heavy Swansea pressure - Gibbins making a marvellous goal-line clearance off a Harris header and Trick shooting against the foot of a post when Alan Curtis's mishit free-kick inadvertently found the full-back.

Early in the second half, Raynor's pass found Curtis. He cut past Perry to hit a powerful drive that Hansbury did well to push round his right-hand post. Cohen Griffiths went closest to adding a second goal for the Bluebirds with a brilliant solo effort. He cheekily chipped Harris but his powerful rising drive smacked against the crossbar.

SWANSEA CITY: R.Freestone, D.Trick, C.Coleman, A.Melville, K.Walker, S.Thornber, M.Harris, A.Curtis, J.Hughes, P.Raynor, A.Legg.
Subs: T.Hutchison, S.Phillips.
CARDIFF CITY: R.Hansbury, I.Rodgerson, R.Daniel, L.Barnard, J.Perry, R.Gibbins, J.Morgan, C.Griffith, C.Pike, A.Lewis, S.Lynex.
Subs: M.Scott, R.Haig.

Scorers: Swansea City (-)
Cardiff City (Barnard)
Attendance: 12,244

Slick Swans win relegation battle

16th April 1990 Football League Division 3

CARDIFF CITY 0 SWANSEA CITY 2

The noon showdown between Cardiff and Swansea, both fighting for survival, was only five minutes old when the visitors took the lead. John **HUGHES** latched on to Andy Legg's corner to steer his downward header past Roger Hansbury and into the far corner.

It was a blow the Bluebirds could ill afford and they struggled to recover as Swansea's midfield troop of Alan Curtis, Robbie James and Steve Thornber enjoyed the freedom of Ninian Park. The Swans could have gone further ahead on 27 minutes as Curtis set up Raynor, but he shot straight at Hansbury when it seemed easier to score.

Cardiff did force Swansea to back-pedal during the early stages of the second half but, even with Kelly instigating every move they made, it was hard to see where the equaliser would come from. Then with just a quarter of an hour to go, Cohen Griffith had the best chance of the match but his glancing header from substitute Nathan Blake's centre was woefully wide - from that moment, the points were virtually in Swansea's bag.

Paul Raynor had a couple of stinging shots palmed clear by Hansbury but the experienced keeper could do nothing about Swansea's second goal in the 85th minute. Andy Legg, who had been kept quiet for much of the game by Rodgerson, found an inch of room to work his cross from the left and Bryan **WADE** did the rest in beating Hansbury from close range.

It was a crucial strike which could well send the Bluebirds down!

SWANSEA CITY: L.Bracey, D.Hough, C.Coleman, A.Melville, M.Harris, S.Thornber, P.Raynor, R.James, J.Hughes, A.Curtis, A.Legg.
Subs: T.Hutchison, B.Wade.
CARDIFF CITY: R.Hansbury, I.Rodgerson, R.Daniel, J.Morgan, S.Lynex, R.Gibbins, M.Kelly, C.Griffith, C.Pike, J.Perry, C.Fry.
Subs: N.Blake, M.Scott

Scorers: Swansea City (Hughes, Wade)
Cardiff City (-)
Attendance: 8,350

Gilligan hands former club an FA Cup knockout

15th November 1991
FA Cup 1st Round

SWANSEA CITY 2 CARDIFF CITY 1

It was ex-Cardiff City favourite Jimmy Gilligan whose stunning goal helped Swansea turn the tables on their arch rivals in this FA Cup first round tie.

The early exchanges were disappointing with neither side creating much and both goalkeepers unemployed for much of the opening quarter of the game. Then, on 25 minutes, the visitors took the lead when Chris **PIKE** scored with a powerful downward header from their third corner taken by Neil Matthews. Cardiff's lead lasted just four minutes when Steve Thornber outjumped Cardiff's industrious Paul Ramsey for winger Andy Legg to hook the ball through to **GILLIGAN**. The Swansea striker needed just one touch as he beat Hansbury with a superb 25-yard strike.

The remainder of the first half territorially belonged to Cardiff but their good work was undone by a series of wasted opportunities, several of which fell to Carl Dale.

It was a vastly different story in the second half as the Swans took control. The Cardiff defence had its work cut out dealing with the aerial threat of the wily Gilligan and the unorthodox wing play of John Williams. Both were involved in the 57th minute match-winner to punish Cardiff's slack marking at a set piece.

Gilligan flicked on Agboola's free-kick to Williams, whose back header found Mark **HARRIS** free to run on and net from close range with an emphatic left-foot shot. With much steadier finishing, Legg would have added two or three more goals to emphasise the Swans' second half control, although Carl Dale almost earned a replay for the Bluebirds in the last minute when his snapshot flew into the side-netting with Freestone beaten.

SWANSEA CITY: R.Freestone, S.Jenkins, R.Agboola, R.Coughlin, M.Harris, K.Walker, J.Williams, S.Thornber, J.Gilligan, J.Bowen, A.Legg.
Subs: S.Chapple, P.Chalmers.
CARDIFF CITY: R.Hansbury, N.Matthews, D.Searle, R.Gibbins, L.Baddeley, J.Perry, P.Ramsey, C.Griffith, C.Pike, C.Dale, N.Blake.
Subs: P.Millar, A.Lewis.

Scorers: Swansea City (Gilligan, Harris)
Cardiff City (Pike)
Attendance: 9,315

Ramsey off in Vetch Field flare-up

19th November 1991
Autoglass Trophy

SWANSEA CITY 0 CARDIFF CITY 0

Violence flared again at Swansea's Vetch Field but this time it was on the pitch. Cardiff City's tenacious midfielder Paul Ramsey was sent off after using an elbow on Swansea's Reuben Agboola in retaliation to a foul tackle by the full-back.

The first of several firecrackers was hurled from a Swansea section of the terraces, exploding close to Cardiff keeper Roger Hansbury just before the woodwork denied Carl Dale. Damon Searle's free-kick was flicked on by Nathan Blake but Dale's shot struck the bar with Freestone beaten.

From the first of two huge Andy Legg throws, Hansbury failed to claim and John Williams had a cross-shot blocked before the stalwart Cardiff keeper had to dive at full stretch to prevent Steve Thornber's well-struck drive giving Swansea an 18th minute lead. On 25 minutes the Swans had a narrow escape when a six-pass move ended with Lee Baddeley beginning a counter-attack from which Chris Pike broke forward to hit a low drive that cannoned off a post.

Then in the 32nd minute came the game's flashpoint as Ramsey received his marching orders, but before he went he protested that Agboola, Swansea's recent signing from Sunderland, had feigned injury and angry team-mate Nathan Blake had to be pulled away from the incident by Swans centre-half Mark Harris.

Despite being down to 10 men, the Bluebirds battled tremendously hard to prevent the Swans from scoring and in fact, with just minutes remaining, they could have snatched a winner. Cardiff captain Roger Gibbins lobbed his shot wide with Swans' hesitant keeper Roger Freestone stranded yards off his line.

Swansea City: R.Freestone, S.Jenkins, R.Agboola, S.Thornber, M.Harris, D.Brazil, J.Williams, S.Chapple, J.Gilligan, J.Beauchamp, A.Legg. Subs: A.Davies, P.Chalmers.
Cardiff City: R.Hansbury, N.Matthews, D.Searle, R.Gibbins, L.Baddeley, J.Perry, P.Ramsey, A.Lewis, C.Pike, C.Dale, N.Blake.
Subs: P.Millar, A.Gorman.

Scorers: Swansea City (-)
Cardiff City (-)
Attendance: 2,955

Swans pay for missed chances

18th February 1992
Welsh Cup 5th Round

SWANSEA CITY 0 CARDIFF CITY 1

The decisive goal which kept Cardiff City firmly on course for a promotion and Cup-winning double would have been ruled out in a normal game! But this match, like all others in Welsh competitions, was played with an experimental rule in which a player cannot be offside when he receives a pass from inside his own half.

Within three minutes of the kick-off, delayed for over a quarter of an hour to await the late arrival of hundreds of Cardiff fans travelling by train, Jimmy Gilligan had a chance to give Swansea the lead. But his header passed narrowly outside Gavin Ward's left hand post. Only eight minutes had been played when Russell Coughlin provided Andy Legg with a good chance but he stabbed his shot wide and then, five minutes later, Gilligan headed Paul Raynor's cross into the arms of Ward.

The home side were made to pay for these misses four minutes before the break. Paul Ramsey was lurking behind the Swans defence when Damon Searle hoisted a high through-ball from well inside his own half. Under the experimental rule, Ramsey was not offside but as he shaped to shoot he was well tackled by Harris. The loose ball broke to Chris **PIKE** and the tall striker coolly made space to pick his spot from 10 yards out.

For the first twenty minutes of the second half, the Swans laid siege to the Cardiff goal and in the 57th minute, the Bluebirds goal had a remarkable double let-off. The ball hit a post when Ward dropped Raynor's cross under a challenge from Legg and then Williams saw his shot, hit from barely a yard out, ricochet off Gareth Abraham's legs and on to the crossbar!

SWANSEA CITY: R.Freestone, R.Agboola, S.Thornber, K.Walker, M.Harris, J.Ford, J.Williams, R.Coughlin, J.Gilligan, P.Raynor, A.Legg. Subs: J.Bowen, S.Chapple.
CARDIFF CITY: G.Ward, J.Perry, D.Searle, R.Gibbins, G.Abraham, E.Newton, P.Ramsey, G.Harrison, C.Pike, C.Dale, N.Blake. Subs: C.Griffith, A.Lewis

Scorers: Swansea City (-)
Cardiff City (Pike)
Attendance: 7,303

Hayes is super Swans hero

19th January 1993
Autoglass Trophy

CARDIFF CITY 1 SWANSEA CITY 2

This full-blooded Autoglass Cup tie crackled with a tension that produced several heated exchanges and there was drama after 22 minutes when Cardiff skipper Paul Ramsey and Swansea's Steve Jenkins had to withdraw from the action after being hurt in a crunching tackle.

The atmosphere was electric and fans who were still flocking through the turnstiles missed the opening goal of the game after eight minutes. Switched to partnering Phil Stant up front, Nathan **BLAKE** lifted himself out of the cloying mud to meet Nick Richardson's in-swinging corner with a firm header that went in off the underside of the crossbar. Then Roger Freestone had to be alert to keep out a Phil Stant header before Harris was cautioned for a blatant foul on Blake as the Cardiff striker burst through a flat-footed Swansea defence.

Midway through the second half Gavin Ward was thankful to clutch a cross by Hayes after failing to hold Keith Walker's 35-yard shot. But with just two minutes of normal time to play, the Cardiff keeper made a glaring misjudgment to let in Swansea's equaliser. Stranded on the edge of his penalty area, **LEGG** pounced to drive the ball home despite Jason Perry's attempt to stop it on the goal-line.

The Swans took the lead in the ninth minute of extra-time. Legg's low cross found Cornforth and although Damon Searle hacked his shot off the line, Martin **HAYES**, the winger signed on a free transfer from Celtic, smashed home the rebound.

With the game drawing to a conclusion, scores of Cardiff fans invaded the pitch after what they thought was an equaliser by Phil Stant but the striker was adjudged to have been offside!

SWANSEA CITY: R.Freestone, D.Lyttle, S.Jenkins, K.Walker, M.Harris, S.Chapple, M.Hayes, P.Wimbleton, C.West, J.Cornforth, A.Legg.
Subs: J.Ford, A.MacFarlane.
CARDIFF CITY: G.Ward, R.James, D.Searle, N.Matthews, J.Perry, K.Ratcliffe, P.Ramsey, N.Richardson, P.Stant, N.Blake, C.Griffith.
Subs: A.Bird, D.Brazil.

Scorers: Swansea City (Legg, Hayes)
Cardiff City (Blake)
Attendance: 13,516

Thompson goal settles derby

22nd December 1993
Football League Division 2

CARDIFF CITY 1 SWANSEA CITY 0

Garry Thompson clinched victory for the Bluebirds in a seething South Wales derby that saw the Ninian Park club leap-frog a Swansea side that had lost its last four league games

Swansea's best opportunity of the whole match came early in the first half when a rapid break down the right ended with Steve Torpey crashing unnecessarily into Cardiff keeper Mark Grew. As the ball broke free, Torpey seemed certain to score but Derek Brazil came from nowhere to clear the danger. This clash was the first of several in a match that began with as bad an atmosphere on the pitch as there was off it!

Loan signing Chris Burns also could have given Swansea the lead but his header went inches wide of Grew's right-hand upright, but at least he did produce Swansea's only shot on target with a rasping drive that was aimed directly at Grew.

The only goal of the game was scored after 52 minutes when **THOMPSON** moved on to an incisive pass from Nicky Richardson, held off John Ford's challenge and hit a superb shot that went beyond Roger Freestone and rolled into the corner of the net. Nathan Blake came close to adding another seconds later as he split the Swansea defence down the middle before shooting just wide of Freestone's post. And Phil Stant should have made the game safe when he fired over an empty goal after Freestone had saved Thompson's first shot

Cardiff's victory, which extended their unbeaten League run to eight matches, lifted them to 17th in the table, one place and one point ahead of the Swans with a game in hand.

SWANSEA CITY: R.Freestone, S.Jenkins, A.Cook, J.Ford, M.Harris, C.Burns, J.Cornforth, S.Chapple, J.Bowen, S.Torpey, D.Perrett.
Subs: A.MacFarlane, M.Clode.
CARDIFF CITY: M.Grew, D.Brazil, D.Searle, M.Aizlewood, L.Baddeley, J.Perry, G.Thompson, N.Richardson, P.Stant, N.Blake, C.Griffith.
Subs: A.Bird, P.Millar.

Scorers: Swansea City (-)
Cardiff City (Thompson)
Attendance: 9,815

Penney's penalty clinches victory for Swans

2nd April 1994
Football League Division 2

SWANSEA CITY 1 CARDIFF CITY 0

The game was poorly controlled by one of Britain's so-called top officials. Five bookings and a sending-off suggested an ill-tempered needle match, which it certainly was not. In fact it was a tame, drab affair lacking atmosphere and watched by the smallest local derby crowd because of the ban on Cardiff fans.

Bowen should have given Swansea the lead from one of the few flowing moves involving captain John Cornforth and full-back Steve Jenkins, while Damon Searle scooped another Hodge shot off the goal-line.

However until Mark Aizlewood received his marching orders after 40 minutes by Solihull referee Vic Callow for using foul and abusive language, the game had all the makings of a scoreless stalemate as defences dominated.

The decisive goal of the game came on 67 minutes when David Penney, released by Bowen's clever through-pass, was tripped by Kevin Brock. **PENNEY** probably Swansea's best midfield player on the day, got up to score with a fiercely struck straight penalty that cannoned down off the underside of the crossbar onto the goal-line and bounced into the roof of the net.

Penney, on-loan from Oxford United, almost gave the game away in the closing stages when in attempting a back-pass to Freestone, he underhit the ball allowing Cardiff's Wayne Fereday to nip in. He took the ball round the Swansea keeper but his shot rolled inches wide. Then with almost the last kick of the game Paul Millar who had replaced Bird on 78 minutes, drilled in a shot that Freestone did well to turn over the bar.

SWANSEA CITY: R.Freestone, S.Jenkins, M.Clode, J.Ford, M.Harris, C.Pascoe, J.Bowen, D.Penney, S.Torpey, J.Cornforth, J.Hodge.
Subs: S.Chapple, A.MacFarlane, L.Jones.

CARDIFF CITY: S.Williams, D.Brazil, D.Searle, M.Aizlewood, L.Baddeley, J.Perry, N.Wigg, K.Brock, A.Bird, C.Griffith, W.Fereday. Subs: N.Richardson, P.Millar, P.Kite.

Scorers: Swansea City (Penney pen)
Cardiff City (-)
Attendance: 3,711

Stant's 'Double' has Swans reeling

14th April 1994 Welsh Cup semi-final 1st Leg

SWANSEA CITY 1 CARDIFF CITY 2

Phil Stant hit his 16th and 17th goals of the season to steer the Bluebirds towards a third Allbright Bitter Welsh Cup Final in a row in this Vetch Field encounter.

The Swans, bidding for an Autoglass Trophy and Welsh Cup double, had a chance to open the scoring in their first attack of the game as Mark Harris headed Colin Pascoe's free-kick across the face of the goal, but neither Jason Bowen nor Andy MacFarlane could convert. Swansea wasted promising approach play usually involving Cornforth, and their only genuine first half strike came from MacFarlane which Kite saved easily.

It was Cardiff who opened the scoring a minute before half-time after Cornforth had spurned a chance from Wayne Fereday's poor clearance by pulling his shot yards wide. From the resultant goal-kick by Phil Kite, Garry Thompson knocked down a header for the unmarked **STANT** to steady himself before placing a great right-footed volley beyond the reach of the diving Roger Freestone.

The Cardiff striker doubled his side's lead on 54 minutes as he punished Harris for a bad back pass. Freestone tried to clear the danger under a challenge from Thompson but the ball rebounded straight to **STANT** who coolly stroked it into an empty net.

CORNFORTH put Swansea back into the game with a 20-yard special from Mark Aizlewood's misguided clearance and then Clode hit the angle of the bar and post with a tremendous 35-yard shot.

A recurring calf injury forced Cornforth to be replaced by Barnhouse with a little under a quarter of an hour remaining and though the Swans continued to go in search of an equaliser, the Bluebirds held out and should have felt confident of completing the job in the return leg of the semi-final a fortnight later.

SWANSEA CITY: R.Freestone, S.Jenkins, M.Clode, J.Ford, M.Harris, C.Pascoe, J.Bowen, S.Chapple, A.MacFarlane, J.Cornforth, J.Hodge.
Subs: K.Ampadu, D.Barnhouse.
CARDIFF CITY: P.Kite, W.Fereday, D.Searle, M.Aizlewood, J.Perry, P.Millar, K.Brock, N.Richardson, P.Stant, G.Thompson, C.Griffith.
Subs: N.Wigg, D.Adams.

Scorers: Swansea City (Cornforth)
Cardiff City (Stant 2)
Attendance: 3,286

Swans shot down as Bluebirds go for a hat-trick

28th April 1994
Welsh Cup semi-final 2nd Leg

CARDIFF CITY 4 SWANSEA CITY 1

Swansea had over 18,000 fans at the Twin Towers to see them win the Autoglass Trophy, but there were just 200 fans at this Welsh Cup semi-final second leg at Ninian Park.

The Swans' enterprising start saw them take a shock lead after 23 minutes courtesy of Cardiff keeper Steve Williams. Perry played a back pass and the keeper tried to find him with a return as MacFarlane closed in. Instead he hit the ball straight to **MACFARLANE** who coolly touched it past and ran round the keeper to add an easy goal to the one he had scored in Swansea's success at Wembley. Minutes later though, Cardiff's teenage keeper made amends with a fine diving save from Ampadu before the Bluebirds drew level on 36 minutes.

Ampadu's pass for Bowen was intercepted by **FEREDAY** who broke quickly from his own half before beating Freestone with a glorious drive from fully 30 yards.

BIRD scored Cardiff's second goal on the hour mark, firing home from 12 yards out after Stant had headed down Millar's corner to him.

Ampadu forced the ball into Cardiff's net after 78 minutes but the effort was disallowed for a push on Williams. With just eight minutes remaining John Ford was punished for a bad mistake, his back-pass finding **STANT** who veered wide of the advancing Roger Freestone to score the Bluebirds' third goal from a difficult angle.

There was no way back for the Swans and Paul **MILLAR** completed Cardiff's emphatic victory with a fourth goal from the penalty spot three minutes from time after Mark Clode had brought down Stant.

SWANSEA CITY: R.Freestone, S.Jenkins, M.Clode, J.Ford, M.Harris, C.Pascoe, J.Bowen, K.Ampadu, A.MacFarlane, J.Cornforth, J.Hodge. Subs: D.Perrett, S.Torpey.
CARDIFF CITY: S.Williams, T.Evans, W.Fereday, M.Aizlewood, J.Perry, P.Millar, G.Thompson, A.Bird, P.Stant, C.Dale, D.Adams. Subs: N.Wigg, S.Young.

Scorers: Swansea City (MacFarlane)
Cardiff City (Fereday, Bird, Stant, Millar pen)
Attendance: 5,606

Penalty miss costs Bluebirds dear

3rd September 1994
Football League Division 2

CARDIFF CITY 1 SWANSEA CITY 1

Neither side had possessed a regular goalscorer this season and this showed in a match where there could have been a lot more goals.

The Bluebirds should have beaten the Swans and probably would have done if they had converted a penalty after Cohen Griffith was brought down by keeper Roger Freestone. Carl Dale was the delegated penalty-taker but Searle confidently elected to take it with his first kick in competitive football since his ill-fated Welsh Cup Final appearance against Barry Town. He struck the shot well but close enough to Freestone for him to make an excellent save.

Cardiff went ahead through Nick **RICHARDSON**, who controlled a long through-ball from Brazil before shooting past the advancing Freestone. The Swansea keeper was in action again just after the interval when he turned Thompson's powerful header over the bar.

Swansea drew level midway through the second half when good work on the left by Cornforth and Hodge made an opening for Martin **HAYES** to side-foot past Williams from close range. Hayes almost added a second moments later but his well struck shot hit the unsuspecting Oatway and bounced to safety. Swansea continued to pile on the pressure but the Cardiff defence, including Mark Aizlewood in a surprise return from injury, held firm.

Garry Thompson's recovery from an ear injury gave the Bluebirds greater aerial strength up front while fit again Carl Dale almost won the game for Cardiff in the final minute. His fine effort rebounded off a post into Freestone's hands after he burst clear with a glimpse of his old sharpness.

SWANSEA CITY: R.Freestone, S.Jenkins, M.Clode, J.Ford, M.Harris, K.Ampadu, D.Penney, S.Torpey, M.Hayes, J.Cornforth, J.Hodge.
Subs: C.Pascoe, D.Perrett.
CARDIFF CITY: D.Williams, T.Evans, A.Scott, M.Aizlewood, D.Brazil, A.Oatway, C.Griffith, N.Richardson, G.Thompson, C.Dale, D.Searle.
Subs: L.Baddeley, P.Millar.

Scorers: Swansea City (Hayes)
Cardiff City (Richardson)
Attendance: 5,523

Triple blast lifts Swans' promotion hopes

7th March 1995
Football League Division 2

SWANSEA CITY 4 CARDIFF CITY 1

Three goals in the space of nine minutes fired the Swans to the fringe of the promotion play-off places and the Bluebirds closer to the relegation zone.

Swansea chairman Doug Sharpe joined the club's groundstaff to fork the Vetch for hours to drain surface water and make the match playable after a lunch-time inspection. Police had also mounted a strict surveillance to enforce the Swansea chairman's ban on Cardiff fans, although a number of the club's regular followers were spotted in the main stand.

A heavy hail storm before the kick-off turned to snow and as the players came out the pitch was a white carpet and an orange ball had to be introduced.

John **WILLIAMS** opened the scoring in what was probably his last appearance for the club before returning to Coventry at the end of a month's loan. He delivered a great pass out to Hodge and then met the winger's cross with a sweeping close range drive which the Cardiff keeper could only help into his net. The Cardiff keeper was at fault for Swansea's second goal from a free-kick. Jason Perry lined his defence up to guard the near post but David **PENNEY** promptly angled a low drive past the end of the wall to beat the poorly-positioned Bluebirds keeper.

Two minutes later, Swansea went 3-0 up when Hodge was the provider for Colin **PASCOE** to sweep the ball home with the Cardiff back-four in total disarray.

The Cardiff defence played much better in the second half and it wasn't until the 85th minute that they scored, when substitute Shaun **CHAPPLE** slid home the rebound after an effort by Torpey had been blocked on the line.

Nathan **WIGG** claimed a consolation goal for Cardiff three minutes from time with a rising half-volley that Freestone got a hand to but couldn't keep out.

SWANSEA CITY: R.Freestone, S.Jenkins, M.Clode, K.Walker, M.Harris, C.Pascoe, J.Williams, D.Penney, S.Torpey, K.Ampadu, J.Hodge. Subs: S.Chapple, J.Bowen.
CARDIFF CITY: D.Williams, C.Honor, D.Searle, M.Aizlewood, L.Baddeley, J.Perry, N.Wigg, C.Griffith, J.Pearson, N.Richardson, W.Fereday. Subs: D.Brazil, P.Millar.

Scorers: Swansea City (Williams, Penney, Pascoe, Chapple)
Cardiff City (Wigg)
Attendance: 3,942

Millar magic silences Swans

11th April 1995
Welsh Cup semi-final 1st Leg

SWANSEA CITY 0 CARDIFF CITY 1

Substitute Cardiff City keeper Steve Williams saved a penalty in the Allbright Bitter Welsh Cup semi-final first leg and then Paul Millar snatched victory for the Bluebirds with a somewhat bizarre goal just two minutes from time.

Swansea had the better of the opening exchanges but still failed to open up the Cardiff defence. The visitors suffered a blow on the half-hour mark when David Williams sustained an injury after contesting a high ball with Swansea striker Steve Torpey. He was taken to hospital with suspected broken ribs and a damaged left ear. His namesake Steve Williams took over and was well protected by a Cardiff defence in which Jason Perry and Lee Baddeley were in commanding form.

However, just after half-time Keith Walker went close to breaking the deadlock with a 30-yard snapshot that smacked against a post with the substitute keeper beaten. The Bluebirds' sterling defensive display looked like being undone when the referee awarded the Swans a penalty for a foul by Perry on Jason Bowen. Torpey took the spot-kick but Steve Williams dived to his left to beat it out and then scrambled away Torpey's second attempt to force the ball over the line.

The save stunned the sparse crowd - Cardiff fans having been banned from the ground - and when Cardiff scored the winner in the 88th minute there was complete silence.

Carl Dale chased a slack back pass from Keith Walker, forcing Roger Freestone to make a hurried clearance which clipped Cohen Griffith and was picked up by **MILLAR**. From fully 35 yards out the midfielder hoisted a shot which floated over the stranded Freestone and just under the Swansea crossbar.

SWANSEA CITY: R.Freestone, S.Jenkins, A.Cook, K.Walker, J.Ford, C.Pascoe, J.Bowen, K.Ampadu, S.Torpey, J.Cornforth, J.Hodge.
Subs: M.Hayes, D.Perrett.
CARDIFF CITY: D.Williams, D.Brazil, D.Searle, N.Wigg, L.Baddeley, J.Perry, P.Millar, N.Richardson, A.Bird, C.Dale, C.Griffith.
Subs: S.Young, S.Williams.

Scorers: Swansea City (-)
Cardiff City (Millar)
Attendance: 2,654

No goals but Bluebirds through to final

2nd May 1995
Welsh Cup semi-final 2nd leg

CARDIFF CITY 0 SWANSEA CITY 0

Much of this game was played in a subdued atmosphere which lacked the usual electricity sparked by rival fans; Swansea fans had been barred from Ninian Park as a consequence of Cardiff fans being banned from the Vetch Field first leg in the interests of crowd safety.

Swansea could have wiped out the Bluebirds' lead as early as the third minute when Mark Clode's near-post cross found Colin Pascoe, but Williams made a brave smothering save at the midfielder's feet.

Cohen Griffith flashed a shot from the edge of the penalty area inches over the top before wasting a 40-yard pass from Paul Milsom. Millar sliced a 25-yard shot well wide, then forced a fine save from Roger Freestone with a better strike on the turn from similar distance.

For all their possession and territorial advantage the Swans could not penetrate a tight Cardiff defence. Although a mistake by Derek Brazil allowed Pascoe to run onto Cornforth's pass, the full-back recovered well to block his shot.

Paul Millar almost gave Cardiff the lead with an angled drive that forced another fine save out of Freestone and then the Swansea keeper made a fantastic reflex save to deny Carl Dale a goal with a close-range header eight minutes from time.

Swansea went agonisingly close to forcing extra-time in the last two minutes when substitute Martin Hayes, on for Mark Clode, slid his shot just wide, Scott Young headed just over his own crossbar and keeper Steve Williams kept out a close-range Steve Torpey effort.

SWANSEA CITY: R.Freestone, S.Jenkins, M.Clode, K.Walker, J.Ford, C.Pascoe, J.Bowen, S.Chapple, S.Torpey, J.Cornforth, K.Ampadu. Subs: M.Hayes, D.Perrett.
CARDIFF CITY: S.Williams, D.Brazil, D.Searle, N.Wigg, L.Baddeley, J.Perry, P.Millar, C.Dale, P.Milsom, N.Richardson, C.Griffith. Subs: S.Young, A.Bird.

Scorers: Swansea City (-)
Cardiff City (-)
Attendance: 4,227

Swans turn on style

3rd December 1996
Football League Division 3

CARDIFF CITY 1 SWANSEA CITY 3

The lowest Cardiff crowd for a league derby of 3,721 witnessed a contest high on both passion and incident as Swansea's relentless `march` into play-off contention continued. This victory, Swansea's sixth in seven outings, took them to within two points of the Bluebirds, although the Ninian Park club had a game in hand.

The few Swansea fans who had slipped through the turnstiles could hardly contain themselves as **AMPADU** gave them an 11th minute lead, beating Tony Elliott from fully 30 yards. The linesman raised his flag but referee David Allison allowed the goal, ruling that neither Carl Heggs or Steve Torpey had obstructed Elliott's line of vision. Coates should have added a second moments later but was unable to connect with Steve Jones's teasing cross.

At the other end, Swansea were their own worst enemies. Christian Edwards sliced two clearances in as many minutes, Carl Dale sending a looping header from the first over the crossbar. The second miscue provided almost great embarrassment to the Welsh Under-21 defender as the ball ballooned inches wide with Freestone beaten.

Then Cardiff were punished in the 37th minute as Heggs's cutback found Torpey and though Tony Philliskirk blocked his effort, the impressive **JONES** curled a sweet left-foot shot beyond Elliott. The Bluebirds were handed a lifeline in the last minute of the first half when Steve **WHITE** found space in a crowded six-yard area to head Jason Fowler's shot-cum-cross into the net off the underside of the bar.

Swansea's bar was struck again three minutes into the second half but this time Freestone saw Jimmy Gardner's 30-yard effort bounce to safety.

Four minutes from time, the Swans scored a third goal when substitute David **THOMAS** outsprinted Jeff Eckhardt to score from a tight angle. Unfortunately, that was the signal for a couple of Cardiff fans to invade the pitch and swing on a crossbar until they were eventually removed by stewards.

SWANSEA CITY: R.Freestone, K.Ampadu, M.Clode, K.Walker, C.Edwards, S.Jones, L.Jenkins, D.Penney, S.Torpey, C.Heggs, J.Coates. Subs: D.Thomas, R.Appleby.
CARDIFF CITY: T.Elliott, J.Perry, T.Philliskirk, J.Eckhardt, S.Young, J.Fowler, K.O'Halloran, C.Middleton, S.White, C.Dale, J.Gardner. Subs: S.Haworth, L.Jarman.

Scorers: Swansea City (Ampadu, Jones, Thomas)
Cardiff City (White)
Attendance: 3,721

Haworth goal is match-winner

2nd March 1997
Football League Division 3

SWANSEA CITY 0 CARDIFF CITY 1

This victory saw Cardiff City join Swansea in the Division Three play-off places as 19-year-old striker Simon Haworth, who had been likened to a young John Toshack, struck the winning goal against a club that enjoyed its most successful era when Toshack was the manager.

Swansea failed to capitalise on a forceful start during which Jonathan Coates fired wide, Brayson just failed to reach a Richard Appleby cross and Hills shot straight at keeper Tony Elliott.

Cardiff's only response before the goal came after seven minutes when a Jason Perry header from Lee Jarman's free-kick was deflected for a corner. The decisive goal came in the 18th minute against the run of play. Lee Jarman moved on to a slanting pass by Jason Perry. His cross was headed out to Scott Partridge who glided past Steve Jones to hit the post with a rising drive. **HAWORTH** was the first to the rebound, hooking in his fifth goal in eight games.

Jan Molby's men would have turned the deficit into an interval lead but for two extravagant misses and Tony Elliott's superb save from Brayson. Steve Torpey was off-target with a free header from six yards in the 25th minute and David Penney spurned a penalty chance seven minutes later when Jeff Eckhardt handled a goalbound shot from Torpey.

Then Brayson, put through by Molby who decided to bring himself on, forced Elliott into making another quality save. Torpey finished the game as he had started with another header off target.

But Cardiff twice went close to increasing their lead in the closing stages. Haworth rode two tackles to shoot wide and supplied the pass for Carl Dale to hit the bar with a deflected drive.

SWANSEA CITY: R.Freestone, S.Chapple, J.Hills, K.Walker, C.Edwards, S.Jones, P.Brayson, D.Penney, S.Torpey, R.Appleby, J.Coates.
Subs: J.Molby, D.Thomas, R.Casey.
CARDIFF CITY: T.Elliott, L.Jarman, J.Perry, J.Eckhardt, G.Davies, J.Fowler, C.Middleton, S.Partridge, S.White, S.Haworth, T.Philliskirk.
Subs: C.Dale, J.Rollo.

Scorers: Swansea City (-)
Cardiff City (Haworth)
Attendance: 4,443

Walker's Sunday punch KO's Blubirds

2nd November 1997
Football League Division 3

CARDIFF CITY 0 SWANSEA CITY 1

A memorable goal by Keith Walker settled this fierce South Wales derby after Scott Young had undermined Cardiff's chances of transforming the game by being sent off after just a quarter of an hour for the second of two reckless tackles within the space of seven minutes.

The decisive goal came after 11 minutes as **WALKER** met Jon Hallworth's punched clearance of a Jonathan Coates corner waist-high with his right foot to propel the ball through a cluster of players and past the helpless keeper.

Swansea's recent signing from Fulham, Nick Cusack, hit the bar with a powerful header and then had a drive touched away for a corner.

Scott Young, who had been cautioned in the seventh minute for a rash tackle on Walker, was shown a second yellow, then inevitably the red one for another crude challenge on Bird in the 15th minute. Bird then spurned an opportunity to score, kneeing the ball over the bar from an O'Leary cross flicked on by Steve Watkin. Crowe squandered the Bluebirds' best first-half chance, scuffing his shot from an accurate lay-back by Mark Harris.

In the second half the loan signing from Wolverhampton Wanderers, from a deep Hallworth clearance, rolled just wide before Roger Freestone foiled him with a superb reflex save. The Swansea keeper had another let-off when he allowed O'Sullivan's cross-shot to slip under his body but managed to turn and claim the ball as it came back off the base of the upright. Andy Saville should have earned Cardiff a seventh successive league draw from a measured 87th minute cross by O'Sullivan but his glancing header went wide.

Swansea's second successive away win under new manager Alan Cork lifted them to within a point of Cardiff who haD now gone nine league games without a win.

SWANSEA CITY: R.Freestone, J.Price, M.Clode, K.Walker, C.Edwards, J.Coates, N.Cusack, S.Watkin, T.Bird, R.Appleby, K.O'Leary. Subs: A.Newhouse, D.Lacey, L.Jenkins.
CARDIFF CITY: J.Hallworth, C.Middleton, C.Beech, S.Young, M.Harris, J.Fowler, W.O'Sullivan, D.Penney, A.Saville, G.Crowe, A.Carrs. Subs: G.Stoker, S.Partridge, S.White.

Scorers: Swansea City (Walker)
Cardiff City (-)
Attendance: 6,459

Bluebirds denied by Coates' late strike

8th March 1998
Football League Division 3

SWANSEA CITY 1 CARDIFF CITY 1

This was a match of poor quality which illustrated just why both clubs are languishing near the foot of the Third Division.

Strong winds had dried a pitch passed as playable by former referee Keith Cooper, but there was precious little goalmouth action to excite a crowd swollen by over 750 Cardiff fans at the Mumbles End.

Hallworth sprinted out of the penalty area to head away a deep clearance by his opposite number, Roger Freestone, but neither keeper had a difficult save to make in a nondescript first period lacking the usual passion of a South Wales derby. Appleby spurned the best first half chance, pulling his shot wide after being put through by Christian Edwards, whose timely block-tackle a minute later denied Saville a shooting chance.

The best piece of first half skill applauded by both sets of fans was provided by Swansea assistant-manager Alan Curtis as he cleverly controlled a ball that went out of play! Matthew Bound brought a moment's light relief in what was a dire first half when his clearance removed the helmet of one of the policemen on the touchline.

Cardiff, whose fans had been allowed into the Vetch for the first time in five years, took the lead after one of the game's most fluent moves. Fowler's pass started the attack and when White headed down Saville's far post cross from the right, **FOWLER** was in position to beat Freestone with a low left-footed drive from 12 yards.

Swansea were struggling to penetrate Cardiff's defence until the 84th minute when Jason Price began the move which led to the goal that enabled them to finish with honours even. Jonathan **COATES** ran on to a cross from substitute Dave O'Gorman to beat Jon Hallworth with a glancing header from the edge of the six-yard box.

SWANSEA CITY: R.Freestone, C.Hartfield, D.Lacey, K.Walker, C.Edwards, M.Bound, N.Cusack, J.Price, T.Bird, R.Appleby, J.Coates.
Subs: D.O'Gorman, K.O'Leary, L.Jenkins.
CARDIFF CITY: J.Hallworth, L.Jarman, C.Beech, J.Eckhardt, S.Young, D.Penney, J.Fowler, D.Hill, A.Saville, S.White, W.O'Sullivan.
Subs: C.Roberts, C.Middleton, A.Carrs.

Scorers: Swansea City (Coates)
Cardiff City (Fowler)
Attendance: 5,621

Bounds' late strike seals Swansea win

22nd November 1998
Football League Division 3

SWANSEA CITY 2 CARDIFF CITY 1

Matthew Bound's dramatic last-minute match-winner, his first League strike in 46 successive appearances since his £55,000 switch from Stockport County twelve months earlier, completed Swansea's rousing second half recovery.

Outplayed in every aspect, the Swans clung on by their fingertips as the visitors tried and failed to apply the finishing touch to a first half performance full of commitment and goalscoring opportunities.

Cardiff took the lead after just four minutes through Swansea old boy John **WILLIAMS**, who hooked the ball home from close range following untidy Swansea defending. The Bluebirds could have extended their lead on a number of occasions but Middleton, Ford and Nugent all failed to hit the target. But it was not simply Cardiff's finishing which let them down. The turning point came on the half-hour mark when Roger Freestone made the first of two superb reaction saves to prevent Smith putting through an own goal. Then just before the break, his save from Nugent was equally critical.

After the interval, the arrival of Julian Alsop transformed Swansea from no-hopers to heroes. Though they forced Cardiff on to the back foot, they had to wait until the 69th minute before equalising. Cardiff keeper Jon Hallworth made the first of two saves from Jason Smith when Martin **THOMAS** latched on to an Alsop header, raced away from two defenders and slotted the ball past the advancing Cardiff keeper.

By then, the Bluebirds had lost Williams, stretchered off with a damaged arm and his departure weakened Cardiff's effectiveness up front.

With the game in its last minute, Appleby swung in a corner which Cusack helped on to Matthew **BOUND**. The big defender kept his composure before drilling the winner beyond Hallworth's reach.

SWANSEA CITY: R.Freestone, S.Jones, M.Howard, N.Cusack, J.Smith, M.Bound, J.Price, M.Thomas, A.Newhouse, S.Watkin, R.Appleby. Subs: J.Alsop, L.Jenkins, S.Roberts.
CARDIFF CITY: J.Hallworth, M.Delaney, M.Ford, G.Mitchell, S.Young, R.Carpenter, J.Fowler, W.O'Sullivan, J.Williams, K.Nugent, C.Middleton. Subs: D.Hill, C.Allen, J.Eckhardt.

Scorers: Swansea City (Thomas, Bound)
Cardiff City (Williams)
Attendance: 7,757

Williams delivers knockout blow

2nd March 1999
FAW Premier Cup quarter-final

CARDIFF CITY 3 SWANSEA CITY 2

Former Swansea strikers Dai Thomas and John Williams scored a goal apiece to help knock their old club out of the FAW Premier Cup.

Dai Thomas gave the Bluebirds a 10th minute lead with his first goal for the club since his £60,000 signing from Watford. He will probably never score an easier goal. Matthew Gregg had ample time to clear a back pass from Casey but the 20-year-old keeper, on loan from Crystal Palace, completely mis-kicked, allowing **THOMAS** to stroke the ball into an empty net. He immediately peeled off his shirt and after waving it in front of the Cardiff fans, was promptly booked!

Alsop almost levelled the scores moments later but his curling shot, which was heading for the top corner, was brilliantly saved by Kelly who had to arch backwards before tipping it over. However, Kelly, deputising for Jon Hallworth, was powerless to prevent **ALSOP** claiming the equaliser with a free header from a perfectly flighted corner by Casey.

Hill was then off target with a cross-shot and Kris O'Leary fired wide from a rehearsed free-kick. Jonathan Coates, involved in some of the Swans best first-half moves, went closest to giving his side an interval lead with a curving shot but was just wide.

Captain Jeff **ECKHARDT** restored the Bluebirds' lead after 65 minutes, tapping in from close range after Lee Jarman had headed down a deep in-swinging corner from Legg. Swansea drew level again after 77 minutes when Ryan **CASEY** beat Seamus Kelly with a low left-footer from 25 yards. But as the match seemed to be heading for extra-time, Thomas supplied the pass for **WILLIAMS** to net the 88th minute winner.

SWANSEA CITY: M.Gregg, D.Lacey, J.Coates, N.Cusack, K.O'Leary, J.Smith, S.Roberts, L.Jenkins, J.Alsop, S.Watkin, R.Casey.
Subs: T.Bird, J.Davies, G.Phillips.
CARDIFF CITY: S.Kelly, W.O'Sullivan, A.Legg, G.Mitchell, J.Eckhardt, M.Bonnor, D.Hill, L.Jarman, J.Williams, D.Thomas, C.Middleton.
Subs: J.Bowen, C.Roberts, R.Carpenter.

Scorers: Swansea City (Alsop, Casey)
Cardiff City (Thomas, Eckhardt, Williams)
Attendance: 2,333

Promotion shoot-out finishes goalless

18th April 1999
Football League Division 3

CARDIFF CITY 0 SWANSEA CITY 0

With so much at stake for both clubs, it was not a footballing classic, but both sides gave it everything. Once the tribal chanting by both sets of fans had subsided, the minute's silence for the 96 who died in the Hillsborough tragedy 10 years ago was observed.

But the heat of the battle soon became evident as the giant Julian Alsop was booked after only two minutes for the use of his elbow in an aerial challenge with Jeff Eckhardt. Two minutes later the referee, who was obviously determined to stamp his authority early, booked Cusack for throwing the ball away to delay a Cardiff free-kick.

Middleton might well have given Cardiff the lead on the half-hour mark as Swansea were caught out by a route one attack. Seamus Kelly's deep clearance was helped on by Nugent and Williams to Middleton, running clear on the right, but the midfielder hooked his shot wide.

Although the Bluebirds had the attacking edge, particularly after the break, neither goalkeeper had a difficult save to make. Freestone was kept the far busier of the two, making clearances from corners and crosses by Legg or safely catching a stream of high balls. Nugent and Williams were both off target with headers from accurate crosses by Danny Hill and Jason Fowler swept a low drive narrowly wide.

Swansea were less of a threat going forward. Their best efforts came from Steve Watkin with a volley that just cleared the bar and an angled drive by Thomas after he had been put through by Watkin.

Then in stoppage time Kevin Nugent and Jason Bowen combined to put Danny Hill through on the left for a cross-shot that beat Freestone but Matthew Bound got back and cleared the ball off the line.

SWANSEA CITY: R.Freestone, S.Jones, J.Coates, K.O'Leary, J.Smith, M.Bound, R.Appleby, M.Thomas, J.Alsop, S.Watkin, N.Cusack.
Subs: T.Bird, D.Lacey, R.Casey.
CARDIFF CITY: S.Kelly, W.O'Sullivan, A.Legg, G.Mitchell, J.Eckhardt, M.Bonner, J.Fowler, M.Ford, J.Williams, K.Nugent, C.Middleton.
Subs: D.Hill, J.Bowen, D.Thomas.

Scorers: Swansea City (-)
Cardiff City (-)
Attendance: 10,809

Kavanagh special decides last meeting

13th May 2002
FAW Cup Final

CARDIFF CITY 1 SWANSEA CITY 0

Cardiff City finished what was a rollercoaster campaign with the FAW Trophy and a £100,000 cheque after beating local rivals Swansea City. Bluebirds captain Graham Kavanagh decided the last competitive meeting between the two sides with a terrific 25-yard free-kick early in the second half.

Cardiff started quite lethargically but they nearly opened the scoring in the 27th minute when Jason Bowen headed Kavanagh's free-kick against a post. At the other end, Swansea forward Steve Watkin was presented with a fine opportunity to break the deadlock courtesy of Layton Maxwell's suicidal square-pass, but the former Wrexham player failed to punish the error.

Jeanne was having an excellent game and almost beat Freestone with the outside of his right boot after latching on to Jason Bowen's through-ball.

Cardiff went ahead in the 56th minute when Swansea defender Kris O'Leary was penalised for pulling down Fortune-West. Up stepped Cardiff skipper Graham **KAVANAGH**, who bent his shot past Freestone before watching the ball go in off the post.

Swansea introduced substitute Steve Brodie and he came close to making an immediate impact by engineering his team's first real chance of the second half. The ex-Scarborough forward forced his way to the by-line but Howard failed to reach his low cross. Another Swansea substitute, John Williams, made his way on to the field with just eight minutes remaining and he was immediately involved in the action, crossing for Watkin whose dipping header bounced off the crossbar!

SWANSEA CITY: R.Freestone, G.Phillips, M.Howard, N.Sharp, J.Smith, K.O'Leary, N.Cusack, A.Mumford, M.Sidibe, S.Watkin, J.Coates. Subs: S.Brodie, J.Williams, C.Todd, J.Thompson.

CARDIFF CITY: M.Walton, R.Weston, S.Prior, J.Collins, A.Legg, L.Maxwell, G.Kavanagh, W.Bolard, L.Fortune-West, L.Jeanne, J.Bowen. Subs: C.Hughes, M.Bonnor, G.Jones, M.Simpkins.

Scorers: Swansea City (-)
Cardiff City (Kavanagh)
Attendance: 6,629

THE STAR PLAYERS

Ivor Allchurch
Len Allchurch
Billy Baker
Colin Baker
Joe Bonson
Terry Boyle
John Charles
Mel Charles
Brian Clark
Chris Coleman
Alan Curtis
Len Davies
Phil Dwyer
George Edwards
Brian Evans
Tom Farquharson
Mike Ford
Roger Freestone
Jimmy Gilligan
Harry Griffiths
Alan Harrington
Mark Harris
Barrie Hole
Brian Hughes
Tommy Hutchison
Robbie James

Leslie Jones
Fred Keenor
Johnny King
Peter King
Billy Lucas
Danny Malloy
Andy Melville
Wilf Milne
Stan Montgomery
Don Murray
Mel Nurse
Colin Pascoe
Jason Perry
Brayley Reynolds
Alf Sherwood
Nigel Stevenson
Ron Stitfall
Joe Sykes
Derek Tapscott
Geoff Thomas
Len Thompson
Keith Todd
John Toshack
Nigel Vaughan
Colin Webster
Herbie Williams

IVOR ALLCHURCH

Cardiff and Swansea

Known as the 'Golden Boy of Welsh Football' he began his league career with his home-town club Swansea and made his debut in the local derby against Cardiff City on Christmas Eve 1949. Allchurch soon developed a fine under-standing with Welsh international wing-half Billy Lucas and was soon capped himself when he played against England at Roker Park in November 1950.

Allchurch netted the first of seven hat-tricks for the Swans against Brentford in April 1953 and his second twelve months later against Fulham. In 1954-55 he was the club's leading scorer with 20 goals including a treble in the defeat of Ipswich Town and the following campaign scored his fourth hat-trick at Notts County. Another hat-trick followed in the 7-0 defeat of Derby County and in September 1958 he scored four of Swansea's goals in a 5-0 win over Sunderland.

He was a fixture in the Welsh team, missing only a handful of games through injury. One of his best games for Wales was against a combined United Kingdom side for the 75th Anniversary of the FA of Wales when he scored twice in a 3-2 win. After he had appeared for Wales in the 1958 World Cup Finals in Sweden, he received great praise from the World's Press and it was obvious he would soon get the chance to show what he could do in the First Division.

He had scored 123 goals in 330 league games for the Swans when Newcastle United signed him for £27,000 in October 1958. Shouldering much of the club's attacking burden, he scored 51 goals in 154 games for the Magpies before leaving to join Cardiff City for £18,000.

His debut for the Bluebirds came in a 4-4 home draw against his former club Newcastle United and after scoring 12 goals in 35 games in that 1962-63 season, he was the club's top scorer for the next two campaigns. In 1964-65 he scored a hat-trick in a 5-0 demolition of Swansea but at the end of the following season Allchurch, who had won his 68th and last Welsh Cap, moved back to Swansea for £6,000. Also in 1966, the Queen presented him with the MBE for his services to Welsh football. In 1967-68, his last season of league football, he netted his seventh hat-trick for the Swans against Doncaster Rovers and remarkably, at the age of 38, ended the campaign as the club's leading scorer with 21 League and Cup goals.

After leaving Swansea, for whom he scored 166 goals in 446 league games, he played non-league football for Worcester City, Haverfordwest and Pontardawe.

LEN ALLCHURCH

Swansea

Len Allchurch followed his brother Ivor by representing Wales Schoolboys and at the age of 14, after playing for Swansea School-boys, he joined the Vetch Field groundstaff where his older brother was in the first team.

He made his debut for the Swans at the age of 17 in April 1951 in a match against Grimsby Town but it wasn't until he had served two years National Service in the Army that he established himself in the Swansea side.

When he was 21 he won the first of 11 full caps for Wales when he played against Northern Ireland in Belfast, forming a left-wing partnership with his brother Ivor. He had scored 49 goals in 272 league games for the Vetch Field club when, in March 1961, Sheffield United paid £18,000 for his services.

In his first season at Bramall Lane, he helped the Blades win promotion to the First Division but in the summer of 1965, after appearing in 123 league games for the Yorkshire club, he joined Stockport County.

In 1966-67 he played an important role as the Edgeley Park club won the Fourth Division Championship. Two years later, after suggestions that he might move to Newport County, he returned to Swansea where he played out the remainder of his league career. He had scored 60 goals in 342 league games in his two spells with the club. In 1971 he joined his brother Ivor at Haverfordwest, later running a hotel in Swansea and establishing a successful leather goods business.

BILLY BAKER

Cardiff

A former coalminer, Billy Baker had trials with a number of clubs including Arsenal and Wolverhampton Wanderers before joining Cardiff City in 1938. He made his debut for the Bluebirds at outside-right in a 2-0 home win over Northampton Town in February 1939, but had only made three appearances when the Second World War intervened.

After appearing in 22 wartime fixtures in 1940-41, Baker went to fight for his country but was captured by the Japanese and was a Prisoner of War for almost four years.

When League football resumed in 1946-47, Baker was converted to wing-half and over the next nine seasons or so went on to score seven goals in 324 first team appearances. In 1948 he was capped by Wales in the match against Northern Ireland and in 1951-52 was instrumental in helping the Bluebirds win promotion to the First Division. His only goal in that campaign came in the 3-0 home win over arch rivals Swansea Town.

Baker, who was the only Cardiff player to have played before the Second World War and enjoy a lengthy career after it, severed his ties with the Ninian Park club in 1955 when he signed for Ipswich Town. He spent two seasons at Portman Road, making 20 league appearances before returning to

Wales to play non-League football for Ton Pentre.

COLIN BAKER

Cardiff

One of the greatest wing-halves in the history of Cardiff City, Colin Baker replaced his namesake Billy Baker in the Bluebirds side, making his debut in a 2-2 draw at home to Sheffield Wednesday on the final day of the 1953-54 season. He had to wait until the 1955-56 season before winning a regular place in the City side and over the next ten seasons made 352 first team appearances, including being an ever-present in 1961-62.

The winner of seven full Welsh international caps, he played his first match against Mexico in the 1958 World Cup Finals in Sweden.

Though he was not a prolific scorer, finding the net on just 19 occasions during his Bluebirds career, he did score two goals in the 5-1 home win over Charlton Athletic in January 1960.

Colin Baker very rarely suffered from injuries but it was he who was the injured player to come off when David Summerhayes became the Ninian Park club's first substitute in the opening match of the 1965-66 season against Bury!

JOE BONSON

Cardiff

A big and burly centre-forward, Joe Bonson began his career with Wolverhampton Wanderers and though he did appear in 10 league games during his four years at Molineux, he played the majority of his football in the club's Central League side.

The Bluebirds had just transferred Johnny Nicholls to Exeter City and signed Bonson as his replacement for a fee of £7,000. He made a goalscoring debut in a 1-1 home draw against Ipswich Town in November 1957. That season he scored 12 goals in 25 league games. He formed two formidable striking partnerships, first with Ron Hewitt and then from 1958-59 with Derek Tapscott, following his arrival from Arsenal.

Bonson's best season in terms of goals scored was 1959-60 when he netted 18 goals in 26 matches including two goals in three consecutive games - Lincoln City (Home 6-2), Hull City (Home 3-2) and Leyton Orient (Away 4-3). He also scored in both league games against Swansea that season but at the end of the campaign, Bonson, who had scored 43 goals in 85 games for the Ninian Park club, was exchanged for Scunthorpe United's Peter Donnelly.

Bonson, who scored the majority of his goals with his head, netted 11 goals in 52 games for Scunthorpe before playing for a number of clubs - Doncaster Rovers, Newport County, Brentford and Lincoln City. His best spell was at Somerton Park where he scored 47 goals in 99 games for the Ironsides.

The Barnsley-born centre-forward played in 328 league games for his six clubs and scored 131 goals.

TERRY BOYLE

Cardiff and Swansea

A Welsh schoolboy international, Terry Boyle began his career at Tottenham Hotspur but failed to make the grade with the White Hart Lane club and moved across London to play for Crystal Palace. At Selhurst Park he made 26 league appearances and had a short spell on loan at Wimbledon as well as being capped twice at full international level by Wales before being transferred to Bristol City. He had played in 37 league games for the Ashton Gate club when he was given a free transfer and joined Newport County to ease the club's financial difficulties.

One of the best defenders ever to play for the Somerton Park club, he had scored 11 goals in 166 league games before joining Cardiff City for £22,000, a fee fixed by an independent tribunal.

He made his debut for the Bluebirds in a 1-1 draw at Hartlepool United on the opening day of the 1986-87 season and was ever-present during that campaign in which City finished 13th in the Fourth Division. Boyle was ever-present again in 1987-88 as the Bluebirds won promotion to the Third Division and won a Welsh Cup winners' medal when City beat Wrexham in the final. He went on to appear in 101 consecutive league games from his debut and in 167 first team matches altogether, before leaving to end his league career with Swansea City for whom he made 27 appearances.

JOHN CHARLES

Cardiff

Immense in physique and talent, John Charles proved to be the complete footballer with a calm and unruffled temperament which earned him the nickname of 'The Gentle Giant'.

Charles was plucked from his native Swansea by Leeds United manager Major Frank Buckley in January 1949 and within three months had made his league debut for the Elland Road club. Despite having to undergo two cartilage operations before he had reached 21, his impact and influence on the game were both immediate and lasting.

At the age of 18 years 71 days, he became the youngest international to play for Wales when he took to the field against Northern Ireland in March 1950, the first of 38 full caps.

As the Yorkshire club bid for more goal power in an effort to climb out of the Second Division, Charles was moved from centre-half to centre-forward and in 1953-54 he scored 42 goals in 39 league games to become the first Welshman to top the Football League's scoring lists.

Eventually hard-up Leeds United had to sell John Charles, who had scored 157 goals in 327 games, to Juventus who paid a world record fee of £65,000 to take him to Turin at the end of the 1956-57 season.

In Italy he became an idol overnight, scoring 30 league goals to pick up a Championship medal and the Italian Footballer of the Year award in his first season. He won two more Championship medals plus three Italian Cup medals and Italian League representative appearances. After 108 goals for Juventus he returned to Elland Road in August 1961 in a £53,000 deal but did not settle and when AS Roma bid £70,000 for him, he returned to Italy.

In August 1963 he joined Cardiff City and made the most remarkable debut for the Bluebirds. Charles scored from fully 75 yards as Norwich City were beaten 3-1 at Ninian Park and he went on over the next two-and-a-half seasons to score 19 goals in 88 games including two against Swansea in April 1965 as the Bluebirds won 5-0.

In 1965 he became Hereford United's player-manager, helping to lay the foundations of the club's successful bid for Football League status.

After spells on the Swansea coaching staff, he ended his involvement with football as manager of Merthyr Tydfil.

MEL CHARLES

Cardiff and Swansea

The younger brother of the legendary John Charles, Mel Charles following a trial with Leeds United, signed professional forms for Swansea Town in May 1952. Over the next seven seasons, Charles scored 69 goals in 233 league games including four in a 5-

1 home win over Blackburn Rovers on the opening day of the 1956-57 season.

Though he was never the star that his elder brother John was, Mel Charles was a very good footballer, winning 31 full caps for Wales. He made his debut for his country against Northern Ireland in 1955 when playing at right-half but with typical versatility he also played at centre-half, inside-right and centre-forward. He was voted the best centre-half in the 1958 World Cup Finals but also showed his attacking qualities when he scored all four goals in Wales' 4-0 defeat of Northern Ireland in April 1962.

By this time, Charles had become much sought after and in March 1959 he had joined First Division Arsenal for £42,750 plus David Dodson and Peter Davies. He made his Arsenal debut at centre-half against Sheffield Wednesday in August 1959 but his progress was hampered by a cartilage operation. In 1960-61 a second cartilage operation was required which resulted in him playing in only 19 league matches. The following season he started out as the club's first-choice centre-forward, scoring 11 goals in the first 18 games. He then lost his place to Geoff Strong and in February 1962 he was transferred to Cardiff City for £20,000.

He made his Bluebirds debut in a goalless home draw against Manchester City in March 1962 and over the next three years went on to appear in 103 first team games. When asked to play in attack he always scored goals -

three in the two matches against Swansea in September 1962 - although he equally did a good job in defence.

Eventually displaced by brother John on his return from Italy, he enjoyed a short but highly successful period with Welsh League side Portmadoc before returning to League action with Port Vale at the end of the 1966-67 season.

On his retirement he went into business in Swansea but was soon guiding the fortunes of his son Jeremy, who played league football for Swansea City, Queens Park Rangers, Oxford United and Wales.

BRIAN CLARK

Cardiff

Brian Clark began his career with his home-town club Bristol City and in six years with the Ashton Gate club, scored 83 goals in 195 League appearances. At the end of the 1965-66 season, he was allowed to leave and joined Huddersfield Town. Unable to settle at the Yorkshire club, he was snapped up by Cardiff manager Jimmy Scoular for the bargain fee of £8,000.

He scored twice on his debut when the Bluebirds won 4-3 at Derby County and then netted again the following week on his home debut against Preston North End. Forming a formidable partnership with John Toshack, he netted 17 league goals in 1968-69 and won the first of three successive Welsh Cup winners' medals before being one of three

ever-presents in 1969-70. That season Clark topped the club's League scoring charts and in the Welsh Cup tie against Barmouth and Dyffryn scored five goals in City's 6-1 win. In 1970-71 Clark again headed the club's scoring charts with 15 league goals, but it was his goal that defeated Real Madrid 1-0 in the European Cup Winners' Cup quarter-final first-leg that ensured his place in the history of the club.

The following season he was the club's leading scorer for a third successive term with a total of 21 league goals. In 1972 he and Ian Gibson were somewhat surprisingly allowed to leave Ninian Park and joined Bournemouth for a combined fee of £100,000. After twelve months at Dean Court, he joined Millwall before returning to play for the Bluebirds.

In that 1975-76 season, he helped the club win promotion to the Second Division and win his fourth Welsh Cup winners' medal but, after scoring 108 goals in his two spells with the club, he left to end his league career with Newport County.

CHRIS COLEMAN

Swansea

Swansea-born Chris Coleman joined his home-town club from Manchester City juniors in September 1987 and in his first season with the Swans, helped them win promotion to the Third Division via the play-offs. He also won Welsh Cup winners' medals in

1989 and 1991 but after four seasons at the Vetch, in which he appeared in 196 first team games, he left to join Crystal Palace for a fee of £275,000.

At Selhurst Park, Coleman won the first of his 32 full caps for Wales when he played against Austria in 1992 and went on to appear in 190 games for the Eagles in a four-year stay with the London club.

In December 1995 he signed for Blackburn Rovers for £2.8 million and though he took a little time to settle in alongside Colin Hendry in the heart of the Blackburn defence, he improved rapidly as the season progressed. However, in 1996-97 an Achilles tendon injury reduced his number of appearances and when Roy Hodgson became manager at Ewood Park, Coleman did not figure in his plans and after appearing in only 32 games, he was allowed to join Kevin Keegan's Fulham for £2.1 million.

In an impressive first season at Craven Cottage, he was voted by his fellow professionals into the PFA award-winning Second Division team before helping them win the Second Division Championship in 1998-99. Coleman was also a member of the Fulham side that won the First Division Championship two seasons later but in January 2001 he was involved in an horrific car accident that was to end his playing career. Now after a spell as caretaker-manager, Chris Coleman has replaced Jean Tigana as Fulham's manager on a permanent basis.

ALAN CURTIS

Cardiff and Swansea

A nephew of former Swansea, Manchester City and Welsh international Roy Paul, he joined the Vetch Field club straight from school. After making his debut against Charlton Athletic in the final game of the 1972-73 season, Curtis quickly emerged as a first team player of imagination, skill and vision and a quite prolific marksman. He netted his first senior team hat-trick in a 4-1 Welsh Cup win over Newport County in January 1977 and ended the season with 14 league goals. His first league hat-trick came in a 5-0 win over Crewe Alexandra in November of that year, whilst on 1 April 1978 both Curtis and Robbie James scored hat-tricks as the Swans recorded their biggest-ever win, defeating Hartlepool United 8-0.

In May 1979, Curtis joined First Division Leeds United for £350,000 but his time at Elland Road was blighted by injury and loss of form.

He was soon back at the Vetch Field in December 1980 as the Swans paid £165,000 to take him back to South Wales. In his first game with the Swans in his second spell, he scored the only goal of the game from the penalty-spot against Watford. He went on to be an important member of the Swansea side that won promotion to the First Division for the first time in the club's history.

A regular for Wales, Curtis left the Vetch for a second time in

November 1983, following the club's relegation from the top flight. He joined Southampton for £85,000 to ease the Swans' financial plight. He failed to show his best form at The Dell and after a short loan spell at Stoke City, returned to South Wales to play for Cardiff City on a free transfer.

Capped 35 times by Wales, Curtis returned to his old stomping ground at Swansea for a third time in October 1989 after helping the Bluebirds win promotion to the Third Division and the Welsh Cup where he scored one of the goals against Wrexham. Retiring at the end of the 1989-90 season, having scored 96 goals in 364 league games, he joined Barry Town as player-coach before signing for Haverfordwest. After a spell as assistant-manager to John Hollins, Curtis is still at the Vetch as the club's coach

LEN DAVIES

Cardiff

The only Cardiff City player to have scored over a century of League goals for the club, Len Davies joined the Bluebirds in 1919 before they were elected to the Football League. He played in just one Southern League fixture in that 1919-20 season when City drew 2-2 at Luton Town. He made his Football League debut in the club's inaugural season in the competition in a 2-0 win at Barnsley but it was 1921-22, the club's first season in Division One following their promotion, that he came to the fore. Replacing Fred

Pagnam, he scored 17 goals in 25 league games including a hat-trick in a 6-2 home win over Bradford City. That season he won a Welsh Cup winners' medal after scoring four goals in a 7-1 defeat of Newport, a hat-trick in a 5-0 win over Merthyr Town and one of he goals in the final as Ton Pentre were beaten 2-0.

In 1922 he won the first of 23 caps for Wales when he played against England.

In 1922-23 he headed the club's league goalscoring charts with 19 goals in 27 games including scoring a hat-trick in a 6-1 defeat of Chelsea. Also that season he won another Welsh Cup winners' medal and netted another hat-trick in a 10-0 win over Oswestry. In 1923-24 he again topped the scoring list with 23 league goals including all four in a 4-2 win at West Bromwich Albion. At the end of that season, he missed a late penalty at Birmingham. Had he converted it, it would have given City the League Championship. Topping the scoring charts for the third consecutive season in 1924-25, he netted another treble in a 4-1 home win over Bury.

Following the arrival of Hughie Ferguson, Davies found himself playing out wide and though the goals dried up, he was still in sparkling form. In 1926-27 he helped the club win both the FA Cup and Welsh Cup, scoring one of the goals in the 2-0 win over Rhyl in the final of the latter competition.

He continued to be a virtual ever-present for the club until 1930-31 when, after scoring 184 goals in 369 games, he left Ninian

Park to play for Thames Association. The following season he was in the Thames side City defeated 9-2 to record their best league win but, shortly afterwards, Davies returned to Wales to become player-manager of Bangor City.

PHIL DWYER

Cardiff

One of the Cardiff City greats, Phil Dwyer holds the club record for the greatest number of appearances with a total of 573.

A member of the successful Bluebirds youth team of 1971, the former Welsh schoolboy international made his debut for the City first team in a goalless draw at Orient in October 1972. He held his place for the rest of the season and ended the campaign with his first Welsh Cup winners' medal when Bangor City were beaten over two legs. An ever-present in 1973-74, he won another Welsh Cup winners' medal and played in 76 consecutive league games from his debut until injury forced him to miss a game.

In 1975-76 he missed just one game - a 4-1 defeat at Hereford United - as the Bluebirds won promotion to the Second Division. At the end of that season he won his third Welsh Cup winners' medal, scoring two goals in the first leg against Hereford United, a tie City won 6-5 on aggregate.

Never one to shirk a challenge, he won Under-21 and Under-23 honours before winning the first of 10 full caps for Wales against Iran in 1978.

Despite a series of niggling injuries, he missed very few games and in 1983-84, he was an ever-present. Though the majority of his 573 games were played at full-back or in the centre of defence, he still managed to score 50 goals. City manager Alan Durban let him leave Ninian Park towards the end of the 1984-85 season and he joined Rochdale, where he appeared in just 15 league games for the Spotland club.

GEORGE EDWARDS

Cardiff and Swansea

One of football's outstanding wingers of the 1940s, George Edwards began his career as an amateur with Swansea and made his first team debut towards the end of the 1938-39 season. Before the outbreak of the Second World War, he won a Welsh amateur cap against England. During the war years he continued to play for Swansea whilst studying for a Degree at Swansea University, but when he was called up for the RAF he was stationed in the Midlands and 'guested' for Coventry City.

In 1945-46 he played for Wales in the Victory Internationals and in October 1946 he won his first full cap against Scotland.

By now Edwards was a Birmingham City player and though he only scored nine goals in 84 league games for the St Andrews club, they were usually very important goals.

In December 1948 he joined Cardiff City for a fee of £12,000 and made his debut in a 2-2 draw at Leicester City. An ideal replacement for Roy Clarke who had left Cardiff for Manchester City in 1947, he was a member of the Bluebirds team that won promotion to the First Division in 1951-52, providing a number of chances for both Chisholm and Grant. He went on to score 34 goals in 194 league games but netted hat-tricks in the 7-1 Welsh Cup win at Bangor in March 1951 and in a 6-1 win against the Jersey Saturday League in a friendly two months later.

When he made the decision to leave the game in 1955, he was still Cardiff's first choice and playing well. He was later invited to join the Ninian Park club's Board of Directors, a position he held for nearly thirty years.

BRIAN EVANS

Swansea

A winger in the old-fashioned mode, Brian Evans joined Swansea from Abergavenny in the summer of 1963, when the Vetch Club's manager Trevor Morris paid the Welsh League club just £650 for his services.

Over the next ten seasons, Brian Evans was to give the Vetch Field club great service, missing very few games. Very quick off the mark, he soon won Welsh Under-23 honours and in 1972 won the first of seven caps at full international level when he played for Wales against Finland. Just prior to that, he,

along with goalkeeper Tony Millington and Dave Gwyther, was selected to tour New Zealand with an FA of Wales party.

Evans went on to score 58 goals in 355 league games, including Swansea's goal in a 1-1 draw at Ninian Park in October 1963, before manager Harry Gregg felt obliged to sell him to Hereford United for a fee of £7,000 as he had to off-load before he could buy.

The flying winger scored nine goals in 48 league games for the Edgar Street club before leaving to play non-league football. He now runs a successful painting and decorating business in Swansea.

TOM FARQUHARSON

Cardiff

Without doubt the greatest goalkeeper in the history of Cardiff City, Dublin-born Tom Farquharson joined the Bluebirds from Abertillery and made his debut in a 3-1 home win over Manchester United on the final day of the 1921-22 season. The following season he shared the goalkeeping duties with Ben Davies but in 1923-24 he became the club's first-choice keeper, a position he held for the next 12 seasons. Also in 1923-24 he won the first of seven full caps for Northern Ireland when he played against Scotland. Six seasons later he won the first of four caps for the Republic of Ireland.

He was in goal when Cardiff lost 1-0 to Sheffield United in the FA Cup Final and when they beat Arsenal, also at Wembley in 1927.

The law that made sure that the goalkeepers' feet remained on the goal-line when a penalty-kick was being taken is down to the antics of Cardiff keeper Tom Farquharson. He would quite often advance from the back of the net as the penalty-taker came in to take the kick!

Farquharson went on to play in 521 first team games for Cardiff City, his last appearance for the Ninian Park club being in a 4-0 defeat at Bristol City on the final day of the 1934-35 season.

MIKE FORD

Cardiff

The son of Tony Ford, who was a full-back with both Bristol clubs, he served his apprenticeship with Leicester City before becoming a full-time professional at the age of 18. After being released by the Filbert Street club, he moved into the Western League with Devizes Town but within a matter of months he joined Cardiff City and made his debut in a 1-1 draw at Leeds United.

He proved himself to be a fine utility player at Ninian Park, appearing at full-back, central defence and midfield. In the club's promotion-winning season of 1987-88 he scored seven goals in 45 appearances and was one of the mainstays of the Bluebirds team. Ford went on to score 13 goals in 145 league games for Cardiff before leaving the club to join Oxford United in 1988.

He remained at the Manor Ground for ten years, captaining the club in many of his 338 first team appearances before rejoining Cardiff. Frank Burrows' most crucial signing, his ability to lead, organise and inspire meant that he was soon appointed captain. The key figure in City's promotion campaign, when he was playing City did well but when he was injured they struggled. He struggled even more with injuries in 1999-2000 and was forced to retire after taking his total appearances in his two spells with the club to 232.

Keen to become a coach or a manager, he went on to complete his UEFA 'A' coaching course.

ROGER FREESTONE

Swansea

Goalkeeper Roger Freestone joined his home-town team Newport County as a trainee in 1986 but within nine months he had moved to Chelsea for a fee of £95,000. An excellent shot-stopper, he went on to appear in 53 games for the Stamford Bridge club when, after loan spells with Swansea and Hereford United, he joined the Swans on a permanent basis in September 1991.

One of the club's most consistent goalkeepers, he did not miss a single league game until April 1995 when he was called up to the Welsh international squad for the match against Germany. In 1995-96 he converted a couple of penalties for the Swans during the first month of the season and missed just one game.

During his first few seasons at the Vetch, Freestone was one of the best keepers outside of the Premiership and his consistency for the Swans was a major factor in the club reaching the play-offs on three occasions and winning the Autoglass Trophy.

In 1998-99, for the first time in his career, a ruptured disc forced him to miss a number of league games through injury. Following his 500th League and Cup appearance for the Swans he broke the club's 368 league appearance record held by the legendary Johnny King.

In 1999-2000, Roger Freestone broke record after record as the club won the Third Division Championship. He kept 22 clean sheets and was recalled to the Welsh international squad after his first call up in 1995 and made his belated international debut against Brazil at the Millennium Stadium.

Awarded a testimonial for his long service to the club, Roger Freestone has now played in over 600 first team games for the Swans.

JIMMY GILLIGAN

Cardiff and Swansea

A former England youth international, Jimmy Gilligan began his career with Watford but in six years at Vicarage Road, the bustling centre-forward scored just six goals in 27 league appearances. After a loan spell at Lincoln, he joined Grimsby Town for £100,000 but within twelve months he had left Blundell Park to sign for Swindon Town for £40,000. Gilligan was soon on the move again, this time to Lincoln City after a loan spell in South Wales with Newport County. When the Sincil Bank club lost their league status in 1987, Gilligan moved to Cardiff City for what proved a bargain fee of £17,500.

He scored City's goal on his debut in a 1-1 draw at home to Leyton Orient and ended the season as the club's top scorer with 20 league goals as the Bluebirds won promotion to the Third Division. One of two ever-presents in that 1987-88 season, he also won a Welsh Cup winners' medal, scoring the second goal in a 2-0 win over Wrexham. He was ever-present again the following season and the club's top scorer with 14 goals. In the European Cup Winners' Cup he netted a hat-trick in a 4-0 home win over Derry City and in matches against Swansea, no matter what competition, when he scored - which he usually did - the Bluebirds didn't lose.

Having scored 49 goals in 131 first team games he followed former City manager Frank Burrows to Portsmouth before returning to South Wales to see out his career with Swansea City, where he once again scored regularly including one against Cardiff in the FA Cup. He went on to score 23 goals in 62 league games for the Swans before a painful back condition forced him to retire.

HARRY GRIFFITHS

Swansea

One of the club's most popular and loyal servants, Harry Griffiths represented Swansea Schoolboys in their first season directly after the Second World War. He joined the Swans groundstaff at the age of 15 and signed professional forms two years later.

He made his Football League debut against Chesterfield in 1948-49 at outside-right and after establishing himself as a first team regular in 1951-52, rarely missed a game in the next 11 seasons.

Griffiths was one of the club's greatest utility players, appearing in every position in the Swansea side, except centre-half and goalkeeper. He won one full cap for Wales when he played against Northern Ireland at Windsor Park, Belfast in April 1953 in a match the Welsh side won 3-2. He left the club in 1964 after scoring 68 goals in 424 league games including hat-tricks against Leicester City in March 1956 and Doncaster Rovers in October 1956.

He became player-manager at Merthyr and remained there for two seasons before returning to the Vetch as the club's trainer under former manager Billy Lucas. Griffiths was appointed the Swans manager in January 1975 and almost led the club to promotion from the Fourth Division in 1976-77, missing out by just one point after a fine run-in. He left the club through ill-health before the Swans went up the following season.

He had returned to help the club out when he died at the early age of 47 whilst working in the treatment room at Vetch Field, prior to Swansea's match against Scunthorpe United on 25 April 1978, a match they won 3-1.

ALAN HARRINGTON

Cardiff

Alan Harrington joined his home-town club Cardiff City from Cardiff Nomads in October 1951 but he had to wait until midway through the 1952-53 season before being given a chance in the Bluebirds first team. Playing at wing-half he made an impressive debut in a goalless draw at home to Tottenham Hotspur. Harrington went on to appear in 10 league games that season and in the first six of those matches, the opposition failed to score!

It was 1954-55 before he established himself as a first team regular and, with the exception of missing the entire 1963-64 season with a broken leg, he was a virtual ever-present in the Cardiff side for the next 12 seasons.

Harrington was capped at full international level by Wales 11 times, winning his first cap against Northern Ireland in 1956.

He had appeared in 405 first team games for the Ninian Park club when he was forced to give the game up following another broken leg in a 1-1 draw at Leyton Orient in January 1966.

197

MARK HARRIS

Cardiff and Swansea

Defender Mark Harris was a late entrant into League football, signing for Crystal Palace in 1988 aged 24 from Wokingham Town of the Vauxhall Opel League. After a very brief introduction to First Division football, he joined Burnley on loan at the start of the 1988-89 season but at the end of his loan period, he was immediately transferred to Swansea for £22,500.

Harris made his debut in a 6-1 defeat against his home-town club Reading but despite this inauspicious start, he was almost a fixture in the Swans defence for the next six seasons.

In 1993-94, Harris was ever-present in a mid-table Second Division campaign but in April 1994, he helped the Swans to victory in the Autoglass Trophy Final at Wembley. Huddersfield Town were finally overcome in a penalty shoot-out following a 1-1 draw after extra-time.

In September 1995, after scoring 18 goals in 288 games for the Swans, he moved to Gillingham and was a regular in the side that gained promotion to the Second Division, scoring the club's goal in the 1-1 draw against prospective champions Preston North End. Released in the summer of 1997 he joined Cardiff City but, after just one month at Ninian Park in which the Bluebirds struggled, he was given a free transfer.

BARRIE HOLE

Cardiff and Swansea

The son of pre-war Welsh international Billy Hole, one of the first league stars produced by Swansea, his two older brothers Colin and Alan both followed in their father's footsteps and played for their home-town club.

Barrie Hole did not follow the family tradition, preferring Cardiff City to his home-town club. He made his first team debut for the Bluebirds at the age of 17 years 170 days in a 4-3 win at Leyton Orient in February 1960, a season in which the club won promotion to the First Division. After getting another first team chance the following season he quickly established himself as a creative wing-half and inside-forward and rarely missed a game. He went on to win five Welsh Under-23 caps before winning the first of 30 full caps against Northern Ireland in 1963. Hole had scored 16 goals in 211 league games for the Bluebirds when in the summer of 1966 he joined Blackburn Rovers for a fee of £40,000.

Although tall and slight in build, Hole was an extremely gifted ball-player. His intelligent positional play and constructive use of the ball made him one of the most exciting midfield players of his day. He had scored 15 goals in 88 League and Cup games for Rovers when in September 1968 he was transferred to Aston Villa for £60,000.

He left Villa Park midway through the 1969-70 season after a difficult time under Tommy Docherty's management. In fact, Hole turned his back on the game and went into his father's business.

During the summer of 1970 Roy Bentley, the Swansea manager, persuaded him to make a comeback, willingly paying Villa £20,000 to bring the Welsh international to the Vetch Field. He went on to play in 78 league games for the Swans before deciding to retire from the game in May 1972. Like his father, Barrie Hole then became a shopkeeper in Swansea.

BRIAN HUGHES

Swansea

Tough-tackling wing-half Brian Hughes worked his way up through the ranks at the Vetch Field before making his first team debut for the Swans during the 1958-59 season. Hughes, who won two caps for Wales at Under-23 level, was a member of the Swansea side when they created a little bit of history in January 1959, when they played Fulham at Craven Cottage. Eight of the Swansea side were full internationals while three, of which Hughes was one, had won Under-23 or Youth caps.

Over the years, Brian Hughes had a number of outstanding games, but perhaps none more so than when the Swans beat the mighty Liverpool 2-1 at Anfield in the FA Cup sixth round tie of 1963-64.

Hughes was an important member of the Swansea side for over ten seasons but in January 1969 after he had scored six goals in 231 league games he left the club to join Atlanta Chiefs in the United States.

TOMMY HUTCHISON

Swansea

One of the most naturally gifted players of the post-war era, Scottish international Tommy Hutchison began his career with Alloa before Blackpool brought him into League football in 1968.

In 1969-70 he helped the Seasiders win promotion to the First Division, laying on countless chances for his team-mates. However, success was short-lived and Blackpool were relegated after just one season in the top flight. Hutchison continued to impress with his close control, pin-point crosses and his ability to beat a player with skill and pace and it came as no surprise when he joined Coventry City in October 1972.

In 1973 he won the first of 17 full Scottish caps, all whilst with the Highfield Road club. In an eight-year stay with the Sky Blues, Hutchison scored 24 goals in 314 league games before leaving to join Manchester City.

One of John Bond's most influential signings, he helped the Maine Road club to the semi-final of the League Cup and the epic FA Cup Final against Tottenham

Hotspur in 1981. During that match he headed City into a first-half lead only to have the misfortune to score a late equaliser for Spurs when he deflected Glenn Hoddle's shot past Joe Corrigan. He left Maine Road in the summer of 1982 to spend a season in Hong Kong before signing for Burnley. Never fully accepted by the Turf Moor crowd, he joined Swansea in July 1985.

He made his Swans debut against Wigan Athletic on the opening day of the 1985-86 season, later becoming player-coach, but he also played his part in the Vetch Field club's promotion to the Third Division in 1987-88. During that season he had a brief spell on loan at Blackpool, almost twenty years after he first played for the Seasiders. In 1988-89 he was virtually an ever-present and competed in the European Cup Winners' Cup in 1989-90 at the age of 42, the oldest player ever to play in a European tie. In March 1991 he played in the last of his 178 league games for the Swans at the age of 43 years 171 days and, at the end of the season, received a PFA Merit Award for his services to football after 860 league appearances for his five clubs.

ROBBIE JAMES

Cardiff and Swansea

It was Swansea manager Harry Gregg who signed Robbie James on amateur forms and after the talented youngster had impressed in Welsh League and Football Combination games, he was given his first team debut in the final match of the 1972-73 season against Charlton Athletic. James, who was just 16 years old, starred in a 2-1 win for the Swans.

The driving midfielder was instrumental in the club's rise from the Fourth Division to the First Division and in 1979 his form led to him winning the first of 47 full caps for Wales when he played against Malta.

Within the space of twelve months during the club's successive promotions, James netted three hat-tricks against Hartlepool United in the Football League (Home 8-0 on 25th April 1978), Newport County in the League Cup (Home 5-0 on 15th August 1978) and Kidderminster Harriers in the Welsh Cup (Home 6-1 on 29th January 1979).

He had scored 99 goals in 394 league games for Swansea when in July 1983, after the club had lost their place in the top flight, he joined Stoke City for £160,000. Never quite able to produce the goods, he left the Potters in October 1984, signing for Queens Park Rangers for a fee of £100,000. At Loftus Road, he was used successfully as a full-back before moving to Leicester City where he provided valuable experience to the Foxes' young defence. In January 1988, with his pace waning, he was released and returned to the Vetch Field for a second spell.

He captained the Swans to promotion to the Third Division in 1987-88 but, after taking his total of league goals to 115 in 484 appearances, he left the Vetch a second time to join Bradford City. After leaving Valley Parade, he had a spell with Cardiff City before playing non-league football but died tragically while playing for Llanelli in a Welsh League match, aged just 40.

LESLIE JONES

Cardiff and Swansea

Inside-forward Leslie Jones began his career with his home-town club Aberdare Athletic before joining Cardiff City in 1929. After making his debut in a 1-0 defeat at the Vetch Field in February 1930, he struck up a formidable left-wing partnership with Walter Robbins. Over the next five seasons he played in 161 League and Cup games with his most prolific season being 1932-33 when he scored 16 goals. His performances during that campaign led to him winning the first of 11 Welsh caps when he played against France. His all-action displays in the Christmas matches of 1933 persuaded Coventry City manager Harry Storer to pay £2,000 for him. In nearly five years at Highfield Road, he scored at a rate of a goal in every other game (74 in 144). In 1935-36 he won a Third Division (South) Championship medal and though Coventry resisted a £7,000 bid from Tottenham Hotspur, they could not refuse Arsenal's offer in 1937.

He helped the Gunners win the League Championship in 1937-38 and in the last season before the Second World War, he won an FA Charity Shield winners' medal against Preston North End.

During the hostilities he continued to play for the Highbury club and won five wartime caps. On the return of peace, he was granted a free transfer and moved to Swansea Town as player-coach. His stay at the Vetch was short-lived and he became player-manager of Barry Town, before returning to League football with Brighton where in 1948-49 he finished his long career. He later managed Scunthorpe United.

FRED KEENOR

Cardiff

After having been capped at outside-right in 1907, the first schoolboy international between England and Wales, he joined Cardiff City as an amateur inside-forward four years later. He turned professional in 1912 and made his Southern League debut in a 1-1 home draw against Exeter City in December 1913. At the outbreak of the First World War, he joined the 'Footballers Battalion' (17th Middlesex) and was twice wounded in action. At the end of the hostilities he returned to Cardiff and made his first appearance for Wales in the Victory internationals.

When City entered the Football League, he scored in the club's first League game in a 5-2 win at Stockport County. Succeeding Charlie Brittan as captain, he led both his club and country to success. He led Wales to the Home

201

International Championship in 1924 and was part of the 1925 Bluebirds team that lost to Sheffield United in the FA Cup Final. He returned to Wembley two years later as victorious captain in the 1-0 defeat of Arsenal.

Keenor, who made 32 appearances for his country, was an inspirational captain. His will to win, coupled with his uncompromising tackling, made him a tough opponent. He went on to appear in 436 League and Cup games for a club he had done much to establish before leaving to join Crewe Alexandra after 19 years at Ninian Park.

In three years at Gresty Road he made 116 League appearances before going into non-league football, first with Oswestry and then as player-manager of Tunbridge Wells. A serious illness ended the career of a man who had become a legend in Welsh football.

JOHNNY KING

Swansea

Until overtaken by Roger Freestone, Johnny King held the Swansea appearance record for a goalkeeper with 368 league appearances under his belt between 1950 and 1964.

He made his Swans debut as a 17-year-old amateur in a 5-0 defeat at Birmingham City on 16th December 1950. After his National Service, King proved himself to be one of the best keepers outside the top flight and in 1955 won the only full international cap of his career when he played in a 2-1 win over England at Ninian Park.

Up until the arrival of Noel Dwyer in 1960, King was a virtual ever-present in the Swansea side but, following the Irishman's performances when he deputised for King, he had to be content to share the goalkeeping duties. In February 1961, King was awarded a £1,000 benefit following a superb performance against Preston North End in the fourth round of that season's FA Cup.

The popular keeper later emigrated to Australia where he died aged just 49 in 1982.

PETER KING

Cardiff

Peter King played his early football for his home-town team Worcester City before joining the Bluebirds in 1960. One of the most versatile players in the club's history, he made his City debut in a 2-1 defeat at Burnley in October 1961 in a First Division match.

He kept his place for most of the remainder of that season but then missed the majority of the 1962-63 campaign with a chest illness. The following season he had fully recovered and scored both Cardiff's goals in a 2-0 Welsh Cup Final replay win over Bangor City.

In 1964-65 King scored his only Football League hat-trick for the club in a 6-2 home win over Middlesbrough and netted the Bluebirds' first goal in Europe when he scored the only goal of the two-legged tie against Esjberg.

He missed very few games over

the next few seasons and in 1967-68 was ever-present, the club's top scorer with 12 League goals and six more in Cup competitions.

In 1970-71 he missed just one game as Cardiff finished third in Division Two, but an Achilles tendon injury forced him to quit the game in 1974 after this most loyal of Cardiff City clubmen had scored 108 goals in 469 first team games in 13 seasons at Ninian Park.

BILLY LUCAS

Swansea

Billy Lucas began his league career with Swindon Town and had just established himself in their first team when war broke out and interrupted his career. He had compensations, as he played in several wartime and two Victory internationals for Wales. When the hostilities ended he resumed his career with the Wiltshire club.

In March 1948, Swansea manager Bill McCandless paid a club record transfer fee of £11,000 to bring Lucas to the Vetch Field as the missing link in a side that would claim the Third Division (South) Championship the following season.

His early displays for the Swans led to him winning the first of seven full caps for Wales when in October 1948 he played against Scotland at Ninian Park. Able to play at both wing-half and inside-forward, he went on to score 35 goals in 203 league games for the Swans including the only goal of the South

Wales derby at the Vetch in November 1950, before leaving to become player-manager of Newport County. The value of his leadership qualities were only really noticed when he left the club.

At Somerton Park, Lucas was in charge of one of the smallest squads in the Football League and had to sell to survive. He resigned his post in April 1961 but was re-appointed less than a year later when Bobby Evans was sacked.

In February 1967 he returned to the Vetch as manager but the Swans were struggling to avoid relegation from the Third Division. Unfortunately, he was unable to save them but he was instrumental in bringing in a good number of young players to the club.

He resigned in March 1969 but returned to Somerton Park for a third spell and in the first six months of this period worked without wages. In 1972-73 County missed out on promotion on goal average but Lucas, who later became the club's general manager, left in 1975 to spend more time on his business.

DANNY MALLOY

Cardiff

Signed from Dundee for £17,500, centre-half Danny Malloy had already been capped by Scotland at 'B' international level when he joined Cardiff City in 1955.

He made his debut in a 3-1 home win over Charlton Athletic, a match in which Neil O'Halloran, also making his debut, scored a hat-trick.

An ever-present in 1956-57 when he scored his only league goal for the club from the penalty-spot in a 3-1 defeat at Manchester United, he went on to appear in 69 consecutive league games from his debut. Malloy was also ever-present in 1958-59 and 1960-61 and missed just one game in 1959-60. In that 1959-60 season, Malloy was captain and led the club back to the top flight as runners-up to Aston Villa. That campaign also saw the Scottish defender score two own goals in the opening match when City beat Liverpool 3-2.

In 1960-61, Malloy did score another goal in Cardiff colours as Knighton Town were beaten 16-0 in a Welsh Cup tie!

In the summer of 1961 Malloy, who had appeared in 262 first team games, failed to agree terms for the coming season and left to become player-coach of Doncaster Rovers.

ANDY MELVILLE

Swansea

Swansea-born Andy Melville began his career with his home-town club and progressed from the youth training scheme to make his senior debut as a substitute in a 3-1 home defeat by Bristol City in November 1985. In his early days with the Swans there was something of a problem in that his best position was not readily apparent. He was tried in most positions before settling into the back four. He won a permanent place in the Swansea side in 1986-87 and helped the Vetch club win promotion the following season.

He was appointed Swansea captain at the age of 20 but in July 1990, after scoring 29 goals in 213 games for the Vetch Field club, he joined Oxford United for £275,000 plus a percentage of any future transfer fee. In three seasons at the Manor Ground, he appeared in 159 games before being transferred to Sunderland in the summer of 1993.

The Welsh international, who has won 54 caps for his country, made a disastrous debut for the Wearsiders in a 5-0 defeat at Derby County on the opening day of the 1993-94 season. His first three seasons at Roker Park were spent in relegation battles but in 1995-96, Melville played in 40 league games as the Wearsiders won the First Division Championship.

Powerful in the air and always dangerous at set pieces, he acquitted himself well in the Premiership before an injury ended his virtual monopoly of a back-four position. Following a loan spell with Bradford City, Melville joined Fulham and in 2000-01, he helped the Cottagers win the First Division Championship.

The following season he captained both club and country and despite approaching his 35th birthday, he remains a regular for both Fulham and Wales.

WILF MILNE

Swansea

Wilf Milne is the club record-holder for the greatest number of appearances in a Swansea shirt, having played in 657 first team games between 1920 and 1937.

He played in the club's first-ever Football League game when the Swans lost 3-0 at Portsmouth on 28th August 1920 and was a member of the Swansea side which won the Third Division (South) Championship in 1924-25. The following season Milne played his part in the club's run to the FA Cup semi-finals where, after beating Arsenal in the sixth round, they lost 3-0 to the eventual winners Bolton Wanderers.

Famous for his sliding tackle, Milne went on to make club history with a record 585 league appearances. He scored his first goal for the Swans in his 501st league match - from the penalty-spot - and then added another in the final match of the 1933-34 season; had he missed, the Swans would have been relegated!

In 1936-37 when the Swans were travelling to play Leicester City at Filbert Street, the club's keeper Stan Moore had a swollen knee and was unable to play. The only available replacement was Wilf Milne - in his 17th season with the club - who performed heroics and kept a clean sheet in a goalless draw. Because the club were playing two games in three days in the Midlands, Milne kept his place for the next match but the Vetch Field side lost 6-1!

Milne left Swansea at the end of that season but not before a special benefit match had been played on behalf of this loyal servant.

STAN MONTGOMERY

Cardiff

The son-in-law of Jimmy Nelson, one of the famous Scotland 'Wembley Wizards' who appeared in 240 league games for the Bluebirds, he began his career with non-league Romford before joining Hull City during the Second World War. After 'guesting' for Southend United during the 1945-46 season he returned to Boothferry Park for the first peacetime Football League campaign in 1946-47. After just five league appearances he moved to Southend on a permanent basis. He had two seasons at Roots Hall in which he made 96 appearances before, on Nelson's recommendation, he joined Cardiff City in 1948 for a fee of £6,000.

The giant centre-half scored on his debut in a 2-2 draw at Grimsby Town in January 1949 and played in the remaining 17 league games. He was only on the losing side twice as City finished fourth in Division Two.

Over the next six seasons, Montgomery missed very few matches and was a tower of strength in the club's promotion-winning season of 1951-52 when his only goal of the campaign secured a point in a 1-1 draw at Notts County. He went on to play in 260 first team games for the Bluebirds before leaving Ninian Park to play non-league football for

Worcester City in 1955. However, his stay was short and he returned to League action with Newport County before playing for Ton Pentre.

He returned to Ninian Park as the club's trainer before becoming Bristol Rovers' South Wales' scout, a position he held for a good number of years. He then became involved with the Bluebirds again when Alan Durban asked him to take charge of the club's triallists.

DON MURRAY

Cardiff and Swansea

One of the greatest centre-halves in Cardiff City's history, Don Murray was just 17 years 113 days old when he made his first team debut for the Bluebirds in a 3-2 defeat at Middlesbrough in May 1963. After playing in half of the club's games the following season, he established himself as the club's first-choice pivot at the start of the 1964-65 campaign, a position he held for ten seasons.

He was ever-present for three consecutive seasons - 1968-69 to 1970-71 - and holds the club record for the most consecutive appearances at Football League level when he played in 146 games from 4th May 1968 to 20th November 1971.

Despite being in trouble with the referees during the early stages of his career, he became a player who led by example and gave his all. The winner of nine Welsh Cup winners' medals during his time at Ninian Park, he was also instrumental in

the club reaching the semi-final of the European Cup Winners' Cup in 1967-68. His performances around this time led to offers from the game's top clubs but Murray remained loyal to Cardiff and though his play was often worthy of full international honours, the Scottish-born centre-half had to be content with just one Under-23 cap.

In October 1974, after appearing in 532 first team games for City, he had a five-match loan spell with Swansea before returning north of the border to play for a season with Hearts. He then returned to South Wales to see out his career at Newport County where former Cardiff boss Jimmy Scoular was in charge.

MEL NURSE

Swansea

Mel Nurse, who scored the only goal of the March 1959 South Wales derby at Ninian Park from the penalty spot, also scored two own goals in the meetings with Cardiff, notably in the Welsh Cup Final of 1969.

The Welsh Schoolboy international centre-half was linked to the Swans via the juniors and signed professional forms for the Vetch Field club in June 1955. Over the next seven seasons, Nurse gave many outstanding performances at the heart of the Swansea defence and in 1960 after winning two Welsh Under-23 caps, he made his full international debut against England at Wembley. It was the first of 12 full caps for his country, nine of them whilst with the Swans.

Though he didn't score too many goals, when he did they were usually spectacular efforts and perhaps none more so than his 35-yard thunderbolt against Burnley in a fourth round FA Cup replay at Turf Moor, which the Swans lost after holding their First Division opponents to a goalless draw at the Vetch. Mel Nurse was an inspirational captain of Swansea but as the club struggled in the lower reaches of the Second Division, he requested a transfer on a number of occasions, all of which were turned down.

Eventually the Swans had to release him and in September 1962 he joined Middlesbrough for a fee of £25,000. A commanding figure in the Boro defence, he was soon appointed captain and was a virtual ever-present in his three seasons at Ayresome Park. One of his biggest regrets though was scoring the goal which sent the Swans crashing into the Third Division!

Nurse's wife wanted to return nearer to South Wales and in the summer of 1965 he joined Swindon town for £15,000. He spent three seasons at the County Ground before renewing his association with Swansea in June 1968. He went on to score 11 goals in 256 league games in his two spells with the club before entering non-league football with Suffolk club Bury before finishing his career with Merthyr Tydfil, for whom he was playing when he suffered a broken leg.

COLIN PASCOE

Swansea

Colin Pascoe joined Swansea as a 16-year-old apprentice in 1981 when the Vetch Field club were members of the First Division of the Football League. After making his debut as a substitute for the injured John Mahoney against Brighton in March 1983, he played his first full game against Liverpool at Anfield.

During his first season with the Swans, he represented the Welsh Youth side and in 1983-84 he was chosen for the Welsh Under-21 side on four occasions. Two years after winning his Welsh Youth cap he was selected for the Wales senior side against Norway. Pascoe had played in 201 first team games for the Swans when he was transferred to Sunderland for £70,000 in March 1988.

After scoring the Wearsiders' goal in a 2-1 defeat at York City on his debut, Pascoe netted the winner against Chesterfield in a 3-2 win for the north-east club. He also scored in his third game for Sunderland in a 4-1 win at Southend United. He helped Sunderland reach the First Division via the play-offs even though it was at the expense of Swindon Town, who were found guilty of financial irregularities and relegated from the top flight. Pascoe went on to score 26 goals in 151 games before returning to Swansea for £120,000 after a loan spell with the Vetch Field club.

He took his total of goals for the Swans to 67 in 324 League and Cup games before being released by the club after suffering damage to his ankle ligaments.

JASON PERRY

Cardiff

Newport-born Jason Perry made his debut for the Bluebirds in a goalless draw at home to Exeter City in March 1987, though it was midway through the 1989-90 season before he ´ established himself as a regular first team member.

After winning Under-21 and 'B' international honours, the strong-tackling defender was capped at full level when he played against Norway in 1994. After helping Cardiff win promotion in 1992-93 he hardly missed a game until 1995-96 when he suffered the worst injury crisis of his career. He bounced back the following season and missed very few games in helping the Bluebirds to the play-offs. After spending almost ten years at Ninian Park and appearing in 344 first team games, he was offered a free transfer and left the club to join Bristol Rovers.

After just one season with the Pirates he moved on to Lincoln City on a free transfer but his stay at Sincil Bank was again brief. Moving to Hull City, much of his time at Boothferry Park was spent on the substitute's bench and after suffering a bad ankle injury he left to play non-league football for his home-town club, Newport County.

BRAYLEY REYNOLDS

Cardiff and Swansea

After playing his early football with Lovells Athletic, Brayley Reynolds began his Football League career with Cardiff City after joining the Bluebirds in the summer of 1956.

Though on the smallish side for a centre-forward, he scored 15 goals in 54 league games for the Ninian Park club before signing for Swansea for a four-figure fee in May 1959.

During the 1959-60 season, he scored 16 goals in 37 games but his best season in terms of goals scored for the Swans was 1961-62 when he found the net 18 times in 33 matches. Included in this total was a hat-trick in a 5-1 home win over Plymouth Argyle on 24th April 1962 and the all-important goal in the 1-1 draw against Sunderland, which ensured that the club remained in the Second Division after coming perilously close to relegation.

Reynolds scored in four consecutive South Wales derby matches for Swansea before, in March 1964, he netted twice in the Second Division meeting at the Vetch.

He went on to score 57 goals in 151 league games for the Swans before leaving to play non-league football.

ALF SHERWOOD

Cardiff

During the early years of the Second World War, Alf Sherwood played for Aberdare Town and Aberaman. It was whilst playing against Cardiff City in a Wartime League game that he impressed the Ninian Park club and he signed for them in 1941. Having been switched from half-back to full-back, he appeared in 140 wartime games for the Bluebirds before making his Football League debut in a 2-1 defeat at Norwich City on the opening day of the 1946-47 season. He missed just one game that season as City won the Third Division (South) Championship.

Having played for Wales in a Victory international against Ireland, it came as no surprise when he won his first full cap against England at Manchester in 1946. Over the next six years he hardly missed an international and won 41 caps. He also had a spell as captain of the team including the famous win over England in 1955.

After Fred Stansfield had left Ninian Park to join Newport County, Alf Sherwood was given the captaincy of the team. He was ever-present in 1949-50 and in 1951-52 led the side in promotion to the First Division.

The master of the sliding tackle, he was also a stand-in goalkeeper for both Cardiff City and Wales. When the Bluebirds travelled to Anfield for an end-of-season game in April 1954, the home side had to win to keep their First Division status. Sherwood had taken over in goal following an injury to Ron Howells and faced a penalty from Scottish international Billy Liddell. He saved it and Liverpool were relegated! He replaced the injured Jack Kelsey for Wales against England at Wembley in 1956 and though he made some outstanding saves, Wales lost 3-1.

At the end of the 1955-56 season, after he had played in 383 first team games, he left to join Newport County, where he scored 21 goals in 205 games before becoming manager of Barry Town.

NIGEL STEVENSON

Cardiff and Swansea

Nigel Stevenson joined Swansea City as a schoolboy and remained with the club during their dramatic rise and fall through the Football League. He made his first team debut for the Swans in a Fourth Division match at Southport in 1976 and thereafter became an established member of the Vetch Field side.

The tall centre-half was instrumental in the club winning promotion in three out of four seasons and when they played in the top flight his form was such that he was awarded his first full international cap when he played for Wales against England at Ninian Park. He made further appearances against Scotland at Hampden Park, Northern Ireland at the Racecourse Ground and finally Norway at the Vetch Field.

After ten seasons with the Swans, 'Speedy', as he was known to friends and fans alike, was awarded a testimonial match against Real Sociedad of Spain, managed by his former boss John Toshack. It was around this time though that he lost his place in the Swansea side and had loan spells at both Cardiff and Reading before returning to the Vetch Field to complete 259 league appearances for the club.

In the summer of 1987 he joined Cardiff City on a free transfer and played in 68 league games for the Bluebirds before hanging up his boots.

RON STITFALL

Cardiff

In a playing career which spanned two decades, Ron Stitfall joined his home-town club Cardiff City as a schoolboy during the Second World War and played his first game for the club in wartime competition whilst only 14 years of age!

He appeared in a number of wartime games for the club before serving in the Army for four years. It was 1947 when he returned to Ninian Park and in October of that year he made his Football League debut at left-back in place of Alf Sherwood, who was on international duty, in a goalless draw at Brentford. For the next 18 seasons, Ron Stitfall was a virtual ever-present in the Bluebirds side, although in his first few seasons with the club he played in a variety of positions.

In 1949-50 he had a spell playing centre-forward and scored in each of his first five appearances in that position. Considering he only scored eight goals in the 454 first team games in which he played, it was a remarkable performance.

Surprisingly he won only two full international caps for Wales, against England in 1952 and Czechoslovakia in 1957. He partnered Alf Sherwood at full-back for nine years and joined Newport County's training staff in 1970.

JOE SYKES

Swansea

Joe Sykes began his Football League career with Sheffield Wednesday but in five years with the Hillsborough club made only 28 league appearances. The 26-year-old joined Swansea in the summer of 1924 and made his debut at centre-half in a 2-0 win against Merthyr, replacing the injured Jimmy Collins.

Standing just 5ft 9ins, Sykes was rarely beaten in the air, whilst his timing was immaculate and his passing outstanding. In November 1924, Sykes was made captain for the visit of Brentford, a game which Swansea won 8-0 and went on to lead the club to the Third Division (South) Championship.

Joe Sykes played for the Swans until 1935, appearing in 313 league games. It was a sad day for the Vetch Field club when he played his final game, for Joe Sykes, who felt he was too old to continue, was only 35.

After the war he returned to the club as assistant-trainer, later being appointed chief trainer. Sykes was to have a great influence on the club and it was he who spotted Ivor Allchurch playing on a public park and took him to Swansea's manager Haydn Green when the youngster was only 15 years old.

During the 1955-56 season, following the death of Billy McCandless, he led the side back into the Second Division and introduced a number of talented youngsters. When Roy Bentley took over as team manager, Sykes, along with Ivor Allchurch remained on the three-man selection committee. In 1966 he became caretaker-manager but as the season wore on he relinquished the post after feeling the pressure of the team's poor results.

One of the club's most loyal servants, Joe Sykes was a gentleman and one of Swansea's greatest players.

DEREK TAPSCOTT

Cardiff

Derek Tapscott joined Arsenal from Barry Town where he was a prolific goalscorer in October 1953. He made his League debut for the Gunners against Liverpool at Highbury in April 1954, scoring twice. During that summer he won the first of his 14 Welsh caps when he played against Austria.

He won a regular place in the Arsenal league side in 1954-55, scoring 13 goals in 37 games. In 1955-56, Tapscott was the Gunners' leading scorer with 21 goals and the following season he scored 25 league goals, the most since Ronnie Rooke netted 33 in 1947-48. Tapscott sustained a number of injuries to his knee and ankle, resulting in him missing the majority of the 1957-58 season. After regaining full fitness he couldn't reclaim his first team place and was sold to Cardiff City for £15,000.

Though he failed to score on his debut in a 4-1 home win over Grimsby Town, he was the club's leading scorer with 20 league goals in 1959-60 as the Bluebirds won promotion to the First Division. He was the club's top scorer again the following season with 21 goals in 39 league games, including his first hat-trick for the club as West Bromwich Albion were beaten 3-1. That season also saw him score in both legs of the Welsh Cup semi-final against Swansea.

Though City were relegated in 1961-62, Tapscott netted his second hat-trick for the club in a 3-2 home win over Birmingham City. He netted his third league treble the following season in a 4-2 win at Charlton Athletic.

Tapscott continued to score on a regular basis and in seven years at Ninian Park, he netted 99 goals in 233 first team games, including six in the 16-0 Welsh Cup defeat of Knighton in 1960-61 - still the individual scoring record of any Cardiff player in a first team fixture. In July 1965 he joined Newport County before later moving into non-league football.

GEOFF THOMAS

Swansea

A product of the Swansea Schools, Geoff Thomas worked his way up through the ranks before making his first team debut for the Vetch Field club during the 1965-66 season. Over the next ten seasons, Thomas missed very few games and always gave his best wherever he was asked to play.

Capped three times by Wales at Under-23 level, Thomas scored two hat-tricks for the club, the first in October 1972 when the Swans beat table-topping Grimsby Town 6-2. His second treble was also the club's next hat-trick when he scored three goals in the defeat of Doncaster Rovers in September 1974.

During his penultimate season at the Vetch, Geoff Thomas, who had played most of his games in midfield, was converted to a sweeper, though it has to be said, not to much effect. Thomas, who was a great servant of the Welsh club scored 52 goals in 365 games.

LEN THOMPSON

Swansea

Len Thompson had played for Sheffield and England schoolboys prior to the outbreak of the First World War before joining Barnsley as an amateur in 1917. He turned professional when he moved to Birmingham the following year. Thompson spent three seasons at St Andrew's before being transferred to Swansea in 1922.

By the end of his first campaign with the club, he had established himself as the Swans first-choice inside-left, a position he was to hold for six seasons. During the club's Third Division (South) Championship winning season of 1924-25, Thompson scored four of the Swans' goals in an 8-0 home win over Brentford, tormenting the Bees defence whenever he got the ball.

When Swansea played Wolverhampton Wanderers during the 1925-26 season, Len Thompson had the distinction of scoring the club's fastest-ever goal when he netted after just 10 seconds of the clash against the Molineux club, which the Swans won 3-2. Later that season he netted a hat-trick in a 6-1 home win over Blackpool. He was the club's leading goalscorer with 26 goals in 1926-27 but missed the start of the following season with an injury to his left knee. Shortly after making a full recovery, Thompson, who had scored 86 goals in 187 league games, joined Arsenal for a fee of £4,000.

At Highbury, Thompson became the club's penalty king, though he was later hampered by a recurrence of his knee injury and spent the bulk of his time with the Gunners in their Combination side. He joined Crystal Palace in 1933 before retiring from football a year later. He then became reserve team manager of Tottenham Hotspur before becoming a scout for Arsenal.

KEITH TODD

Swansea

Welsh Under-23 international Keith Todd made his Swansea debut as an 18-year-old in 1960, scoring the winning goal in a 2-1 defeat of Derby County. The young centre-forward also made the Swans' other goal for Len Allchurch. Over the next eight seasons, the Swansea-born player proved himself to be quite a prolific goalscorer.

He netted his first hat-trick for the Swans in the win over Walsall in November 1962, his performance earning him international recognition at Under-23 level. Todd's next hat-trick for the club came in December 1963 as Swansea beat Swindon Town. That season he scored some important goals in the club's run to the FA Cup semi-finals, including two against Stoke City to earn a draw and another in the 2-0 replay win.

Todd's third and final treble for the Swans came in September 1964 as Manchester City were beaten 3-0 at the Vetch.

Todd, who went on to score 76 goals in 199 league games, also netted twice for the Swans in the infamous Welsh Cup match against Cardiff that saw the Bluebirds beaten 5-3 after extra-time. He suffered from a series of injuries towards the twilight of his Swansea career and, at the end of the 1967-68 season, he left league football.

JOHN TOSHACK

Cardiff and Swansea

One of the greatest names in Welsh soccer history, John Toshack came off the bench on 13th November 1965 to score the final goal for Cardiff in a 3-1 home win over Leyton Orient - he was just 16 years 236 days old.

A week later he netted twice in a 4-3 win at Middlesbrough and ended the season with six goals in seven games. Over the next few seasons he continued to find the net and on 16th January 1968 he netted his first hat-trick for the club in an 8-0 Welsh Cup win over Ebbw Vale. After teaming up with Brian Clark he netted 31 goals in 1968-69, including scoring in both legs of the Welsh Cup Final in a 5-1 aggregate win over Swansea, and was the Second Division's leading scorer. In 1969-70 he scored his first League hat-trick for the Bluebirds in a 4-2 home win over Queens Park Rangers and followed it with another early the next season as Hull City were beaten 5-1.

When he left Ninian Park to sign for Liverpool for £110,000 in November 1970, he had scored 100 goals in 203 games and was already a Welsh international, having been capped against Scotland in 1969.

He quickly endeared himself to the Liverpool fans by helping the Reds come from two goals behind to beat Everton 3-2. He went on to play an important role in winning six major trophies, yet for most of his Anfield career in which he scored 95 goals in 245 games, he was dogged by a nagging thigh injury. His most prolific term was 1975-76 when he found the net 23 times including three hat-tricks on his way to a League title and UEFA Cup double.

In February 1978 he joined Fourth Division Swansea as player-manager and made his debut the following month in a 3-3 home draw against Watford. Toshack, who scored 24 goals in 63 league outings, bought freely and took Swansea from the Fourth Division to the top of the First Division in four seasons. In fact, in each of their promotion seasons, the Swans had to win their last game to clinch their place in the higher division and succeeded each time.

It all began to go wrong and in October 1983, Toshack resigned, but in a rather strange turn of events, he was invited back by the directors two months later! The club's results did not improve and in March 1984 came the final break.

Toshack then took over the Portuguese side Sporting Lisbon, where he proved yet again that he had the magic touch. He later took Real Sociedad to their first Spanish Cup success and then took Real Madrid to a Spanish League Championship in his first season with the club. Despite this, the club sacked him and he returned to Real Sociedad as General Manager. In March 1994 he had a spell as Welsh national team manager but it lasted a mere 44 days and one game. Toshack, who had been awarded the MBE for his achievements in the game, returned to Spain to take over at Deportivo La Coruna before rejoining Real Madrid.

NIGEL VAUGHAN

Cardiff

Nigel Vaughan began his Football League career with Newport County and went on to score 32 goals in 224 League appearances for the Somerton Park club. Whilst with Newport he won the first of his 10 Welsh caps when he played against Yugoslavia.

He arrived at Ninian Park in September 1983 as part of an unusual five-man exchange deal between the two clubs, but suffered an unhappy debut as the Bluebirds lost at home to Barnsley 3-0. He then played in all the remaining 36 games of the season as the club finished 15th in the Second Division. In 1984-85 he was City's top scorer with 16 league goals but, despite his efforts, the club were relegated to the Third Division. He was the club's top scorer again the following season, including netting the only goal of Cardiff's home game against Swansea, but the Bluebirds were relegated for a second successive season and dropped into the League's basement. In 1986-87 he became dissatisfied with Fourth Division football and played on a weekly contract until, after scoring 54 goals in 178 games, he left to join Wolverhampton Wanderers for a fee of £12,000.

He made his debut for the Molineux club at Ninian Park when he came on as a substitute and scored in a 3-2 win for the Bluebirds. He went on to score 10 goals in 93 league outings for Wolves before ending his career with Hereford United.

COLIN WEBSTER

Swansea

Cardiff-born Colin Webster joined his home-town club as a 17-year-old in 1949 but failed to make the grade with them and signed for Manchester United in 1952. On his arrival at Old Trafford he was too old to take part in the club's FA Youth Cup success and had to serve his apprenticeship in the club's Central League side.

After making his first team debut at Portsmouth towards the end of the 1953-54 season, the versatile forward, who was also able to play at wing-half, played enough games in the club's League Championship-winning side of 1956 to qualify for a medal. With United he won four full caps for Wales, the first against Czechoslovakia in 1957, the other three in the 1958 World Cup Finals.

After the Munich disaster, he established himself as a first team regular and played in the club's 1958 FA Cup Final defeat against Bolton Wanderers. He had scored 31 goals in 79 League and Cup games when he joined Swansea for £6,000 in September 1958.

Webster soon made an impact at the Vetch and in 1959-60 was the club's leading scorer with 21 goals. Included in his total were hat-tricks against Plymouth Argyle and Charlton Athletic. The first goal of this latter threesome was scored after just 30 seconds. He was the Swans' top scorer in 1960-61 when he found the net 18 times, but in March 1963 after scoring 65 goals in 159 league games, he left the club to see out his career with Newport County.

HERBIE WILLIAMS

Swansea

Herbie Williams was a member of the Swansea schoolboys team that beat Manchester in the final of the English Schools' Trophy in 1954, a year in which the side won the Welsh Shield. In 1955, Williams captained the Swansea schoolboys as they won the Welsh Shield for a second time.

After leaving school he was learning a trade at Swansea Docks but decided to give this up on being offered professional terms by Swansea.

Williams was just 17 when he made his first team debut for the club in September 1958 in a 5-0 home win over Sunderland in which Ivor Allchurch scored four of the goals. His first goals for the club came at Leicester City when he scored twice in a 6-3 win for the Swans.

In 1964 he was a member of the Swansea side that lost 2-1 to Preston North End in the FA Cup semi-final and, the following season, his performances led to him winning two Welsh caps when he played in both matches against Greece. Seven years later he added another cap to his collection when he played against Romania.

Williams was a great club man and when Roy Bentley became manager in 1969, he was appointed

215

captain. He went on to appear in 513 league games scoring 104 goals including four against York City, a hat-trick against Southampton from left-half and a magnificent treble in a 4-0 win over Oldham Athletic during the club's promotion-winning season of 1969-70. Later in his career he settled at centre-half, although he played in a variety of positions for the club.

A skilful and whole-hearted player, Herbie Williams, who had played under seven managers, left the Vetch Field in January 1975 to go and live in Australia.

THE STATISTICS

SWANSEA CITY

	P	W	D	L	F	A
Football League	48	18	14	16	63	61
FA Cup	2	2	0	0	4	1
League Cup	4	2	0	2	5	5
Associate Members Cup	4	2	1	1	4	3
Welsh Cup	36	7	8	21	45	67
Southern League	4	1	2	1	3	3
Wartime Competitions	42	6	6	30	55	126
Jubilee Benevolent Fund	2	0	2	0	4	4
Friendlies	8	3	2	3	15	15
TOTAL	**150**	**41**	**35**	**74**	**201**	**286**

CARDIFF CITY

	P	W	D	L	F	A
Football League	48	16	14	18	61	63
FA Cup	2	0	0	2	1	4
League Cup	4	2	0	2	5	5
Associate Members Cup	4	1	1	2	3	4
Welsh Cup	36	21	8	7	67	45
Southern League	4	1	2	1	3	3
Wartime Competitions	42	30	6	6	126	55
Jubilee Benevolent Fund	2	0	2	0	4	4
Friendlies	8	3	2	3	15	15
TOTAL	**150**	**74**	**35**	**41**	**286**	**201**

All the following statistics exclude wartime matches - these are covered at the end of this section.

ATTENDANCES

Highest Football League Attendances

1. 60,855 at Ninian Park   27th August 1949
2. 46,003 at Ninian Park   26th December 1951
3. 42,482 at Ninian Park   24th August 1957
4. 41,074 at Ninian Park   24th March 1951
5. 34,881 at Ninian Park   7th November 1959
6. 29,093 at Ninian Park   5th October 1929
7. 27,264 at Vetch Field   24th December 1949
8. 26,224 at Vetch Field   4th November 1950
9. 24,687 at Vetch Field   5th September 1962
10. 24,450 at Ninian Park   7th March 1959

Average Home League Gate for South Wales Derbies

Swansea City 14,841
Cardiff City 20,690

Lowest League Gate

Swansea City 3,711 2nd April 1994
Cardiff City 3,721 3rd December 1996

FOOTBALL LEAGUE

LEADING APPEARANCES

1=	Ivor Allchurch	Cardiff City and Swansea Town	11
	Roger Freestone	Swansea City	11
	Ron Stitfall	Cardiff City	11
4	Alan Curtis	Cardiff City and Swansea City	10
5=	Alan Harrington	Cardiff City	9
	Brian Hughes	Swansea Town	9
	Johnny King	Swansea Town	9
	Andy Melville	Swansea City	9
	Colin Pascoe	Swansea City	9
10=	Harry Griffiths	Swansea Town	8
	Tommy Hutchison	Swansea City	8
	Herbie Williams	Swansea Town	8
13=	Terry Boyle	Cardiff City	7
	Danny Malloy	Cardiff City	7
	Jason Perry	Cardiff City	7

LEADING GOALSCORERS

1	Jimmy Gilligan	Cardiff City	5
2	Brayley Reynolds	Swansea Town	4
3=	Ivor Allchurch	Cardiff City	3
	Mel Charles	Cardiff City	3
	Billy Lucas	Swansea Town	3
	Herbie Williams	Swansea Town	3
7=	Jason Bowen	Cardiff City	2
	John Charles	Cardiff City	2
	Keith Ellis	Cardiff City	2
	George Kelly	Cardiff City	2
	Peter Kitchen	Cardiff City	2
	Sam McCrory	Swansea Town	2
	David Penney	Swansea City	2
	Paul Raynor	Swansea City	2
	Mike Tiddy	Cardiff City	2
	John Toshack	Cardiff City	2
	Nigel Vaughan	Cardiff City	2
	Colin Webster	Swansea Town	2
	Ralph Williams	Cardiff City	2
	Ronnie Williams	Swansea Town	2

WELSH CUP

LEADING APPEARANCES

1=	Don Murray	Cardiff City	9
	Geoff Thomas	Swansea Town	9
	Herbie Williams	Swansea Town	9
4=	Brian Evans	Swansea Town	8
	Barrie Hole	Cardiff City and Swansea Town	8
	Peter King	Cardiff City	8
7=	Ivor Allchurch	Cardiff City and Swansea Town	6
	Jason Bowen	Cardiff City and Swansea City	6
	Brian Clark	Cardiff City	6
	Tom Farquharson	Cardiff City	6
	Roger Freestone	Swansea City	6
	Alan Harrington	Cardiff City	6
	Mel Nurse	Swansea Town	6
14=	Colin Baker	Cardiff City	5
	Dave Carver	Cardiff City	5
	Roy Evans	Swansea Town	5
	John Ford	Swansea Town	5
	Harry Griffiths	Swansea Town	5
	Brian Harris	Cardiff City	5
	Wilf Milne	Swansea Town	5
	Ron Stitfall	Cardiff City	5
	Keith Todd	Swansea Town	5
	Alan Williams	Swansea Town	5

LEADING GOALSCORERS

1=	George Johnston	Cardiff City	4
	Brayley Reynolds	Swansea Town	4
	John Toshack	Cardiff City	4
4=	Len Thompson	Swansea Town	3
	Herbie Williams	Swansea Town	3

THE STATISTICS

OVERALL APPEARANCES IN SOUTH WALES DERBIES

(Including Football League, FA Cup, League Cup, Associate Members Cup, Welsh Cup, Southern League, Benevolent Fund and Friendly games, but excluding all wartime fixtures).

1	Roger Freestone	Swansea City	19
2=	Ivor Allchurch	Cardiff City and Swansea Town	17
	Alan Curtis	Cardiff City and Swansea City	17
	Herbie Williams	Swansea Town	17
5	Ron Stitfall	Cardiff City	16
6	Alan Harrington	Cardiff City	15
7=	Barrie Hole	Cardiff City and Swansea Town	14
	Colin Pascoe	Swansea City	14
9=	Harry Griffiths	Swansea Town	13
	Tommy Hutchison	Swansea City	13
	Robbie James	Swansea City	13
	Jason Perry	Cardiff City	13
13=	Brian Hughes	Swansea Town	12
	Johnny King	Swansea Town	12
	Peter King	Cardiff City	12
	Don Murray	Cardiff City	12
17=	Colin Baker	Cardiff City	11
	Brian Evans	Swansea Town	11
	Mark Harris	Swansea City	11
	Andy Melville	Swansea City	11
	Mel Nurse	Swansea Town	11
	Geoff Thomas	Swansea Town	11

LEADING GOALSCORERS IN ABOVE COMPETITIONS

1	Brayley Reynolds	Swansea Town	8
2	Ronnie Williams	Swansea Town	7
3=	Jimmy Gilligan	Cardiff City	6
	Herbie Williams	Swansea Town	6
5=	George Johnston	Cardiff City	4
	John Toshack	Cardiff City	4
7=	Ivor Allchurch	Cardiff City	3
	Bobby Ball	Swansea Town	3
	Tommy Bamford	Swansea Town	3
	Mel Charles	Cardiff City	3
	Billy Lucas	Swansea Town	3
	Phil Stant	Cardiff City	3
	Len Thompson	Swansea Town	3

WARTIME FOOTBALL

BIGGEST WINS

For Swansea Town: 5-2 on 24th April 1943
For Cardiff City: 8-0 on 26th October 1940

HIGHEST AGGREGATE SCORE

Swansea Town 1 Cardiff City 8 on 21st February 1942

MOST GOALS

Beriah Moore of Cardiff City with 29 goals including 10 in five consecutive games.

HAT-TRICKS

3 - Beriah Moore
1 - Bill Rees (scored 4 goals)
Bill James
George Wright
David Weir
Colin Gibson

All players performed the feat whilst playing for Cardiff City.

THE SOUTH WALES DERBIES